MATTERS OF LIFE AND LONGING

Critical anthropology

Volume 1

Edited by Michael Jackson
University of Copenhagen

Critical Anthropology
explores life on the margins
of the modern world,
and demonstrates
the power of ethnography
to provide new insights
into the human condition.

MATTERS OF LIFE AND LONGING

FEMALE STERILISATION IN NORTHEAST BRAZIL

Anne Line Dalsgaard

MUSEUM TUSCULANUM PRESS
UNIVERSITY OF COPENHAGEN
2004

Matters of Life and Longing
© Museum Tusculanum Press 2004 and the author
Cover design by: Pernille Sys Hansen
Copy editor: Menaka Roy
Composition by: Narayana Press, Gylling
Set in: Aldus
Printed in Denmark by Narayana Press, Gylling
ISBN 87 7289 901 8
ISSN 1811-0665

Published in the series *Critical Anthropology*
Series editor: Professor Michael Jackson, University of Copenhagen

Cover illustration: Mother and son posing for the author, Camaragibe 1997.

Published with support from
The Danish Research Council for the Humanities
and
The Danish Council for Development Research

Museum Tusculanum Press
Njalsgade 94
DK-2300 Copenhagen S

www.mtp.dk

Contents

Acknowledgements

Nesta rua, nesta rua, tem um bosque	*On this road there is a forest*
que se chama, que se chama solidão	*which is called solitude*
dentro dele, dentro dele mora um anjo	*Within it lives an angel*
que roubou, que roubou meu coração	*That has robbed my heart.*

(Traditional children's song from Nordeste)

This book is based on a research project financed by the Research Council of the Danish International Development Agency (DANIDA) whom I wish to thank for their unreserved support, without which the rest would not have been possible. Having said this, I am left with a gratitude that I do not know how to express properly, except as a long list of names. For me they are memories of shared experiences, sorrows and joys.

Above all I want to thank people in the neighbourhood, where I worked, especially the women who accepted their role as my informants. Names and lifehistories have been changed in my stories about their lives, but that does not change my deep gratitude towards these women, whom I do not mention by name out of some – perhaps totally misunderstood – concern for their privacy. The crèche *Vivendo e Aprendendo* always received me and my family with open arms, enthusiasm and a good feast. The *agentes comunitárias de saúde* deserve my warmest thanks for the part they took in the research. And I could not have done what I did without Josenita Duda's wholehearted engagement in my work. I thank her from the bottom of my heart.

In Recife I want to thank Betania Ávila and SOS Corpo for the support they gave me. Parry Scott from the Federal University of Pernambuco assisted me with research arrangements, anthropological insight and advice. Carla Batista and Pedro Nascimento gave me their help as colleagues, assistants and friends. Alexandre Andrade's computer assistance for the surveys was invaluable. Joachim Kock and Andrea Penaforte let me stay in their home and gave me company on days of hard work and homesickness. Wellington da Silva helped us find friends in the interior Pernambuco and became a friend himself. Jacirema Bernardo, Nathan and their children have a particular place in my heart as my substitute family in Olinda. I wish to thank them all.

In Salvador I want to thank Tereza Rizério, her family and Marcel Horande for the questions and days they shared with us. In São Paulo I owe much to Daphne Rattner and Sonia Nussenzweig Hotimsky, who both work to improve the conditions for childbirth in Brazil and willingly lent me a bed, a patient ear and their expertise, while I was there.

In Copenhagen I have received much help, inspiration and encouragement from colleagues and students at the Institute of Anthropology. I want to single out my Ph.D. supervisor professor Susan Reynolds Whyte, associate professor Tine Gammeltoft, and professor Michael Jackson, who all in different ways and at different times have been prominent figures in the development of my work. I also want to thank my Ph.D. colleagues Cecilie Rubow, Hanne Mogensen, Karen Valentin, Lotte Meinert, Tina Jensen, and Tine Tjørnhøj Thomsen. I have enjoyed their company and their helpful comments after readings of drafts. The Prologue has been enriched by comments from volume editors Richard Jenkins, Hanne Jessen and Vibeke Steffen, as it forms part of the chapter "Birth Control, Life Control" in a forthcoming volume published by Museum Tusculanum Press. Morten Nielsen has read and commented, too, and been a good partner for discussion. In addition, my gratitude also includes Ph.D. secretary Jørgen Pedersen, who has helped me patiently through the years.

Throughout the whole process my neighbour, Ole Carsten Pedersen, has been indispensable with critique and statistical expertise. I am also indebted to Eunice Kårsberg, Ana Melim and Tine Lykke, who have all assisted me with the Portuguese language and turned what could have been a difficult learning process into a joy.

With the publication of my work I owe much to Michael Jackson, who as a series editor has inspired and supported my preparation of the manuscript. The Museum Tusculanum Press has been unreservedly interested and helpful. I also thank Menaka Roy, who, as language and copy editor, assisted me in finalizing my manuscript.

Of course, in spite of all the help and support, the responsibility for shortcomings is mine.

My nearest and dearest deserve more than I can say or give in return. My mother-in-law, Lene and my parents, were always ready to help, when I was away or too busy. And my husband and children have had to go far, geographically as well as emotionally, to follow me. "Thank you" does not fully express my feelings here.

I dedicate this book to my father, Mogens Dalsgaard, who lived a life full of books and passed his appreciation of a well told story on to me.

Tubal ligation

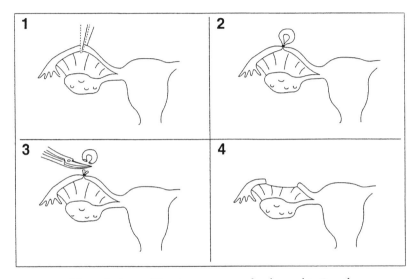

The technique of ligation most prevalently used in Brazil.

The tubal ligation is a surgical contraceptive method to prevent the woman from having more children. Being surgery, a tubal ligation needs anaesthesia, and therefore it has to be performed at a hospital by specialised health professionals. The most common ligation method presently in use in Brazil is the following (see illustration above): The doctor makes an incision in the abdomen of the woman to reach the tubes (1), which thereupon are tied (2) and cut (3); the passage of the egg through the tube to the uterus is hindered (4). Thus, a barrier is created that prevents the meeting between egg and sperm and fertilisation is no longer possible.

(Carloto et al 1994:75, my translation)

Prologue

Motherhood in the midst of poverty and violence

I already saw many, I knew many, good boys, calm boys and suddenly something enters them and they become monsters. Because a friend calls them, "let's do this, let's do that" and suddenly the guy is stealing. I already knew many, they are killed, young, young, young, younger than my sons. All friends... sons of my friends, whom I saw being born, saw grow up, because they were good boys....

(Sonia, mother of 7 children)

In 1997 and 1998 I did fieldwork towards a doctoral degree in anthropology in Camaragibe, a municipality adjoining the city of Recife in northeast Brazil. With my husband and children I had moved into what to us was a small and rather simple house in the middle of a so-called *bairro popular* (popular neighbourhood). I was there to study the prevalent use of female sterilisation and, being an anthropologist, I looked for the meaning of fertility and birth control on the micro-level, that is, among people in their everyday life. Everyday life is, however, an elusive and diffuse category. It exists only as a background condition against which particular events stand out (Lewis 2000:539).

Hence, the 'everyday life' that I came to know was deduced from the
extraordinary. Not that I did not chatter, buy food, wash clothes, fetch
water and share the lazy midday in the shade of a tree or a house with
my neighbours. I did all this, but it was the moments of feast and crisis
that gave meaning to these everyday activities. Likewise, some violent
events which took place while I was there came to be central to my
understanding of people's valorisation of controlled fertility.

The place we lived in was a low income neighbourhood, like so many
others in Brazil. Some families were miserably poor, most were poor
in the sense that they earned just enough for daily subsistence, and
a few families were a bit better off. The internal social hierarchy was
never stable, as conditions and situations were always fluctuating. Unemployment, illness, divorce and other misfortunes could change a
fairly stable family economy into a misery. Nevertheless, despite these
fragile family economies several months had passed before I fully
realised the pain behind the fluid and flexible way of survival that
people practised with such skill. The days were full of good company,
and there was a sense of competence around in the bright sunlight
that made me overlook the defeats. "There is always a *jeitinho* – a
way out", Brazilians use to say with a captivating smile and indeed
there was. The *jeitinho* is usually understood as a "fast, efficient,
and last-minute way of accomplishing a goal", with the help of one's
social network (Barbosa 1995:36) and the competence I found in the
neighbourhood seemed to spring from knowing how to get by in this
manner. Relatives, friends, neighbours, all strings were pulled in times
of necessity and solutions found to almost any problem. The reverse
side of the coin was the dependency of others and the vulnerability of
the individual when networks failed. Looking closer into the apparent
strength of the people and how they constructed the viability of their
lives there turned out to be unavoidable moments of *fait accompli*,
when relationships dissolved and no strings could be pulled. At such
times the margin of social life came threateningly near.

In her book *Death without Weeping*, Nancy Scheper-Hughes describes the fear of violence, "of being made to vanish", as all-pervading
in the neighbourhood Alto do Cruzeiro, where she did her fieldwork
(1992:232). Located in Pernambuco, like Recife, but different in terms
of, among others, the years that separated her fieldwork from mine, and

the difference in access to urban facilities, Scheper-Hughes' Alto do Cruzeiro does not fully resemble the neighbourhood where I worked. However, one main feature running through her description resonates with my experience: the fear of violence and its social consequences. People on the Alto feared the indifference and violence from the state to which they were subject. At public clinics and hospitals, the civil registry office, the cemetery, everywhere, they were treated as 'nobodies' and the police terror directed towards them, epitomised by the so-called 'disappearances', confirmed their sense of being worthless to society. Furthermore, rumours of organ-theft reinforced their fear of anonymous disappearance (ibid.: 216ff).

The people I came to know feared violence in the same way. They would look into the darkness of the night and to my naive comment on its beauty they would reply,"Don't you have *violencia* in Denmark?" I learned, though, that to them *violencia* meant neither police terror nor organ-theft. The violence they feared most was that which was linked to the drug dealing and related criminal activities that increasingly dominated the neighbourhood. But while the background changed, the phenomenology of the fear itself echoed Scheper-Hughes' description: "Consciousness moves in and out of an acceptance of the state of things as normal and expectable – violence as taken for granted and sudden ruptures whereby one is suddenly thrown into a state of shock" (Scheper-Hughes 1992: 233). The ambivalence, the waiting for things to happen, created a constant tension – an atmosphere of "free floating anxiety" (ibid.) in which people experienced themselves as fragile and vulnerable.

However, the fear had an extra dimension in the neighbourhood. In contrast to the threat on the Alto do Cruzeiro, the *violencia* did not stem from exterior forces, but from elements within the neighbourhood. Indeed some of the criminals had moved to the area in order to hide in the biggest squatter settlement, called the 'invasion',[1] but others were sons of well-known local families, young men attracted by the money and excitement available in criminal circles. The threat was fostered among people themselves, yet nobody knew exactly where and in whom the danger lay. In the atmosphere of uncertainty parents had to be on guard in order to keep their children away from bad influences. It was for this that the right upbringing was crucial.

Responsible parenthood

In the neighbourhood, the capacity to bring up children was seen as dependent, first and foremost, on the family's economic situation. Parents should be able to provide for their children: feed them, dress them properly and pay for medicine and schooling. People generally held that a couple could have as many children as they could afford to bring up. Poor people should only have two. "Having one is having none, having two is at least having one", people would say to justify why two children were considered the minimum. Having no children was out of question; having many, "filling the house with children", as people would say, was seen as irresponsibility. As one mother said, "You take it from the television where you see all these hungry children living underneath a bridge. They [their parents] do not do anything to avoid children. They have children just to let them suffer".

Earning money and making ends meet was ideally a joint task for a couple, as was planning for the future. But ideals were not easily lived up to. A man from the neighbourhood explained to me how lack of planning was the stigma and tragedy of the poor. Sitting on a ragged and dirty sofa in his shack of a house he said,

> The strange thing I have observed is that when they [the rich] want to have a child, they plan. For four, five years. They move together and then they prepare themselves for that child to come and then they have more structure [infrastructure] to bring it up. I see it this way, you have a lot of children, and then you buy a thing for one, but not for the other. Sometimes even the food, some times you only have little food and have to divide it, and nobody will be able to fill the stomach. Everybody will be hungry. And then the parents will suffer, because they just let the children be born. I see it like that – it is the curse of the weak class.

Women were confronted with this notion of responsible parenthood when they consulted the health care system: both negatively and positively expressed it pervaded health care providers' attitudes and acts towards the women. Observing a birth at one of the big hospitals in Recife, I overheard an ironic, but casual, remark from a nurse to a woman who had just delivered. The nurse said: "Oh, your husband doesn't work, he only knows how to make children, eh?" In contrast, when asking the local gynaecologist for sterilisation, the women were met with understanding and reinforced in their efforts to be 'responsible'. The gynaecologist told me that she herself had only two children: "It is fine, more than two is expensive and a lot of responsibility in relation to studies, to bring them up properly... two is enough for me." She saw the women who sought her help as suffering from unwanted pregnancies and begging to be rescued. She spoke of a state of emergency that did not leave either time or money for further considerations about the appropriateness of sterilisation, which was the rescue she provided.

The parents' emphasis on responsible adjustment of fertility to their economy was thus part of a general discourse, and so was their perception of urgency in relation to their children's schooling. Literacy rates have always been low in Brazil, especially in North and Northeast Brazil, but since the 1990s school education has become central to both political planning and parents' aspirations, even where illiteracy has been the norm. During my stay there Pelé, the famous Brazilian football player, promoted schooling for children in a television campaign, and there was a billboard at the roadside near the neighbourhood reading "Out of the sugar into the future", showing two children walking hand in hand with their school bags towards the horizon between high walls of sugar cane. While few children worked in the neighbourhood, and none in the sugar cane fields, parents nevertheless concurred with the message. They knew by experience that lack of education was a disadvantage, and they firmly believed that schooling was the way forward.

Illiteracy has long been associated with poverty in Brazil, and was often understood in terms of ignorance. Old Dona Severina, who lived close to me in the neighbourhood, stated that many "ignorants" would still die from hunger in Brazil, because they did not study. Others would say that soon you would need to study in order to get even a simple job. Yet others would state the general assumption that if children did not study, and live a regular life between home and school, they would be lost in the street like the street children one sees on television. 'Loose children' as people called children who did not stay close to their home and their mother, were seen as out of place and dangerous both to themselves and their surroundings. As Tobias

Hecht writes in his book on street children in Recife: "While street children have been used by some to exemplify the vulnerabilities of childhood, they have also been refashioned in another way – as harbingers of the danger posed to society [...] by the unsupervised youth" (1998:173).

Nurtured children stay at home

In Brazil the 'street' is perceived as the place of commerce, of men and of prostitutes, whereas the 'home' is the place of the family, of wife and children (DaMatta 1997). This distinction was completely taken for granted in the neighbourhood, and gave structure to everyday practices and gender relations. Women stayed near home as much as possible, and housework, childcare and ownership of the house was generally ascribed to women. For good and for bad, houses and homemaking were women's domain. Men were supposed to participate in the life of the 'street', to work, and to provide economically for their families. From early childhood, children were brought up according to these gender roles, and boys were allowed to run around more freely than girls during daytime. However, when violence broke out or when a child misbehaved, parents would agree that even boys ought to stay at home with their mothers.

My friend and neighbour Sonia was worried about her adolescent sons. She said that they were lazy, played too much football and did not learn anything in school. At times when I came to see her I found all the doors locked to keep the children in, away from the dangers of the street. On such days she herself would often be furiously pacing around like a lion in a cage. When talking about these situations, she once said: "If just one of my children would sit down and read a book, oh, it would be so beautiful!" Reading a book seemed to epitomise the behaviour of the well educated home-nurtured child. But in Sonia's house I never saw a book, a newspaper or any other reading material, and Sonia herself read only with great difficulty. Another day she told me that she found it difficult to help the children with their schoolwork. Sometimes the child would have written down the exercise so badly that Sonia found it illegible and could not figure out what it was all about. Sometimes, I think, she was just too restless to sit with a child for the time needed. Worries were many and patience difficult to produce.

Quarrels with husbands and economic problems occupied most women and created friction in their homes. Husbands were supposed to show their concern for the family by 'not letting things be lacking at home', but this was an almost impossible task in a situation of widespread unemployment and poverty. A woman could never rely on having her husband provide properly for herself and their children. Husbands who spent their scarce money on other women or alcohol were common, and the women were often desperately trapped. They had to face the children's demands – for interesting food instead of the perpetual cornmeal, for clothes, for a few coins to buy some sweets to break the monotony, or for notebooks and pencils needed in school.

The generally held ideal of motherly patience was often expressed with self criticism, since most mothers felt they could not live up to it. As Rute, who was 25 and a mother of three boys, once put it, "A good mother is one who understands the child, who gives a good education, gives affection. But it is difficult because children make one lose one's mind. I will not lie. Mine exhaust my patience too much. At times I cannot take it and I beat them. Afterwards I get that remorse inside … but the boy did not listen! So I punished him."

The lack of patience posed a serious problem for the women in the long run, as the women knew it might have fatal consequences. Sonia used to say that her sons were so difficult because they were brought up in misery and without affection. When they were small, Sonia lived with them in the interior of Pernambuco under harsh conditions with her husband, their father, who drank too much. Today she lives with another man with whom she has two more children. But she is still worried: "What bothers me is this, because, there is no affection, no affection. Nobody says 'let us talk today,' 'let us sit down here, let us play, let us invent a story.' It doesn't exist, it is only ignorance. The child comes, and then 'Go, go!' The way it is today it is only drugs. Boys who leave their home early, they get involved with some who are older, and start doing wrong things. My fear is this".

In the women's view a child should not only have proper food, a good school and 'all that is best', it should also have affection from its parents in order to become a decent person. The women felt the need to give all this to their children, but at times it was difficult not to 'heat up the head', as Irene said when everything became too difficult. Irene worked at the local health post, and she was one of the more politically engaged people in the neighbourhood. One day when we were discussing the subject, she said:

> The rich child is not brought up given slaps, no, he is not beaten, no. He is filled with caresses, filled with liking [...] From what I see, it is only the sons of the poor who are brought up with slaps, humiliation, beaten, because they do not have anything! Because look: if you do not have...if I do not have proper food to give to my children, if I do not have a good school to give them, if I do not have good clothes to give them, do not have snacks, do not have leisure, and I even beat them? [...] The children of today from the poor class have this vice of revolting. It is due to the fact that the parents do not have jobs, we do not have a good home, no leisure and no good food, isn't it so? And then the children become what? Rebellious. The parents are unemployed, many children walk without shoes because they cannot buy a sandal and when they buy, it is the most fragile sandal that only lasts for a week. Somebody steps on the foot and then it breaks. One has to consider that. I cannot bring up my children properly because I cannot give all that I want to give to them [...] My children, when a notebook [for the school] is missing, it takes me almost a month to be able to buy it, and that is not what I want. I don't want it to be missing.

Even when they saw that they were prey to poverty in a society that did not support them, the women felt that they were the ones who were called on to do the impossible, to love and care for their children in order to keep them away from the dangers of the street. When, as frequently happened, violence and killing suddenly erupted, their worries were further fuelled. The fear of losing one's children, and perhaps oneself, merged with the despair of not being able to educate them. The force of these mixed emotions was revealed to me, when – as people said – "the neighbourhood caught fire". Only then did I understand the depth of the frequent utterance, "We don't have the conditions for bringing up children".

Violence and social exclusion

I was in the neighbourhood, on my second field trip, when a state of shock crept over us all. The events started as something fairly distant. One of the central figures in a drug network was shot within the 'invasion'. Nobody really knew by whom or why and everybody mentioned the murder as little as possible. It was too dangerous to know about it, and it did not directly affect anybody outside the closed circle of criminals. However, a week later in the middle of the night, in a house outside the 'invasion', a young girl was abducted by hooded men. They dragged her away in front of her parents, who did not dare to intervene. The next morning, when the rumours went around, people discussed whether the intruders were the police or the bandits. But soon a part of the 'invasion' was taken over by 'them'. Shots were fired to scare away the curious. My friend Neide, and others who lived nearby, fled to other houses. On the following day the girl was found, thrown on the ground, raped and killed. She had been the girlfriend of the man who was the supposed murderer of the first victim.

From that day an atmosphere of fear spread to almost everybody. Houses were closed in the 'invasion' boards saying, "House For Sale" were seen everywhere, and health workers no longer visited the families there. Then the next, third murder happened within the 'invasion'. A young man was killed in front of his house in the middle of the night. His wife and his mother screamed when it all began, but they were ordered to be silent and stay indoors, which they did until daybreak. The corpse lay outside the house all day long until the police took it away in the afternoon. I was told that it was forbidden to move it before their arrival.

Some days later, the police arrested Miriam, the daughter of Tereza, who once was my neighbour. They came – also hooded – and drove Miriam away in a car without further explanation. She was engaged to a man who apparently had something to do with the drug gang. It was at this point that I got frightened. Not that I had any objective reason for it but the whole atmosphere was just saturated with fear, and suddenly I felt that I had poked my nose into too much. One day soon after I was standing in front of Tereza's house, talking with another of her daughters. Tereza had had a heart attack due to the shock and was hospitalised, and she – the daughter – was afraid of being alone in the house with the children. We were discussing the situation when a man came up the road towards us. He stopped about ten metres away and delivered a message from Tereza's son, Roberto. I found the distance hard to understand until I turned around and saw somebody standing further up the lane, watching us. The whole scenario flashed through my mind: the man watching, me being close enough to Tereza's daughter to receive confidential information, the messenger keeping his distance and speaking very loudly, signalling that no secrets were being passed. I hurtled into the paranoia that gradually overtook us all, a mistrust infecting friendships and otherwise good relations among neighbours.

In this atmosphere my friend Neide had to pay dearly. She was struggling to keep her two sons, Fernando and Fábio, out of the drug network. Much later I learnt that she had borrowed money and sold her radio and a blender in order to provide for her sons, so that they should not be attracted to something 'bad'. On top of these worries she quarrelled with her man, who was not the father of the sons, and who no longer wanted them in the house. And then one day it was announced on the radio that, according to an anonymous source, Neide's sons were the only ones involved in the gang who were still around in the neighbourhood. The police, or whoever it was, showed up, but the sons were not at home, they had fled. Neide was now afraid to stay in her house during the night. "They will return," she said, "and it is better not to be around, for they prefer to kill immediately." With this turn of events Neide became dangerous company. Her best friend Elizia stayed away. Neide once said about their friendship that she could always count on Elizia: "She gives me everything. When I need advice she advises me, and when I am weak because of the children, she calms me down, says, 'Relax, *rapaz*'. She gives me strength. She is an excellent friend." But now Elizia had disappeared; her house was for sale, too. When a family was threatened, everybody seemed to turn their backs on them. Nobody wanted to be involved.

During the following days, when Neide tried to find a safe place for her sons, she was therefore also seeking a solution to her own isolation. She wanted to get them into a home for drug users – to have them out of the house, in a safe place so that they would not be killed, and so that she could stay with her husband and in her social network. I helped her contact a social worker from the municipality. It was during this meeting with the well-intentioned social worker that I realised the cruelty of individualising the responsibility for children's upbringing, without providing the social and economic basis for it. In short, Neide began to explain how she saw the problem of her sons. She had left them with their grandmother when she – Neide – moved to live with her new husband. This is a common practice, and Neide had told me about it before without reflecting upon the moral aspect of it. Now she said, however, that her mother had been ignorant and not very good at bringing up the children, but that she – Neide – had done everything possible for them, while they were growing up, she stated proudly that she had always provided them with food and good clothes. The social worker then said, "But, Neide, don't you think that children need more than good clothes and food?" And while Neide was outside for a moment she continued with a sigh: "Doesn't she understand that she has a responsibility? How could she do it?"

When asked, Neide answered, "Yes": yes, children need more than shoes, clothes and food. Her efforts to provide materially for her children were not recognised and her responsibility for what had happened was left hanging in the air. When I came to Neide's house two days later she had left in the middle of the night with her children. I never saw her again though I later found out where she lives, alone with her children trying to build a new life somewhere else. One of her sons has subsequently been killed. Her husband sold the house and went to live with his mother.

In the neighbourhood, good upbringing was cast in terms of economy. However, economy was a means rather than an end in itself; women's ultimate concern was their ability to produce true mother love. Left without means to provide what was needed, the mothers with whom I talked were worried about the future of their children, their fear reinforced by a persistent focus on violent death in the media – photos in the newspaper of young boys, killed and left in the grass where they fell; early morning radio reports about yesterday's killings; and the omnipresent television broadcasting news about death and misfortune in an emotional tone that presented the subject as a matter of immediate concern. It was a fear of losing everything that confirmed

Recife, segunda-feira, 18 de fevereiro de 2002   **POLÍCIA**   FOLHA DE PERNAMBUCO **3**

Adolescentes são achados mortos

Os três corpos estavam às margens da Estrada Velha do Frio, em Paulista

Matheus Machado

Três adolescentes foram encontrados mortos, na manhã do último sábado, nas margens da Estrada Velha do Frio, que liga o município de Paulista ao bairro de Jardim Paulista. Todos levaram tiros na cabeça, o que caracteriza uma execução, segundo a polícia. A estrada é a que leva até o Lixão da Muribeca e lá é conhecido por ser um local de desova, onde pessoas são mortas e deixadas no lugar. Nenhum dos adolescentes aparentava ter mais de 17 anos. De acordo com o sargento Carlos Silva, do 17° Batalhão da Polícia Militar (PM), é provável que o triplo assassinato tenha ocorrido ainda na manhã do sábado e não na madrugada, hora

preferencial para os matadores. "O sangue não está coalhado, o que indica que o homicídio foi feito há pouco tempo", destacou.

As vítimas estavam trajando bermudas e camisas e todas elas estavam descalças. Segundo o sargento, existe a possibilidade de que dois menores sejam parentes. "Eles são bem parecidos. Podem ser até irmãos", observou. O delegado da Delegacia do Janga, Inácio Vicente, informou que nenhum parente das vítimas foi procurar a DPO caso será investigado pela Delegacia de Paulista. De acordo com o delegado Djalma Raposo, esse triplo homicídio não tem ligação com a chacina dos oito mortos que ocorreu em Rio Doce, na última quarta-feira.

CABO - Um rapaz conhecido apenas pelo apelido de Xoxo, aparentando 20 anos, foi encontrado morto com um tiro na cabeça, no último sábado, por volta das 2h30, na rua Visconde de Porto Alegre, no Centro do Cabo A vítima havia saído do cabaré da Florentina, conhecido ponto de encontro do baixo meretrício do Cabo. Lá, teria havido uma discussão, segundo a polícia, envolvendo a vítima. Após deixar o local, no caminho de volta pra casa, Xoxo foi abordado e executado pelo assassino, que fugiu em seguida. Coincidentemente, na última quinta-feira, o menor A.G.S., 17 anos, foi executado a tiros na mesmo local, a poucos metros de onde foi encontrado o corpo de Xoxo. Os policiais da Delegacia da Cabo ainda não têm pistas com relação aos dois assassinatos.

"Adolescents found dead", *Folha de Pernambuco* 18 February 2002

one's worth as a person: one's loved ones, one's worth as a neighbour or friend worthy of recognition and – due to an indirect linking of irresponsibility and violence – one's worth as a citizen of the modern Brazilian society. It was the fear of being reduced to nothing, as if the corpses lying there decaying, waiting for the police to take them away – these corpses that attracted everybody's morbid curiosity – represented the essence of the situation, the anonymous and worthless product of the poor, who could not control themselves. As Sonia said: "What a pain for a mother to see her son like that!"

Chapter One

Introduction

Creatures of history and habit, to be sure, but in their experience of the world in which they make their way with such blind faith, they are each singular and significant. Each has friends and families for whom the world would be the less without them. Each has a story to tell.

(Jackson 1998:25)

This book is about female sterilisation in a low income neighbourhood in Northeast Brazil.[1] It is about women's motives for accepting – and often actively seeking – sterilisation and centres on the individual subject and her life-world.[2] In this subjective world sterilisation proves to be just the tip of the iceberg of intention, acquiring its particular meaning within a wider context of poverty, disrespect and constrained agency.

My analytical focus is on recognition as a human need. Based on the works of Maurice Merleau-Ponty, William James, George Herbert Mead, Alfred Schutz, Michael Jackson and Nick Crossley – and with Hegel's notion of recognition as the specific point of departure – I interpret women's striving for sterilisation as a search for social acknowledgement. Although the argument is phenomenological in its focus on lived experience and subjective meaning, by situating fertility and sterilisation in the existential dilemma of autonomy and dependency my analysis also includes the contested field of social relations which is shaped by forces of political economy beyond the immediate life-world.

In the prologue I have described fertility and motherhood in a context of everyday violence. Maternal sentiments are prominent in this description as I see emotion as a synthesis of the social and the individual psychological order (Lyon and Barbalet 1994:63), turning collective norms and values into personal matters and bringing motivation into action. I have described how the structural violence of having to act while being powerless is central to local perceptions of motherhood, and how moments of loss and helplessness give direction and force to women's efforts to change their lives and the lives of their children. In the neighbourhood fertility control was not just dictated by the need to make ends meet economically. What was at stake was much more profound and serious than the painful experience of not being able to give one's child what was needed here and now: it was a question about social being in a very fundamental sense. Being fertile in this context was an Achilles' heel, a weakness that under certain conditions was directly associated with death, symbolic as well as real. Sterilisation, for reasons that I will soon describe, had become a means to counteract this weakness; a barrier to block their otherwise fluid and vulnerable life. Where women once used to say "I will have as many children as God will give me, and he who gives us the children will see to our survival" many of them now felt that they had to take on the responsibility themselves.

In the following I move on to describe the structural changes in the Brazilian society through which the women in focus seem to have lost out in all except one area: they have gained the right to define and work upon their lives by means of modern medicine. With this right followed the discourse on individual responsibility and submission to medical authority that ran through the women's reproductive histories.

My argument centres on the inferiority that the women feel in meeting with better-off Brazilians, such as the staff at public hospitals who are also in a position of power that is quite explicit. I link this sense of inferiority to the experience of the body as betraying and without value and I describe how women impose change, symbolic as well as real, upon their bodies in a search for the recognition they are denied by their inferior status. Finally, I argue that the motivation for sterilisation must be understood in the context of the immediate life-world of family and neighbours with its endeavours and frustrations. Within the multiple concerns of a woman's life sterilisation relieves immediate pressures and endows her with recognition as a responsible mother. However, it does not fundamentally alter problematic relationships and leaves her with a longing for more than a surgical intervention in itself can bring.

Rather than seeing sterilisation as simply a method of birth control I argue that for the women in focus it constitutes a hope for control in one's own life.[3]

Female sterilisation in Brazil

Today female sterilisation is the most commonly used method of birth control in the world. Countries like China and India have after many years of persistent and widespread family planning programmes reached levels of female sterilisation at respectively 33.5 per cent and 34.2 per cent of all married women of reproductive age (United Nations 2001).[4] In comparison Brazil ranks high; in 1996 40.1 per cent of married Brazilian women of reproductive age were sterilised.[5] Taking into account that this level of sterilisation has been reached in the absence of large-scale public family planning programmes, the development in Brazil is remarkable as the high use of female sterilisation seems first and foremost to be the result of individual women's choices and actions (Kaufmann 1998:245; see also Berquo and Arilha 1992; Diniz et al. 1998; Andrade 1997; Serruya 1996; Vieira and Ford 1996). What remains to be seen is whether it is an entirely positive development.

Sterilisation has become increasingly widespread since the late 1970s. At a time when women of all income groups were already practising birth control, while better-off women relied on contraception methods such as tubal ligation, delivered by private health clinics, low income women were left with clandestine, precarious abortions and unsupervised use of contraception (mainly the pill) purchased from pharmacies or distributed by private internationally supported family planning organisations. The practice of tubal ligation for birth control was initially a privilege of the rich and associated with the growing use of caesarean sections. In Brazil (as in North America) caesarean sections in the 1970s became a consumer good for those who could afford the expense of a private hospital delivery, and sterilisations were routinely recommended after three consecutive caesarean sections (Mello e Souza 1994; Faundes and Cecatti 1991).[6] Public health units were not meant to deliver family planning services, sterilisations included, but a laissez faire attitude among legal and political authorities to the emerging unauthorised provision of sterilisation within the public health care system soon made the method available for a huge number of lower class women. However, though increasingly common up through the 1980s, sterilisation was surrounded by legal ambivalence and condemned by the Medical Ethical Code[7] until November 1997 (Costa 1995:22). Tubal ligations were therefore often performed under cover of caesarean sections and the individual physician paid 'under the table'. This uncontrolled practice of sterilisation and its effects have been thoroughly criticised in Brazil by women's groups and feminist politicians but continue to be rampant among the poor nevertheless.

Political unease

In a study on contraceptive use conducted in Recife from 1983 to 1985, Maria Betania Ávila and Regina Barbosa describe the growing use of sterilisation in the following terms: "The access to tubal ligation has increased considerably during the last 10 years to a point where we today can talk about the existence of an industry of sterilisation in the periphery of Recife" (1985:149, my translation). In this study Ávila and Barbosa criticise Brazilian doctors for stimulating the growing interlinkage between surgical deliveries and sterilisation due to prospects of personal gains (economic as well as in terms of time). Later studies have pointed equally towards a direct link between the medical preference for caesarean sections and sterilisation and the growing use of these practices in Brazil (Barros et al. 1991; Carranza 1994; Costa 1995; Mello e Souza 1994; Giffin 1994; Hopkins 1998). The Brazilian rate of caesarean section is one of the highest in the world today (36.4 per cent in 1996)[8] and is criticised for being too costly, consuming disproportionate public health care resources, and presenting a risk to mothers' and new-borns' health and survival

(Faundes and Cecatti 1991).[9] Strong critiques within health politics and the feminist movement emphasise the need to reduce the use of surgical deliveries and to restructure the health care system in favour of normal births (Junqueira 1997; *Notas Sobre Nascimento e Parto* 1998; Rattner 1996).

The increased use of female sterilisation has caused debate as well as "political unease" in Brazil (Kaufmann 1998:244). Cast in terms of an internationally financed control of poor black women's reproduction it was opposed by black activists in the late 1980s (Andrade 1997; Thomassen 1992/93).[10] Among others the federal deputy Benedita da Silva fuelled the debate by saying that "Those who have an interest in killing poor black children in Brazil, also have an interest in not allowing these children to be born" (Costa 1995:26). However, a racist tendency in the delivery of sterilisation was difficult to prove. A Parliamentary Inquiry Commission established to uncover any hidden agenda underlying the high sterilisation rates came up with vague results (Costa 1995; Kaufmann 1998), and statistical data has shown no significant difference in sterilisation according to race (Berquó 1998:389).

As the use of sterilisation increased, regret and re-fertilisation became serious issues. Rates of regret are found to be high in Brazil (Costa 1995:21) and seem to be related to the too willingly provided sterilisations. Studies of regret all indicate that low age and few living children at the time of sterilisation are statistically significant risk factors (Hardy et al. 1996; Vieira 1994; Vieira and Ford 1996; Machado 1998), as are poor ounselling and limited knowledge about, or access to, reversible contraceptive methods (Machado 1998 and Hardy et al. 1996).[11] Hence, with the legalisation of sterilisation for both sexes in 1997, a control of the practice was aimed at from political and medical quarters.[12] Certain hospitals and clinics are today authorised to deliver the method under restrictions on age and number of children and with an offer of alternatives. If the negative consequences of the sterilisation practice up till now can be avoided in the future, sterilisation may prove to be unproblematic to the Brazilian state and perhaps even lead to favourable demographic and economic conditions for social improvement (Carvalho and Wong 1998). While sterilisation itself should continue to be one of the options available to women, this may divert attention from why women *so willingly* choose to be sterilised, a question that perhaps more than ever deserves attention and thoughtful consideration.

A question of recognition

Several of the above mentioned studies point towards women's choosing to undergo both caesarean sections and sterilisation as an important factor behind the fertility decline in Brazil (see also Berquo and Arilha 1992; Diniz et al. 1998; Kaufmann 1998; Serruya 1996). However, quite different forces may be at play depending on the social status of the women who seek sterilisation. To my knowledge no studies have been conducted among rich or middle class women in Brazil in order particularly to elucidate their perceptions of sterilisation. In her study of caesarean sections Carranza proposes that rich and middle class women are more unconscious and inexperienced about their bodies than their counterparts in other countries, perhaps due to a strong focus on beauty and outer appearance in Brazil (Carranza 1994:133). The lack of intimate knowledge of their own bodies may be a reason, Carranza suggests, for the preference of sterilisation and the pill – both methods which do not require touching the body. However, a further exploration of better off women's ideas about fertility and femininity would be very interesting in comparison with the existing studies of low income women's motives.

The studies mentioned reveal a complicated and opaque situation in which unequal gender and class relations motivate lower income women to control fertility, while medical authority and disrespecting attitudes push them into sterilisation as a final solution to their reproductive problems (Diniz et al. 1998:65). A few have been conducted with a qualitative approach to the use of sterilisation, varying considerably in their attitude to the women in focus.[13] A quick look at two of them, representing respectively a rather paternalistic and an optimistic, sympathising point of view, will clarify my positioning within this field of research.

In her book *Submissão e Desejo* (*Submission and Wish*) Suzanne Serruya (1996) presents a study on female sterilisation based on interviews with 20 low income women from Belém, the capital of the Amazon region. According to Serruya, the women were generally uninformed about their own bodies, did not use contraceptive pills correctly and valued the medical control of their fertility. Under these circumstances, tubal ligation was both a delight and a relief. Serruya's work gives credit to the Foucauldian notion of docile bodies wishing their own submission, as she concludes that "in a perverse manner, the women feel happier after the tubal ligation. Therefore, when the women decide, definitively, not to have more children, their silence speaks of domination and alienation" (ibid.: 172, my translation).

In contrast to Serruya, Simone Diniz, Cecília de Mello e Souza and Ana Paula Portella present the women in their study *Not Like Our Mothers* as active agents who have chosen to speak up about the unjust burdens of their lives as mothers, wives and patients (Diniz, de Mello e Souza and Portella 1998). The women interviewed in this study were from three different Brazilian sites (rural Pernambuco, Rio de Janeiro and São Paulo), and most of them were engaged in social movements. They all felt entitled to regulate their fertility, but only some were sterilised (numbers are not mentioned). The authors' emphasis on women's agency may be derived from the fact that these women were politically active.

Like Serruya I discuss my data in terms of medicalisation and sub-mission (Chapter Four), but simultaneously, like Diniz et al. I want to stress that the women I met perceived themselves as agents in their own lives. They were not politically active women. Their aspirations for a better future were mainly related to consumption and ideas about 'happiness', and their efforts to change their situation could not be cast in terms of resistance in any traditional sense. Nevertheless, they did not see themselves as dominated or alienated. The women I met knew what they wanted; they just did not have the wherewithal to reach it. Sterilisation was an attempt to create such conditions in their lives.

The argument of this book proposes a mediation of these two apparently mutually exclusive stances. Seeing the oscillation between sub-mission and agency as an existential, rather than analytical dilemma underlying all human endeavour, I will locate the women's endurance and strivings as part of a common human search for recognition in a given social world.

Fertility and intersubjectivity

The recent remarkable fertility decline in Brazil has challenged traditional notions about demographic transition (Faria 1997/98; Martine,
Das Gupta and Chen 1998). Declines in fertility have long been attributed to improved access to contraception or to reductions in number of children wished for as a result of improved living conditions.
Neither availability of contraception nor improved living conditions
have characterised the transition in Brazil. Though it began in a period
of economic improvement, the 'Economic Miracle', the decline accel-
erated in years of impoverishment – the 'Lost Decade' of the 1980s
(Berquó 1998). Simultaneously, induced abortion was the initial means
of fertility regulation for the majority of women in Brazil who could
not afford private health care.

The theoretical distinction between 'supply led' transition (induced
through propagation of contraception) or 'demand led' transition (re-
sulting from structural changes and a reduction of the desired family
size) needs to be modified in order to include developments like the
Brazilian (Faria 1997/98). In his analysis of the fertility decline in
Brazil Vilmar Faria proposes "a mode of analysis that emphasizes the
causal complementarity between structural processes and social action
of individuals, going beyond the false dualism between structural de-
terminism and individual action" (ibid.: 183). However, Faria himself
does not fully realise the mode of analysis that he proposes. I have
made extended use of Faria's excellent analysis and take it further than
he does in applying it to a particular empirical space where structures
and individual lives intersect.

My contribution to fertility studies begins with the emphasis on
the need to include individual experience when reproductive change
is considered and assessed. After all, new patterns of value orientation
and behavioural norms do not happen in the abstract. They come about
for specific actors and may be forced by a certain degree of suffering
and pain as well as by hopes and longings. In order to follow Faria's
proposal, we need to interpret what is at stake for particular participants in particular situations (Kleinman and Kleinman 1996).

However, individual experience is always intersubjectively generated
and the meaning of having children is no exception. Although often
perceived as highly private, procreation is a matter of intersubjectivity,

whether defined as the union of families, God's intervention or the meeting of egg and sperm. "[F]ertility describes a relationship and is not simply an attribute of an individual" (Townsend 1997:108); that is, wanting or not wanting to have children is not an isolated decision, but part of one's view of self and other and reproductive decisions are motivated by a wish to work upon relationships here and now as much as – or perhaps even more than – by plans about future outcome.

In this context, actors are always more than merely reproductive actors. They are "juggling a variety of interdependent concerns" as Anthony Carter puts it in his argument for a focus on agency in fertility studies (Carter 1995:78). Thus, fertility must be considered in its intersubjective embeddedness in order to elucidate its role within these concerns: We exist within intersubjective space and our actions and thoughts cannot be reduced to us alone (Crossley 1996a: 173). They are part of the games we play and the positions we hold – always in relation to others. Fertility is not an individual attribute; neither is life.

My work should be seen as a proposal for a much broader perspective on fertility, one that takes into account the fact that giving life (or not) to new human beings acquires meaning from life as already lived. However, life as lived is not discernible in demographic statistics. Statistical data are necessary and useful, since without measures of fertility or contraception we would remain ignorant of the trends and changes which need explaining (Säävälä 1999:297). But once questions are raised they need to be addressed by a "demography without numbers" that takes into account the multifaceted existential, cultural, medical, moral and political dilemmas (Scheper-Hughes 1997:219) which in life surround any demographic fact. For such a demography to exist, engaged immersion in the "lived phenomenological worlds of anthropology's subjects" is a prerequisite (ibid.:218). Without the contextually rich, life-mirroring approach of anthropology (Wolcott 1995:252) demographic transition cannot be fully comprehended.

A phenomenological perspective

My work has taken place within a highly politicised field. Women's situations and rights to reproductive health and citizenship have long been themes of vivid discussion, research and active, political engagement in Brazil, and I have often doubted whether I should be able to add anything to what had already been said and done. However, somewhere between all the ideas and the political discussions I found a raison d'être for an anthropology of "life as lived" (Paul Riesman cited in Jackson 1996:7) and set out to describe people I met as "going through life agonizing over decisions, making mistakes, trying to make themselves look good, enduring tragedies and personal losses, enjoying others, and finding moments of happiness" (Abu-Lughod 1991:158). This approach may not provide quick answers and may not be immediately translatable into political action, but it may allow us to see our truths from the perspective of the other and call us to ponder what life really *is* and should be about. At least, in this hope I wrote as I did.

I have positioned myself within anthropology by giving priority to lived experience. I have worked in a geographic and thematic field so vividly described by Nancy Scheper-Hughes in her famous book *Death Without Weeping* (1992). Yet one remarkable empirical change separates my work from hers: the recent decline in infant mortality in Northeast Brazil.[14] Scheper-Hughes worked in the shanty town Alto do Cruzeiro in a town in the interior of Pernambuco. On the Alto mothers had many children who died one after the other. Among the women I met most had only two or three children, and expected them to survive. Scheper-Hughes' argument is a materialist one: conditions for survival shape people's priorities in the sense that high infant mortality rates due to hunger and malnutrition influence mothers' attachment to their babies in a negative direction. And the other way around, when infant mortality and fertility rates are lowered, she argues, ideas about human life, the value of the individual, and therefore also the 'appropriate' maternal sentiments are affected and allow for a reproductive strategy based on heavy emotional and economic investment in few children from birth onward (ibid.: 401-2). The ideals about mothering that I have described (see Prologue) seem to echo Scheper-Hughes' argument. I do not say that parents have not always loved their children, but that the dominant discourse on 'love' seems to have changed. Parental aspirations, in the neighbourhood I came to know, had become a matter of good upbringing rather than bare survival, which among other things depended on mothers' capacity to show their children patience, attention and emotional support in addition to providing education and better life chances in general. However, the mothers in my study found it difficult to live up to these ideals due to the economic and emotional pressure they were under.

By focusing on the difficulties in conforming to ideals, the many contesting concerns, and the resultant compromises that people lived with, my work parts from Scheper-Hughes' in its analytical approach. Scheper-Hughes demonstrates how people in impoverished life circumstances are given means to cope with even the most unbearable experiences – be it the common use of 'nerve medicine' or narratives about infants who want to return to God. But in her focus on discourse and power she does not describe subjectively experienced dilemmas and failures to conform to ideals of behaviour. The mothers in her study seem to accept the culturally constructed truth; "angel-baby beliefs not only 'console' *moradores*" she writes, "they shape and determine the way death is experienced" (ibid.:423). In contrast, but not necessarily in dispute, my work emphasises the frustrations and sufferings related to the wish to conform and be acknowledged. I have described the women as active, doubting and self-conscious individuals, who may want to cry but choose to show anger, who may cry with one and laugh with another, or who may be deeply ambivalent about what to do. I argue that to perform in culturally prescribed ways is not always easy, but that people – each from their individual story – do their best in order not to have recognition withdrawn.[15]

It would be a mistake to see these mothers as passively adhering to cultural norms or submitting to social structures. Indeed, they perceived their maternal role in terms of culturally constructed ideas of femininity, and saw themselves as low status citizens, lacking the socially-distributed, status-giving signs but they were not passive victims. They sought ways to cope with the present constraints. Obtaining a sterilisation was not just habitual unreflective behaviour, but a meaningful act from beginning to end, motivated by the pursuit of a goal. The women strategised and manipulated in order to reach what they wanted. However, their choices and actions cannot be understood without the political and economic context of their lives.

I present my work as a combination of facts on societal structures, discussions on historical and political change, women's individual stories and my own personal impressions in an attempt to create an interplay between different ways to approximate understanding. One perspective cannot substitute the other; rather, they seem complementary, and I have painted my picture as generously as possible with the means at hand.

Telling stories

In my writing I have searched for a style of representation that could convey the sense of life as lived in its multifaceted and ever changing form. "The world is never something finished, something thought can bring to a close" (Jackson 1996:4), and the experiential base of knowledge in fieldwork-based writing challenges the way ethnography is represented. Writers are left with a lot of ambiguity to handle when experience has to be mediated by words. And as Susan Whyte notes: "If real life, practice, is not as clear cut as anthropological analysis makes it out to be, then we may need to find other ways of writing and analysing" (1997:226). Confronted with this need in the present work I have made extensive use of storytelling. I have told stories about the field and its persons and about particular moments during fieldwork, in which meaning was revealed to me in one way or another.

The use of stories is a representational means that allows ethnography to be specific and rich, and yet, at the same time, avoids the pitfall of objectification and definite truths. Through vivid descriptions of events as experienced by the fieldworker stories work as means of "cracking open the culture and the fieldworker's way of knowing it so that both can be jointly examined" (Van Maanen 1988:102). The intention is to reveal to the reader the experience from beginning to end, recalled with its details and puzzles not necessarily explained, in order for the reader to relive the experience with the teller and engage in the 'unpacking' of the hitherto unknown or strange (ibid.).

Naturally, the reader will never experience as the fieldworker did. To remember is a certain kind of experience consisting of selected impressions and distinguishable events, while actual experience is "a welter of sights, sounds, feelings, physical strains, expectations, and minute undeveloped reactions" (Langer 1953:263). A narrative of past events represents this sifted material of memory, as Susanne Langer puts it, with an intensity and a vividness that actual experience seldom has. Hence, through stories from the field the reader will not experience on equal terms as the fieldworker, but may by way of imagination share recalled impressions with the teller. In the best case a story provides the reader with a sense of "felt life" (ibid.:292). This sense emerges when that which is told resonates with the reader's own experience of what life can be. And it may transform that which is known into something understood.

Telling stories from the field is to, in no uncertain manner, renounce all claims to a single 'Truth' in the hope of communicating understanding. Positioning is a common condition for all anthropologists, but in the telling of stories this condition becomes crucial. There would be nothing to tell if somebody had not been somewhere with all her senses, feelings and thoughts. Not only do the field and its inhabitants exist for the reader, but also the person who saw it, the anthropologist, and the reader's task is to deduce the relationship between field, field-worker and text. The authority of the story depends on whether the reader accepts it as something that might have happened. It therefore has to strive towards literary standards such as verisimilitude, coherence, generosity, wisdom, honesty and respect which are different from the academic standards we usually apply to our work, but that does not make them second-rate; "when taken seriously, they may require even more from an ethnographer than those formulated by the profession" (Van Maanen 1988: 33). Besides, as Van Maanen points out, they are not exclusionary standards. Readers who read ethnography for pleasure and general knowledge are as able to judge whether they are achieved as those who read for professional reasons (ibid.). I found these considerations important, as I wanted to reach a broad audience and, in addition, wrote into a field, where many knew more than me about local conditions, though from different perspectives. I wanted my work to be convincing and honest in the understanding it conveys without hiding its limitations and necessary subjective basis.

Plan of work

My presentation will never be *the* truth, but hopefully a probable interpretation of what was at stake at a certain moment of history according to my experience. It is partial as ethnographic truths are inherently "committed and incomplete" (Clifford 1986:7); partiality, however, is not a reason for dismissing ethnography. Once accepted, as Clifford writes, and built into the ethnographic work it can in itself become "a source of representational tact" (ibid.: 7), and even the basis for a claim of validity (Sanjek 1990). In fact, ethnography gains validity through a thorough description of the "ethnographer's path" and through explicit accounts of choices made in the field and while writing up, whereby partiality is made transparent (ibid.).

Therefore, in Chapter Two the fieldwork behind this work and the circumstances under which it was done are discussed. The chapter includes an account of the methods used; these were qualitative interviews, surveys, observation at public hospitals and participation in daily life informed and substantiated by secondary sources. In this account I reflect particularly upon the data obtained from interviews, and the relationship between experience and speech that I had to consider after frustrating interview situations. I have written rather lengthily about my position in the field and my relation to the people I interviewed, as I see myself as an instrument in the anthropological process that has to be known by the reader in order to situate the work presented. In continuation, I discuss the particular problem of doing fieldwork under circumstances where status difference between researcher and informant may turn participation in the research project into a matter of prestige or fearful respect, and I consider my public image in the neighbourhood and the influence this may have had on some of the data I collected.

In Chapter Three, 'The Neighbourhood', I introduce the place where I lived and worked, referred to throughout this book as 'the neighbourhood'. It is portrayed as a lived unit structured by experiences of we-ness and otherness and surrounded by a larger world that is known mainly through TV. In this chapter I describe life in the family, the school and the church; the gossip that works as a socially levelling force and a means of negotiating inclusion or exclusion of female networks; and the individualisation of success (and failure) that fosters the nagging doubt whether one could have done better. Life in the neighbourhood is marked by unemployment and economic scarcity, which makes dominant ideals of masculine control hard to live up to.

The vulnerability of a man's reputation and the attempts to perform with masculine grace and generosity are described as prominent features in the neighbourhood.

In Chapter Four, 'Fertility and History', fertility is situated in relation to recent structural changes in Brazil described in the light of Foucault's notion of 'bio power'. Living conditions have changed considerably over the last four decades in Brazil; people have moved to the cities, paid work has replaced rural subsistence survival, and almost everybody has access to a television and the values diffused from better-off Brazilians to the rest of the society through this medium. Alongside all these changes fertility control has become the norm, which people strive to reach mainly through sterilisation. In order to better comprehend subjective experience, in this chapter I describe in detail the medicalisation of reproduction which has taken place in Brazil, with particular focus on the peculiar interlinkage between caesarean sections and female sterilisation practised in the country since the late 1970s. Local patterns of sterilisation are juxtaposed with individual women's contraceptive histories in order to exemplify common practices. Sterilised women's perceptions of their status as neither fertile nor sterile are also examined through an exploration of the use of the word *esterilização*. I conclude by proposing that women through their acceptance of the role of compliant patient have acquired the means to think about and act upon their lives in ways that men do not share.

In Chapter Five, 'Fertility and Recognition', I look into the symbolic construction of the 'second-class citizen' that motivates poor Brazilians to change their lives and, for women, their bodies. The chapter begins with a discussion of recognition as a common human need based on Hegel's early writings. According to Hegel, the subject becomes a subject for itself only when it exists for another, a notion that is paralleled among others by Merleau-Ponty's discussion of the mirror stage, James' notion of the 'social self' and Mead's division of the self into 'I' and 'me'. I argue that people's sense of inferiority springs from the image of themselves that they meet in public life, here primarily described in terms of consumption and medical health care. This inferiority is perceived as integral to the whole person including the physical body. Bodies are therefore targets of change in a search for recognition. As a metaphor for embodied selves, the construction of better houses comes into focus in this discussion and I conclude that sterilisation has become yet another metaphor in the struggle for recognition – a sign of control.

In Chapter Six, 'Fertility and Home', I argue that women's decisions for or against sterilisation have to be seen as results of a constant search for balance in the pushes and pulls of daily relations, among which some carry more weight than others. I describe the women as particularly attached to their mothers, children and husbands, all problematic relations full of contradictory expectations. I employ Mead's image of the 'game' to describe women's involvement in the shared worlds of 'mothers' and 'wives', worlds wherein values and expectations arise. I also use Schutz' hierarchies of projects to explain how choices are made on different levels of urgency and importance. Entangled in all these relationships the women weigh one compromise against another in their striving towards the recognition, autonomy and intimacy they want in their lives. Within the multiple concerns in each woman's life sterilisation proves to be empowering, as through the change of her body she become less subject to the dependence associated with fertility. However, it does not grant her the intimacy she longs for.

I conclude with a summary of the discussion of women's motives for sterilisation as I have seen them, arising from the need to be of value in others' eyes. Bringing together Foucault and Merleau-Ponty I argue for a synthesis of agency and structure in which the notion of recognition constitutes a key element. I discuss the often criticised notion of rational choice within traditional demographic theory and argue that the rationality at play in women's choices and actions *was* rational insofar as it provided a sense of sufficiency in the present and banished uncertainty from the future. The life I describe is full of worry and doubt and not at all controllable. The unpredictability impelled some women to get themselves sterilised, while simultaneously, it baffled others' plans to do the same. I see the significance of my work in its attempt to establish a respect for agency under harsh conditions. The longing I describe does not represent a conscious political stand, but it constitutes a potential for change, when recognised by others and the women themselves. To the extent my work can further such recognition it has fulfilled its purpose.

Chapter Two

The Fieldwork

> *The art of fieldwork is achieved to the extent a field-worker is able to render from research-oriented personal experience an account that offers to a discerning audience a level of insight and understanding into human social life that exceeds whatever might be achieved through attention solely to gathering and reporting data.*
>
> *(Wolcott 1995:251)*

My fieldwork bears witness to the truism that anthropological field-work is often a process of "playing things by ear" (Crick 1989:25). From the very beginning events surprised me, turning out differently to what I had expected, demanding adjustments. I had planned a study of the social context and consequences of the prevalent use of caesarean sections combined with sterilisation in Brazil. However, coming to Brazil in order to prepare for the fieldwork I realised that several research projects on either caesarean sections or sterilisation, even though mainly from a medical point of view, had already been done (though not yet internationally published) or were still in process. This new knowledge forced me to be much more specific in my focus and I chose to concentrate on caesarean sections and the actual experience of giving birth, which complemented a fieldwork I had formerly done in Denmark. As I had already made research arrangements in Recife, I kept my focus on lower income women in that region. However, I found that my expectations made me seek answers in the wrong direction. The women I had interviewed in Denmark had focused on the moment of childbirth as a particular, symbolically meaningful and intense moment in life, central to and embodying their notions of a kind of true, natural femininity. In Brazil a critique, mainly from politically active middle class women, opposed Brazilian obstetrical practice based on technology and medical control in similar terms. Besides arguments on mortality and morbidity this discourse focused on the respect for the individual woman passing through an important moment of her life. However, the focus on birth as significant in itself was not part of women's reflections in the neighbourhood I came to know. I returned home after seven months with lots of interviews stating that what was important in a delivery was the possibility of obtaining a sterilisation at the same time and the avoidance of patronising attitudes in hospital staff. These statements did not contradict the efforts to improve delivery practices, but did nevertheless make me want to change my focus.

When I returned to the field almost a year later I had decided to follow up on these two issues – of patronising attitudes and the wish for sterilisation. What I had learned the year before would now contextualise these particular aspirations of the women. With these decisions I felt much more determined and eager to achieve results, as time in the field was short and the day of reckoning near. This second fieldwork became a combination of focused research (structured interviews and a survey) and social relations that took me in different and often unexpected directions. What dominated the period for me were the violent events that took place in the neighbourhood (see Prologue). People I used to share my days with had to move, and I realised that everything I had learned till then had to be understood within this context of violence and fear. The sterilisation that I focused so hard on emerged to be a crucial, but in itself rapidly passed step in a search for recognition under circumstances I had not comprehended till then.

After the fieldwork a long period of anxious search for the central argument of my writing followed. Texts were written, discarded or put aside as 'not really it'. Not before I committed myself to write a paper on the women's struggle for social recognition, did I feel the nearness of the pain that made the rest of their stories vibrant – the joys, the hard days, and the endless monotony of empty refrigerators

Map 1. Metropolitan region of Recife (Source: Alheiros in Observatório PE 2002)

and nowhere to go. Looking back on my fieldwork with this plot in mind, 'data' appeared that I had previously considered irrelevant, and experiences lined up in stories to be told. It was as Inger Sjørslev writes: the methodological process does not end with fieldwork because only when the working up of the text is well in hand does the anthropologist know which events in the field were important and which were not (Sjørslev 1995). Writing on the process of fieldwork thus includes constructing a narrative that out of the mass of 'life' appears as an ordered, meaningful universe; perceptual experience is structured, memory organised, and 'events' distinguished and made purposeful, as in the narratives we tell of our personal lives (Bruner 1987:15).

This chapter is a look into my doings, thoughts and feelings in the field, told as if I had a choice, as if what happened was not necessary, but could have been done differently. As with any narrative it gives meaning to the past as well as to the present: a desk full of disorderly stacks of books and papers, my computer, and a half-finished cup of cold tea.

Entering the field

Located 14 kilometres from the centre of Recife Camaragibe is part of the so-called metropolitan region of the city. Its geographical location makes it seem like a suburb, while in fact it is an independent municipality with its own political orientation, created as recently as 1982 until when it formed part of the neighbouring municipality São Lourenço da Mata. In 1996 Camaragibe covered 52.9 square kilometres of land with a population of approximately 120,000 individuals (*Secretaria de Planejamento* 1997). I settled near one of the local health posts, and the 'neighbourhood', which I will describe further on, is the area covered by this health post. Around 1500 families live in this area. However, my activities were mainly centred around the place where I lived, which was both near the main road with all its shops and bars and traffic, and close to the 'invasion', the squatter area that constituted the 'margin' of proper 'respectable' family dwellings.

Memories of an arrival

I rode with Josenita the long way from the centre of Recife to Camaragibe. I had met her more or less by accident at a moment of almost
desperate lament about my lack of a 'home' in the big, noisy and dirty
city. Where was I to do my fieldwork? Where was that friendly and
accessible spot on earth where I would live with my husband and our
two children? She invited me to her place and we set out to find a bus.
Waiting in the shadow of the bus stop, all sweaty and already worried about how I should find my way back in the imminent darkness,
I listened absent-mindedly to her description – that Camaragibe was
a municipality next to Recife, that it formed part of the 'metropolitan
region' of the city, that it was governed by the socialist party PT (*Partia
dos Trabalhadores*), and that the *movimento popular* therefore was
actively engaged in local politics. She also told me that she was a lesbian
and considered herself part of the *movimento*. Only half listening to
all this I did not even think about the fact that being introduced to
the area by her put me in a particular position. However, in the dense
web of relations that I entered on this very afternoon, the position as
'Nitas friend' became my initial point of identification.

We drove along the Avenida Caxangá. The bus was yellow and
white with big red letters operated by the company 'Metropolitana'
that runs several lines to Camaragibe and further on: 'Camaragibe-
Derby', 'São Lourenço', 'Alberto Maia', 'Parque Carpiberibe', with
different prices according to the extension of the line. I would soon
acquire the skill of getting around on the cheaper lines, sometimes
frustrated finding myself letting buses pass, as the ticket would be
'expensive', even though I was in a hurry and the difference in price
meant practically nothing to me. Strange situations that arose when
my Danish rationales blended with habits acquired in the field, two
different logics belonging to two very different worlds, but both in
one person.

We passed the Rio Carpiberibe, upon which people have built sheds
on poles although they know that every once in a while the water in
the river rises and sweeps away everything; passed by the place where
they sell big turquoise blue tanks for swimming pools. And then
passed the big, modern hospital Barão de Lucena in front of which

coffee, sweets, soap and other necessities were sold in the stalls under the burning sun; passed the *Bompreço*, the big supermarket where everything can be bought, then all the undertakers, where coffins of all sizes are exhibited almost on the pavement. Seeing the small coffins for babies made me remember that I had entered Nancy Scheper-Hughes' research field – "the land of sugar and sweetness but also of leather and darkness" that she described in *Death without Weeping* (1992). At that time I still considered my project very different from hers. It wasn't till much later that I would realise how closely related my empirical findings would be to hers. Brazil has changed, is still changing, but everyday life seems to have its own inertia. The strange contradicting simultaneity of vulnerability and viability that she described would be what I, too, would have to give life to in my writing.

We continued on our journey. People gradually left the bus and we got a seat. The landscape became greener with palm trees, bushes, flowers. No apartment blocks, no big supermarkets. But road work; the traffic had no space to move in any direction and we had to stop. A bus gets terribly hot when it is standing still and fresh air does not enter the windows.

Passing through the centre of commerce of Camaragibe we saw people everywhere. Brown skinned in varying degrees. Shopping, selling vegetables, waiting for the bus. Almost a crowd. Stores selling everything from clothes and groceries to cement and chickens. Pharmacies, video distributors and bars. Whenever we stopped there would be a lot of white Volkswagen mini buses coming and going. These are the *kombis* – privately owned unauthorised mini buses that drive from bus stop to bus stop at a lower price and a hazardous speed. Old women and men, young timid girls, mothers with babies, men returning from work, boys, lots of bags and boxes. Sometimes a man would pass on a horse. There was certainly an atmosphere of new settlers' life in this place.

We left the bus right in front of the greengrocer's. The smell of decaying fruit met us: beautiful, sensual mangoes gone a bit off in the heat. The smell blended with the smoke from the bus as it went off. We passed the road and headed for Josenita's house. There were people everywhere. Sitting outside the house talking. Going to and from the shops at the road. Plastic bags full of sugar, cuscuz, eggs, coffee and these white loaves of bread that somehow never really fill the stomach. Children playing. Small sheds where sweets were sold. Or vegetables or cakes. Three women around the public telephone. A group of people with hymn books and serious faces on their way to the evangelical church. Always somebody saying: "Oí, Nita!" She often stopped to talk to people, and coming from the bus to her house was a long process. There she was – 'Nita' at her own place.

When we finally reached Josenita's house she handed me a towel, a yellow cotton dress and a pair of plastic slippers and showed me how to take a shower with the water in the bucket. I did as told and showed up some minutes later in my Camaragibean outfit. Tall, pale and strange in these surroundings. I think it was while we sat in the night talking with her friend Sonia that I decided to stay.

At home
Fieldwork is a process from 'here' to 'there'. From 'home' to 'not-home' in the initial phase, but as the process progresses, from 'not-home' to 'home' in a new setting. I sometimes miss the feeling of competency that I acquired in Camaragibe. The satisfaction when I knew how to do things that had once been out of my reach. I experienced a competency in relation to small, daily tasks, that in my Danish everyday life I would habitually do without even registering them. After some weeks I found myself knowing how to approach the gate of a house – clapping my hands loudly and firmly without entering the gate, as a sign of respectful approach, but also because there could be a dog on the other side. I learned how to behave in the bus on the long and hot way to the city of Recife: when sitting, asking people if I should take care of their bag, when standing letting people hold my bag without fearing robbery. I learned how to do the dishes with very little water, pouring it from one pot to another. How to boil *macaxeira* and how to know when the *maracujá* fruit was ripe. I learned how to find my way in the area and settle somewhere in a kitchen or the shade of a house for a small talk or two. And I almost learned how to leave in time, before people got tired of my company, though that was a difficult bit.

My new 'home' was not yet entirely familiar, unlike my Danish home. With the appreciation of my own competence followed the realisation that I was still aware of these actions being new to me. And I was to recognise afresh that being in-between worlds can be a revealing experience for which one cannot help feeling a certain gratitude. As Merleau-Ponty says, we cannot experience ourselves without culture, in a cultural vacuum so to say (Crossley 1995:56), but in the transition from one set of cultural habits to another, we have a chance to see our habituatedness as a shared human condition. It is the experience of this sharing of the common condition of existence that is the ground from which anthropology gains its particular strength (Ardener 1989). It is not by *being* like the other, but by opening oneself to the existence of a different human being that understanding is arrived at. And it seems that in a moment like that a true relationship can be felt. As Edwin Ardener writes: "The human universal lies in the capacity of both sides to gain that experience" (1989:184).

I find that such moments make long term fieldwork worthwhile. Somewhere in between all the practical problems, the boring days and all the embarrassing failures these revealing experiences give meaning to all the mess without which they would not have occurred. At least this is what we as anthropologists believe, and why we still consider fieldwork essential for our production even though out of time with dominant values. As Wolcott writes: "It is fieldwork's time-consuming, slowly focusing, sometimes convoluted and inefficient but always contextually rich, life-mirroring approach that needs to be protected in our age of efficient anxiety" (1995:252).

Since my initial exploratory visit to the neighbourhood I worked in Camaragibe for a total of ten and a half months, seven months in 1997, when I lived in a rented house in the neighbourhood, and three and a half months in 1998, living partly in Recife and partly in Josenita's house. During the first period, my husband and our two children (at that time 4 and 8 years old) were with me for three months. During the second period they shared one and a half months of Northeast Brazilian summer with me. Through the whole process Josenita worked for me as a paid assistant. Others have helped me, too, but I could not have done what I did without the help of Josenita.

The methods

The health post in the neighbourhood was part of the Family Health Programme initiated by the municipality in 1994. At the health post itself were a medical doctor, a nurse, an assistant nurse and an assistant of 'general service' who worked in the reception. Working at the health post were also 11 *agentes de saúde* (ACSs), minimally trained primary health workers, who visited every family in the area once a month, except for families with newborn babies; these were visited once a week. They passed by the houses, called forth whoever was at home, asked about health problems, made sure that cures were followed up, children taken for regular exams and vaccinations at the health post, and that pregnant women had their antenatal care at the post or a hospital.

After having settled in the area I contacted the health post assuming that through the ACSs I could achieve a perfect entry into my field. I was allowed to follow them on their daily rounds. All ACSs were women who lived in the neighbourhood.[1] Thus, walking around with one of the ACSs also meant visiting her neighbours and friends and listening to the gossip and news they exchanged with one another. The ACSs certainly knew what was going on; conversations with them while walking along were therefore always interesting and instructive. I did not find any formal distance between an ACS and 'her' families. People would stop her on the road, or pass by her house to seek advice and she would ask somebody nearby whenever a women she went to meet was not at home. However, I never heard any ACS pass on what I would consider intimate information, and I appreciated the respect for the individual's privacy that they exercised in spite of difficult conditions.

Through the ACSs I contacted the first women for interviews. I searched for pregnant women in order to follow their expectations and experiences through pregnancy and delivery, and interviewed 12 pregnant women either two or three times, preferably both before and after giving birth. Two of these women were Carmen and Luzia, who became central figures in my fieldwork. In these interviews I worked without a fixed question guide but with some central questions from which the conversations developed. Six older women were interviewed

Agentes de saúde (ACSs), January 2000

too (among these were Ana and Dona Lívia) as were some of my personal contacts, be they friends, neighbours or other acquaintances (including Sonia and Neide, among others). Pedro Nascimento, who at that time was a student of anthropology at the Federal University of Pernambuco, worked with me for a while as an assistant. He interviewed husbands of my informants in order to enrich my data with a male point of view (5 men, 1-2 hours each). Besides these interviews Josenita and I conducted a descriptive survey among 192 mothers who had given birth within the latest two years (210 births as some had two children within the period). These women were visited once with a questionnaire (1/2 – 1 hour interview) mainly by Josenita but the first 20 also by me. I visited three public hospitals (spending two full days at each) in order to observe the praxis of birth giving (in total 3 caesareans, 6 normal births and many women in labour). Besides this, I went with Luzia for antenatal examinations at the health post and accompanied her at the hospital when she gave birth.

When I returned to the neighbourhood for my second fieldwork in 1998 I had decided to add more data on sterilisation to the material I had already collected, specifically focusing on how women obtained the operations, and what the sterilisation pattern looked like when seen across generations. Josenita and I therefore conducted structured interviews with survey respondents whom we had previously registered as sterilised (28 women). Besides these structured interviews, we also sought, through word of mouth, women sterilised recently who were either particularly young (so as to know their motives and life circumstances) or who had had the surgery through the help of a political candidate (to know how it came about). Secondly, with the help of the ACSs I collected data on age, number of children, and sterilisation status for 1762 women in the area in order to assert the prevalence of sterilisation in general and across generations. In between these activities I did a few interviews with relevant health care providers: the doctor and the nurse at the health post, the gynaecologist (and vice mayor) Dr. Nadegi and a gynaecologist, Dr. Olímpio, from one of the public hospitals, who had been authorised to provide sterilisations.

We arranged two evening meetings at one of the schools in order to discuss some of my immediate findings with the women. I learned much from these rather improvised meetings, mainly because nobody mentioned their problems on these occasions. What was put forth in response to my interpretations were the 'nice stories', as Sonia said. She, who knew the troubles behind the surface, could hardly bear to listen. I, on the other hand, found it interesting to learn how things were presented in a public forum, as I most often talked with the women face to face and more informally.

In the following pages I will reflect more on the applied methods, as I find that each fieldwork context poses specific, though comparable, challenges for the researcher. I will therefore present some of the questions, barriers and openings that I found in mine.

Interviewing
I did my interviews with the use of a small tape recorder. In the beginning my Portuguese was simple and listening to the tapes after the interviews helped me. What I did not understand at the moment of talking I could afterwards return to, assisted by a dictionary or Josenita. However, as my language skills soon improved the tape recording's main function became the collection of data. I have found

this way of working in the field appropriate. Sitting calmly with just one or two persons and without the need of taking notes allowed me to understand more. In addition, a tape recorder reminds the informant of the situation being 'under research' and I seldom found that it hindered a good conversation – rather on the contrary.

In her essay 'Is Ethical Research Possible?' Daphne Patai writes about conducting interviews in Brazil: "I was surprised, in Brazil, that virtually everyone I approached was willing, even eager, to talk to me, and by the time I had completed several dozen long interviews I became convinced that not enough people are listening, and that the opportunity to talk about one's life, to reflect on its shapes and patterns, to make sense of it to oneself and to another human being, was an intrinsically valuable experience" (Patai 1991:142). Patai's conviction resonates well with my own reflections on interviewing women in Camaragibe. I often felt I met an immense hunger for attention, a need for a listener. To listen and ask a few questions here and there, while the women spoke, became my role in many of the interviews. Initially I found it an appropriate way to learn about everyday life.

I later became aware of what at that time I perceived as a lack of authenticity in the women's narratives. Too often I found myself sitting estranged in front of a person who talked and talked without seeming to be herself directly engaged in what she said. Many notes in my diary are complaints about this seemingly superficial way of talking: a combination of indignation and flimsy hope, while I felt that what she was talking about demanded greater gravity. Halfway through fieldwork I saw these endless flows of words as a methodological problem and concluded that I had to learn to interrupt, change subject or challenge viewpoints.

Maybe I learned, maybe I just learned to listen differently. I became aware of moments containing a different quality in the flow of almost mechanical repetition. As on the day when I visited a young woman who had just lost her baby in birth three days before. She was 18 years old and lived in her mother's house. I started my tape recorder and the woman and her mother explained what had happened. The mother, especially, talked with indignation about the doctors, who were to blame for the death: "They killed my granddaughter and they wouldn't even let us bury her" she said, explaining to me how the staff had hesitated to hand over the dead body to the family while the young woman had to stay on in the hospital for a few more days. The young woman continued after her mother in the indignant tone of voice I had heard so often before. I taped it all, but felt that it was strangely irrelevant to me except for the information in itself; there seemed to be a discrepancy between the way the story was told and the loss and pain they told me about. I did not understand that what was absent, perhaps more in tone than in words, could not be expressed differently. In a moment's silence I became aware of milk seeping out of the young woman's breast. She saw it, looked up into my eyes and said in a low voice with a sudden despair: "And what do I do with this?"

There were feelings that due to their weight and importance for the individual could not be talked about, people just had to cope with them. Irene and I visited a young mother who had two sons, was sterilised, extremely poor and living with a man who beat her regularly. I was shocked by the misery, and after having noted down the story about her early sterilisation, I asked her if she had anybody she could talk with. She just shook her head. I could do nothing except engage in the jokes and the laughter when we left and thank her for having helped me with my research. She had her life, and it was as it was. Why should she share her pain with me?

I learned to be less attentive to words and more attentive to intentions (Wikan 1992). People certainly talked a lot in order to make sense of their lives. It seemed to be as Michael Jackson writes that retelling one's experiences in the presence of others is a way of renegotiating retrospectively one's relation with others (Jackson 1998:23). Through a reconstruction of the past they tried to change the present. They resisted feeling weak and defeated through the indignant complaints about others' ignorance and through their dreams about the future. The pain they were up against was often only discernible in a movement of a hand, a sudden silence or other small signs. I did not notice them in the beginning, but in the end my days were full of these observations.

Unni Wikan writes of the importance of "going beyond words and expressions as well: not in the literal sense of reading deeper meanings into surface behaviour, but to attend to the concerns and intentions from which they emanate" (Wikan 1992:477). Merleau-Ponty puts it differently: "Our view of man will remain superficial so long as we fail to go back to that origin, so long as we fail to find, beneath the chatter of words, the primordial silence, and as long as we do not describe the action which breaks this silence. The spoken word is a gesture, and its meaning, a world" (Merleau-Ponty 1962:184). Both suggest that there is no deeper private or superior world "beyond words" or "beneath the chatter", but that intention and gesture are simultaneous in our relation to the world. In this simultaneity emotion is always implied as a tone or mood, or, in line with Merleau-Ponty, as "a way of being in relation to the world" manifested in all our perceptions, doings and sayings (Crossley 1996a:45-46).

When I 'listened to emotions' I did not search for nor find any private inner worlds. What was apparent was exactly the "situated corporeal attitude" or the "embodied thought" (Rosaldo 1983:143); the communication of social relatedness through the body in which dark eyes or trembling hands expressed what words could not say, while equally indignation or laughter was a resistance to the feeling of weakness. Like Margot Lyon I understand emotional behaviour to be, though a truly embodied phenomenon, yet always relative to another person and comprehensible only in its social context (Lyon 1995:257). I therefore searched in social relations for answers to the questions these emotional expressions (oscillating between weakness and indignation) posed to me. Empathy in itself did not seem to suffice. As John Leavitt writes, empathic recognition is part of human interaction, but rather than being an end to understanding it is the beginning of a search (Leavitt 1996:530). I searched, asked my questions, looked for similarities and differences, and thereby tried to understand what was conveyed to me.

My interview material is a mixture of those of a more superficial character meant to provide facts about one subject or another, others where I have been given some hints to contextualise what is said, and interviews that for some reason or other became a meeting between the two of us, where understanding seemed to arise immediately out of interaction. Some of these interviews are rather taped conversations between a friend and me. I used to talk with, especially, Sonia, Irene, Neide and Josenita about things I did not understand, and they were always willing to explain. When I drew forth the tape recorder from my crumpled supermarket plastic bag, they would say "Oh, that Lini!" and continue the explanation.

Working with surveys

I planned to use quantitative data in my study in order to achieve an overall view of women's reproductive lives. Knowing the number of caesarean deliveries from the area, the prevalence of deliveries performed at private clinics, the general use of different contraceptive methods and other related information would make it possible to situate my field in relation to statistics on Brazil and Northeast Brazil in general.

The first survey consisted of 100 questions about the women's last birth, socio-economic situation and reproductive history. From the health post we obtained names and addresses of all women who were registered as having given birth within the latest two years (192 in total). We began after a small pilot study on 20 women which we did together. Each interview lasted more or less half an hour. Josenita conducted the interviews after the initial phase and for some weeks we met at night and discussed her findings of the day. Some of the data became part of the fundamental knowledge on which the analysis presented in this book is built, some turned out to be irrelevant as my study developed. Most importantly, though, Josenita's participation in my research added, more than information, perspectives and depth.

The following year we conducted a simpler survey with the help of the ACSs authorised by the Municipal Secretary of Health. I provided the ACSs with a questionnaire with five questions to be answered by every woman over 12 years of age: her age, number of children, sterilisation status (yes or no) and in case of affirmation, her age at sterilisation and the type of birth with which she delivered her last child.[2] Out of the 1500 houses of the area our sample of 1762 women does not include all houses. Some houses (2-10 per ACS) were only inhabited by men; some were empty (especially due to the violent events which at that time made many people move out); and some were for one reason or another not visited, either because nobody was at home at the time, or the family did not accept visits from the ACS.[3] Sometimes the ACS forgot a house or registered it wrongly.[4] In total 1130 houses were included in the final material.

This survey provided useful information, though the process was not perfect. There were some problems in having the ACSs do the survey[5] and ethical considerations in relation to informed consent that I had not thought through properly.[6] As the information was not at all private in the neighbourhood (though it would certainly have been so in a Danish setting), and as the ACSs usually note many different kinds of information when visiting the families, my efforts to keep up at least some level of research ethics seemed superfluous, unpractical and rather hysterical in the context. However, we worked upon it, and some of the results will be presented in this work.

In their article 'Combining Qualitative and Quantitative Research in Fortaleza' Kerndall et al. advocate for a dialogue between qualitative and quantitative research as a way to craft a "pluralistic approach which juxtaposes different orders of knowledge in a self-critical environment of an engaged researcher" (Kendall et al. 1999:18). Their point of departure is the quantitative research method. From this position they conclude that qualitative methods provide insights that cannot be reached differently, but that these methods contributed relatively little to the direction of their research programme even though supporting and deepening insights. Read in reverse it approximates my conclusion: the kind of knowledge I have gained through the statistical information was not otherwise obtainable. It has justified some conclusions and led to further investigation of others. We saw the pattern of caesarean sections and sterilisations in the neighbourhood, got a general overview of living conditions, and, what I particularly appreciated, a perspective on childbearing over time.[7]

Observations at hospitals
I made observations at two big hospitals in Recife and at the local hospital, Hospital Geral de Camaragibe, in order to understand first hand what I was told in the neighbourhood, and perhaps to be more alert to what I was not told, to read between the lines. I gained access to these hospitals through the directors, and was free to move around in the maternity wards. I talked with some nurses at each place, and with women in labour or resting after the delivery, holding a hand or bringing a towel. As I had not asked for permission to interview doctors, nurses or patients, and as I felt myself in an awkward position, I

only asked a little here and there, whenever there was a pause. There-fore, I could not always judge if what I presumed, was actually taking place. Did the birth attendants really feel disgust at the women's rough feet, so used to walking without shoes, and now dangling strangely from the stirrups of the delivery table? And did the women really feel humiliated by the birth attendants' conversations on mobile phones right in front of their torn genitals waiting to be sewed?

What I saw was not necessarily what they felt. I know from what I heard in the neighbourhood that women dreaded the hard pressure down upon the belly meant to force the baby out,[8] and of course I did not doubt their screams to be utterances of real pain. And I know that they experienced some doctors to be very haughty. Therefore, when an obstetrician during a delivery was highly preoccupied with a few drops of blood that spotted his perfectly white trousers, I interpreted it as an example of arrogance and neglect. However, I was probably shocked by things that Brazilian women took for granted.

I accompanied my friend Luzia when she went for her antenatal visits at the health post and when she gave birth at the local hospital. Only in her case did I have the possibility of comparing observation with narrative. I learned through this that a narrative is more than recounting what actually happened; it is a way to create sense out of situations (Mattingly 1994:812) and, as in Luzia's case, to regain some control over distorting experiences (Jackson 1998:23). However, this inconsistency is surely informative, and I wish I had more data of that kind.

Being a participant

In retrospect 'doing research' became too time consuming, when measured by the insights I gained by running so busily around. On January 5 1999 I wrote in my diary: "I saw myself entering Josenita's house in a hurry, delivering a message about the work for tomorrow, while picking up my bag in order to run quickly to the bus. Josenita and Jocias sat in her rocking chairs. Legs up. Chatting. The crickets playing their music; the mosquitoes out for the night. The streetlights were on. People sat outside their houses calmly talking. Small boys playing football. And me running through it all. I felt like I'd arrived from Mars. A structured, focused life form meeting a fluid way of living."

I was often caught by the wish to be productive, but I might have learned more from taking it easier. However, the research activities served as a reason for being in the neighbourhood, and a whole life unfolded around them. I soon got to know people, with whom I liked to share some time every day. In addition I had my middle class friends in Recife, where I found rescue when rest was needed, and my friends at the women's organisation SOS Corpo, where I often visited the library, sought advice or just passed by in order to pick up e-mails. After some time I developed more 'professional contacts'. I got to know Parry Scott, associate professor at the Department of Anthropology at the Federal University of Pernambuco, and I attended the seminars of his study group *Família e Gênero* (Family and Gender). I also took part in seminars arranged by the university and NGOs, mainly on women's health and related topics. And I went to the cinema, restaurants or the beach, whenever family life, friendship or fieldwork despair required it.

Besides the more or less structured attempts to collect data, I think I learned as much by living in the middle of everyday happenings. Disturbed, confused, sweating and tired, but often quite happy.

My position in the field

As Richard Shweder states, "the really real truth for us mortal beings is that we can never be everywhere at once (even in a global mind), any more than we can be nowhere in particular." We are always somewhere perceiving the world from a particular position and giving expression to a particular and necessarily incomplete worldview (1991:18-19). When this is taken into account we may escape objectifying the other (Abu-Lughod 1993:15), we may gain some accountability (Sanjek 1990), and by joining other partial views we may find a larger vision through "the connections and unexpected openings situated knowledges make possible" (Haraway 1991:196). For the anthropologist reflecting on her fieldwork, the crucial question will therefore be: which position was mine while collecting my data? And next: how did that position allow or hinder my understanding of the field?

A researcher

I came to the field as a researcher. In preparation for my work I had made contact with the women's organisation and research centre SOS Corpo in Recife, while still in Denmark. Betania Ávila, who heads SOS Corpo and is a well known Brazilian feminist, became my contact person. Betania introduced me to Josenita as a researcher associated with the centre. Josenita introduced me to whoever we met thereafter on equal terms. She would often explain to the women we contacted that my work was partly for the University of Copenhagen and partly for the women's movement, thereby positioning me as well as herself. I found that she always used the moment to emphasise the importance of the women's movement, and I willingly accepted being part of her project as she was part of mine. However, when I introduced myself, I would explain my research in terms of understanding: that as a researcher I was interested in ways of living so different from life in Denmark. I used to mention that both caesareans and sterilisations were rare in Denmark, and that I myself had tried neither. I never expressed moral considerations against these procedures, but due to my many questions and the association with the women's movement I sometimes found myself positioned as sceptical.

The women generally seemed interested in contributing to my research. It seemed as though being seen as interesting by a researcher lead to reflections on their life that they seldom had opportunity to develop. After filling out the questionnaire Josenita always asked for the opinion of the interviewed. "How did you find this interview" she would say. In the beginning I found it a rather artificial procedure, later I began to respect the manner in which she tried to teach both me and the respondent that we were equals and both had the right to give and take, and finally I found the women's replies revealing. Most said that being interviewed was interesting, but remarkably many also saw it as an opportunity to learn. "It is always good to learn something new" as one woman said. I discussed it with Josenita and we both thought it most probable that the interview offered the woman a rare opportunity for reflection. However, we were not the only ones to highlight their reproductive life; at hospital or the health post for antenatal examinations or cancer prevention they would be asked much the same questions, but I think that it was the open and interested attitude more than the theme of our interviews that was instructive. Or perhaps a combination of the two.

My role as a researcher was further strengthened when I began to join seminars and meetings at the university. Likewise, Pedro's introduction to the area as 'my colleague from the university' associated me with the local academic world.[9]

A friend

Besides being a foreign researcher I entered the field, as described earlier, as 'Nitas friend'. Josenita was an ambiguous figure in the social landscape, much discussed, but highly respected. She once started a day care centre for children; she had also been an ACS and helped many in their problematic dealings with authorities. She had even been a political candidate, but though she distributed lots of powdered milk (I always forgot to ask how she got hold of it), only a few friends voted for her. She was crazy, people said, *doida*. She had epilepsy and she talked too much about the things that should not be talked about and in the wrong places. On top of all this she was known to be a lesbian.[10] To me she was an excellent assistant and friend. Apart from knowing the area very well she had a certain flair for political life, and, at her best, had an outstanding tact in personal relations. In addition, she helped me by conducting some of the interviews on her own. Having been with me initially as a facilitator and interpreter (interpreting my Portuguese into something more understandable), she had learned what kind of questions to ask.

However, Josenita had her alliances and enemies and I had to be aware of establishing my independence in relation to her. I felt that she was somewhat possessive about me, but finding my informants through the health post ultimately gave me access to social relations that criss-crossed a variety of social networks. In addition I became friendly with a person that Josenita did not like, which definitively manifested my independence. I found that everybody was interested in talking with me and was pleased but soon exhausted. One day I suddenly found myself complaining about all these people who just wanted to use me, with all their nice words and smiling faces. They just wanted to borrow money that they would never return. Or they would try to become my 'best friend' knowing that I would one day leave my house and then 'Who was going to have all my belongings?' a question I had to answer many times. I remember telling my husband that I felt myself caught up in falseness. I was sick and tired of the demanding web of relations in which I was entangled. But being in the midst of it without an exit I had to search for a different attitude.

Conscience is such a strange factor in human life. It takes time for pondering, reflection and settling. In my Danish everyday life things happen quickly and according to well established habits and I seldom let in questions, but in Brazil I suddenly felt the need to listen to that inner voice in order to find a direction for my life in this morass of social relations. Questions popped up: Who was false? Did I myself not establish relationships just in order to get some rich fieldnotes? Who was using whom? Were they not right to profit in whatever way possible from my intrusion into their lives? Without at that time putting it into words, social relationships changed for me from being matters of morality and thought into lived manifestations of a general human condition. Accepting the fact that we all fulfil our needs by using others, in the field as well as at home, I continued to struggle to find my way, but I no longer felt misused. Neither did I feel that I misused anybody. I began to enjoy the friendships that some of my informants offered me with all the doubts and misunderstandings that this included.[11] I came upon the truth of the simple fact that to be useful to others is a meaningful part of life. How could I have forgotten it?

Exploitation?
However, one could easily argue that considering any of these rela-tionships a friendship would be false. Underneath or within each of them there was always this dissonance, this knowledge that I was rich and would only stay for a short time. It was very evident when on rare occasions I returned home in a taxi with my family or walked up the lane with plastic bags full of exotic goods from the supermarket in Recife with which to feed my choosy children. It was more easily forgotten when I lived alone and could more convincingly play my fictitious role as 'one of them'. As Clifford Geertz puts it: "Usually the sense of being members, however temporarily, insecurely, and incompletely, of a single moral community, can be maintained even

in the face of wider social realities which press in at almost every moment to deny it. It is fiction – fiction, not falsehood – that lies at the very heart of successful anthropological field research. However, the fiction is never completely convincing for any of the participants: at one point or another it will reveal its true self" (Geertz 1968 cited in Ridler 1996:245).

Therefore, calling some of my relationships friendships makes me vulnerable to accusations of 'romanticism', or even exploitation, as intimacy may just as well deepen the symbolic violence inherent in any fieldwork (Hastrup 1995:142).[12] As Daphne Patai writes, inequality and potential treacherousness in the relationship between researcher and research subject is inescapable, as the former can leave the field much freer than the latter, without leaving any intimate revelations behind in exchange for the 'data' she carries away with her (Patai 1991: 142). This inequality may be even more profound when status difference makes participation in the research project a matter of prestige or fearful respect. So-called informants may enter relationships with the ambiguous 'fieldworker friend', without truly knowing in which project and especially to which degree they participate. The attention and "comparatively non-judgemental acceptance" (Stacey 1991:117) that fieldwork research may offer to its informants, can lead them to intimacy on false premises. As Judith Stacey puts it: "The lives, loves, and tragedies that fieldwork informants share with a researcher are ultimately data – grist for the ethnographic mill" (ibid.:113).

I have no answers to such arguments except that as so much else in this study they bear witness to the fact that the anthropological project fundamentally is to "commit oneself to something essentially contestable" (Geertz 1973:29). As both Stacey and Patai did, I chose to find my way between open questions, hoping that the discomfort of not knowing the answers would keep me alert to the pitfalls of my ambiguous position.

An outsider

Every relationship with another human being entails an element of risk. The risk of not being identified as the person one likes to be identified as. The risk of being misunderstood or finding oneself part of a project over which one has no control. One may experience oneself as captured in the experience of the other (Crossley 1996a:61), objectified and estranged from oneself. In anthropological fieldwork the fieldworker plays with this risk with an element of the opportunistic, as the look of the other in itself can convey important insights. Finding herself objectified as 'a wild one' in the local Icelandic world where she did her fieldwork, Kirsten Hastrup indirectly received information on the Icelanders' discourse on wilderness (Hastrup 1995:55). Objectification in the field is the process of being assigned a social role that one most often cannot fully choose oneself as it depends on the merging of personal qualities, available roles in the local world one is entering, and more accidental circumstances in the course of fieldwork. The outcome has a fundamental impact on one's research since particular social roles give access to particular data (Hasse 1995).

As time passed, I became aware of the image of me that the women in the neighbourhood seemed to have. Without wanting anything at all like that, I came to represent the free woman – at least to some of them. I had two children, 'a couple' (a boy and a girl) as was the ideal, and I had a husband who took care of the children, and who did not drink too much nor play soccer as men often did to excess – to women's annoyance. I was educated, rich (relatively), and I 'walked a lot' – I went around from house to house, without my husband confining me to the home. I remember the day when Carmen came to my house and among other things told me that I was her only friend. The only person with whom she could share her wishes for a better life, where she would study and live alone without a husband. We had a good talk and I felt invited to confidence. I wanted to give some intimate information in exchange for all that she told me in order to establish a friendship instead of the informant-anthropologist relationship. So I told her that I was considering having another child. Her reaction was very immediate and precise. She moved her head backward in an attitude of scepticism, her face becoming closed and hard. The admiration and tenderness suddenly disappeared, and I realised that I had betrayed the dream I represented to her.

Looking back on it now, I wonder why this exchange did not make me pose direct questions about their image of me. I only continued deducing from experience their ideas about me as a person; this would have helped me to contextualise their attitudes and utterances in my presence. I often felt that they found me innocent and 'nice'. As I did not want to express any sexual availability I dressed relatively modestly. One day somebody asked me if I was a 'believer' (follower of a Pentecostal Church) as I often wore skirts below the knee. Neide and her friends with whom I spent many afternoons in the shade used to advise me about clothes, lipstick and earrings. Besides, my lack of linguistic competence also made me 'innocent' as I did not understand the often rather subtle slang, giving myself away by not laughing at the right moments. Finally, in order to hear people's own way of expressing things, I often posed simple questions as if I knew nothing, which made me seem like a child, not a 'real adult'. This position of mine opened a space for dialogues that would be impossible with anybody else (they told me, and I felt the truth of it). However, it also precluded my participation in a certain kind of intimacy that I only experienced in rare moments like the afternoon when I engaged in a vivid discussion about how to get lice out of children's hair and demonstrated a certain expertise.

I have asked myself if, for instance, women's utterances in relation to motherly patience were provoked or even determined by my public image as a patient mother. I surely did things that mothers generally did not do in the neighbourhood. My children were very timid, when we were visiting the families together, and I often had one of them on my lap. At other times, visiting without my own children, I enjoyed having some other children on my lap or sitting close to me – a quick caress on the hair or just a moment's special attention to a child in the room. All my Danish middle class habits were exposed in the Brazilian sun, where mothers did not do that. Sometimes they were even embarrassed by my behaviour. I was really naive – to me this was just the way to relate to children and it took me a long time to integrate this behaviour of mine in my reflections. Why were they embarrassed? One woman thought that I would steal her children. Was that the case with all of them? Why did Neide tell her son to get off my lap? Why did Sonia avoid her own children's caress and tell them that they should also leave me in peace? I interpreted what happened as related to the women's mixed feelings about motherhood. In many ways I became a live example of a different way of relating to children, and that created some disturbances and reflections on their part. I do not think, though, that I introduced new ideas. Women in the neighbourhood had already for a long time been exposed to middle class family patterns and their longing for a 'better life' was not changed (though perhaps more easily articulated) due to my 'being around'.

My position as an outsider was an inevitable condition that I as an anthropologist had to cope with. For me as a person, the friend 'Lini', it was at times an insurmountable void, as when one morning Luzia told me about Neide's flight the night before and with tears in her eyes, and said: "Oh, Lini, there are lots of things you do not know". Had I in that moment fulfilled my role as an eager anthropologist, I might have asked: "Which things, Luzia?" I just kept silent, filing her words away as a reminder: No, I do not know a lot of things, but yes, I can learn from questioning over and over again what it is that I do not know.

Chapter Three

The Neighbourhood

A place is not a mere patch of ground, a bare stretch of earth, a sedentary set of stones. [...] Rather than being one definite sort of thing – for example, physical, spiritual, cultural, social – a given place takes on the qualities of its occupants, reflecting these qualities in its own constitution and description and expressing them in its occurrence as an event: places not only are, they happen.

(Casey 1996:26-27)

I had entered a world remarkably different from the middle class world I inhabit in Denmark. Scarcity, physically arduous work or, for the unemployed, lots of spare time – these were the characteristics of life in the neighbourhood. Days were long. Around five o'clock in the morning dogs would bark and the cocks start crowing, one began and others followed. The first radio would soon be turned on. People would wake up, some talking loud enough for neighbours to hear, and soon the first few would walk to the *avenida*, the main road, and take the bus to Recife. Well-dressed in clean and newly ironed clothes, with the scent of light perfume. The buses to Recife were many but still full during the rush hours. Very few people had cars. Pedro, one of the bar owners, had a Volkswagen, a *fusca* as it was called, which he often used to help out people in difficulty – such as taking pregnant women to hospital. And Tonio, the greengrocer, had a smart car with air conditioning and music.

Heading for Recife.

Tonio had come to the neighbourhood more than 25 years ago with nothing and now he had the biggest vegetable stall in the area right in front of the bus stop at the *avenida*. He even had a loudspeaker in front of his shop, so that from his chair at the cash desk he could announce good offers of the day to people passing by, though he had to compete for people's attention with the religious radio channel playing from a loudspeaker on the other side of the road in front of the bakery, as well as the traffic. Tonio had to speak loudly, and he did. He seemed to enjoy all the good offers and his own position as a wealthy merchant. And as one of the very few fathers from the neighbourhood who had managed to send his children to private schools, with both daughters holding university degrees. Tonio's son, however, was not as ambitious as his sisters. He liked the neighbourhood and apparently wanted to continue in his father's footsteps. Perhaps like many others he could not really see himself in other circumstances. As a mirror of oneself the neighbourhood had a certain restraining, but also comforting attraction. For many it was 'home', though not an uncomplicated home. When people talked about themselves they often saw their limited possibilities as directly related to the fact of living in a poor neighbourhood. Tiago, a 23 year old man, expressed the relationship between self and home like this:

> The boys live in the periphery flying kites, playing ball, marbles, going to school but missing class in order to play video games, and they stay like this with the excuse that they are poor. I don't think that the problem is that one is from a *favela* nor the poverty; the problem is that the person isn't proud of himself, because even if he is poor, he can study and get what he wants. But many take the logic from this: It is because I am poor, live in a shack, in a *favela*, that I don't want to study, just do the *maloqueiragem*,[1] play ball, fly kites, do all the things that don't have value, all that fooling around. In my case for instance, I didn't study because of what? Because I did not want; I just wanted to live the life of *maloqeuiragem*.

Tiago had grown up in the *favela* and was proud of himself, but painfully aware of the social barriers that prevented him from living a decent life. He seemed to contradict this in what he explained to me, and yet I knew what he was talking about. Life in the neighbourhood was double-edged. People struggled hard, but with the nagging doubt that one could perhaps have done better mixed with the fact that life so seldom improved; this created a negative version of one's possibilities which at times was difficult to resist.

Play seemed to be a way of ignoring the negative self-image, at least for boys and men. Men played football every Sunday, leaving early and returning in time for lunch, dirty, sweaty and satisfied. Some women like Anita hardly saw their husbands. They worked late every day of the week and on Sundays they would play in the morning and drink in the afternoon. Kites, too, were certainly flown and marbles played. Often when I went to the 'invasion' I passed the place along the road, where boys would always be flying kites over the open land below. The kites were made of coloured silk paper and a kind of very strong straw. Many metres of sewing thread fixed to an empty Nestle powder milk can enabled the boys to steer the movements of the light kites far above. I enjoyed watching them, often boys of different ages showing their skills to passers-by and each other. The powdered glass they had glued onto the thread in order to cut down each others kites was not visible to the naked eye, but once in a while a kite cut loose would drift slowly to the ground.

To me the kites represented both the beauty, the playing out of ideals of graceful, masculine control and the internal, tense hierarchy of the neighbourhood.

An inhabited place

The neighbourhood was not an isolated unit, nor was it homogeneous, self-sufficient or clearly bounded. When I write 'the neighbourhood' I refer to a rather loose and primarily experienced unit that only partly coincided with a geographical area. People called it *o bairro*, which translates into English as 'the district' and on the municipal map it also seemed to have well-defined boundaries. However, the map showed only administrative divisions that did not take hilltops, roads and other separators into account. The lived experience of 'near' and 'far' constituted a sense of co-residence or otherness amongst people, which could not be read from any map.

Living conditions

Looking back at my first impressions of the neighbourhood invites reflection on the understanding of daily life that I acquired later in the fieldwork. In the beginning I saw the settlers' life, the entrepreneurship, the newly constructed houses. History was very present. I learned that the area of the now existing municipality was one of the first to be colonized in the sixteenth century. The sugar mill *o Engenho Camaragibe* was founded in 1549 and became one of the most prosperous in the region during the early years of colonisation. The old *casa grande* (the dwelling of the owner) of the sugar mill now had the status of historic patrimony. It lay at the entrance of the municipality with its pink coloured walls and the palm tree alley reminding one of a feudal past not too far away. Only in 1888 was slavery abolished in Brazil.

I also learned that Camaragibe is a recently created municipality. It had formed part of the neighbouring municipality called São Lourenço da Mata, but when Pernambuco experienced an intense flow of rural-urban migration in the 1970s, along with the rest of Brazil,

Late afternoon somewhere near the *avenida*

the population of Camaragibe increased and in 1982 it was made an independent municipality. Old Dona Benedita related how it had been "one big terrible bush" when she moved to the area thirty years ago: "Everything was forest when I bought this lot. The only houses on this road were that of deceased Ritinha, and, my God, which was the other? A very small one also made of mud belonged to deceased Antonio, the father of Margareta. It is where Lau lives today, on that other road, and another was Dona Lindalva's. It's the one that belongs to Seu Alcides nowadays. Those were the houses."

The more I got to know individual people and became involved in their daily life, the more I lost this view of the present as a direct continuation of the past. The colonial past with slaves and masters, the 'subaltern' past full of droughts and misery in the inlands, and the recent past where the famous economic miracle of Brazil brought only collapse, rootlessness and violence to the Northeast – all this that I knew was superseded by what I experienced here and now. The present absorbed me. I had set myself to learn about everyday life in the neighbourhood and as people did not refer to the distant past I, too, often forgot the historical depth of what I saw and heard. History was somehow not very relevant to the present any of us lived in; only later did I ask myself why.

In her book *Dreaming about Equality* Robin Sheriff points out how silence works as a cultural censorship in Brazil and suppresses talk about racism and other disturbing experiences of humiliation and vulnerability (2001). Her work addresses people's everyday experiences with racism, but the history of racism on which the Brazilian nation is built cannot be separated from this; it, too, is embraced by the silence (ibid.:61-62). Silence is a kind of agency, according to Sheriff, a way of actively trying to forget. However, "the paradox of silence resides precisely in the fact that it implies and objectively constitutes a kind of political accommodation to oppression at the same time that it allows people [...] to let it go, to forget, to at least partially contain the wounds of victimization and carve out a world in which to live with dignity and laughter" (ibid.:75).

I began to see sterilisation in a much broader context when I became aware of the existence of a second class citizenship in Brazil and understood the depth of the humiliation that poor people experience. Nevertheless, racism never came into focus in my study. Brown skin is known to correlate with poverty in Brazil, and like most other Brazilians people in the neighbourhood cast inequality in terms of economy rather than race.[2] Indeed, casual remarks referred to skin colour as an indicator of worth, as when a woman told me about applying for a job and in between other things suddenly said, "Thank God, I am of this colour, but I always have my things in order." Other women sometimes told me how one or another mother-in-law resisted her son's marriage, as the woman of his choice was of the wrong colour – too dark. In one particular, dark-skinned family the two ambitious sons had both married remarkably white, almost pale women and in another family a baby was admired because her skin was so fair.[3] In retrospect I see how the question of race was present in the life I observed and took part in. It was, however, tangled up with poverty and other aspects of appearance and behaviour, and I did not single it out for further exploration.

Generally, people living in the neighbourhood were, as some of them called themselves, *a classe fraca* (the weak class). However, differences in income were considerable. In my survey 70 per cent of the families with children under 2 had two minimum salaries or less per month (at that time one minimum salary of R$ 160 was equivalent

House in the 'invasion'.

to US$ 120).[4] At least ten per cent of these families had less than one minimum salary or no remuneration at all, while seven per cent of the families had between four and five minimum salaries per month and five per cent had more than six. Hence, within the neighbourhood families with absolutely miserable living conditions lived next to families who could afford varied, nutritious food, health insurance and perhaps private schools for their children. It was a neighbourhood like many other Brazilian 'popular' neighbourhoods, where an internal stratification had developed between the less poor, the poor and the miserable, mainly due to some individuals' personal characteristics and success in solving individual economic problems (Mariz 1994:33).

Unemployment was the main reason for the poverty. In the municipality only four major industries offered employment: the textile industry, an industry of glue extraction, another of fertilizer and a fourth of concrete. The latter was located in the area where I lived. During the period of my fieldwork this factory just employed a few people and the work there was hard. Sonia once said, "In this factory not everybody works, only the ones who have courage to really work, because it is heavy, it is really heavy there. There *o pau canta*."[5] Those who didn't work at these industries were employed in 'business' (formal or informal), as drivers, mechanics, servants, watchmen, in construction or in some other unskilled or semi-skilled job. A few were public servants. Some were odd-job workers known as *biscateiros*. Many worked outside the municipality, principally in Recife, returning at night in the overloaded buses always delayed by roadwork. Fourteen per cent of the husbands from the above-mentioned survey were described by their wives as unemployed. They would hang around in the area, ready to help where help was needed in order to earn a few *reais*. The local employment agency was of no use; they would write down your name but never return to you with a job; at least that was what people said. Friends, relatives and better off acquaintances were more reliable paths to jobs.

While young and still unmarried[6] some women had paid work outside the home, but later in life only a few of them would seek employment, generally as maids in middle class families in Recife or in some other job requiring 'unskilled' labour.[7] A few were primary school teachers or hairdressers or worked in one of the shops at the *avenida*. Asked why they did not have jobs, women would usually state that they either had nowhere to leave their children, or that their husbands would not let them leave home. Some, who had already tried getting a job and failed, mentioned lack of employment as yet another reason for staying at home. They simply could not find a job and did not have the contacts that would help them surmount their limited knowledge of where and how to look.

Rates of formal employment are terribly low in Recife and extraordinary resourcefulness is needed, if one is to succeed. Yet another factor may have played a role. As Fonseca observes, a woman who works outside the home may lose in her marriage what she gains through her job. Not only will she probably still have to do all the housework, her husband may also feel less responsible towards her and the children as she can now pay for food, gas and other necessities herself. Seeing himself as the proper head of the household, the husband may even feel threatened by his wife's relative independence and humiliated because he cannot keep her at home.[8] His commitment to her may get diluted and he may spend his money outside the home with other women, or perhaps give money to his mother. Not working outside home can

thus be a tactical means for women to manipulate husband-wife relations (Fonseca 2000:74). Though I did not hear women consider their
situation in these terms, I know that, among many other concerns,
women had to consider their husbands' commitment towards themselves and the children and giving him an opportunity to let go of
responsibility would certainly be running a risk. Neide, for instance,
ran a small lucrative stall at the *avenida* but had to move it to a less
busy place due to her husband's jealousy. A woman could not just be
practical – she had to be tactical as well.

Men in control?

My days were full of talk with women. They were the focus of my
study, they were the ones who were at home, and they were the ones
whom I shared daily tasks with. But there were often men around.
Having my nails done I would sit on Cida's new sofa with my fingers
or feet in a bowl with cold water and dish detergent, while her husband
would hang around, stand in the door, sit next to us watching the TV
half listening or engaging in our conversations now and then. When
I visited Irene, her husband Jairo would be there talking, asking questions and sometimes engaging very actively in our conversations. And
when I sat in Sonia's kitchen night after night, her husband Edilson
would of course also be there, and we would eat, watch TV, talk about
this or that happening, and so on. It was the women's universe that
I came to know best, but the men were always around somewhere as
they generally seemed to be in the women's lives.

The masculine ideal in Brazil is the stereotypical *macho*: in control,
above all of his wife and children, autonomous in relation to other
men, strong and courageous, and provider of the family.[9] 'Bravura,
virility and generosity' are virtues related to this ideal that are still
performable where lack of wealth or autonomy do not allow the display
of other signs of status (Fonseca 2000:26). In the neighbourhood the
men struggled hard to incorporate such qualities, often strongly contested by women's more practical considerations and needs. One day
Sonia's son, Manuel, at that time 12 years old, perfectly demonstrated
this masculine attitude to me. Manuel and I went with his sister to the
centre of Camaragibe to look at people in the street during the day of
elections. Knowing that I would probably buy us all ice creams, their

father gave them one *real* (maybe the only *real* he had) to spend and
the children asked me to keep it in my pocket. We bought three popsicles, and the remaining centavos returned to my pocket. On the way
home I gave them to Manuel, who generously said "No, they're yours.
Keep them." Later that day his sister came to me and, totally aware of
the amount remaining, she asked me "Lini, how many centavos were
left over from the popsicles?" giving me the opportunity to return
the money to the rightful owners. Manuel wanted to be generous; his
sister wanted to use the money. The elements of this small transaction
were repeated over and over again in the homes of the neighbourhood.
Men wanted to be generous, women had to economise.

Being generous was a way of showing that one was in control of
one's life. Things were not missing at home, and wife and children
were all satisfied. A poorly run home, un-cared for children, piles
of unwashed dishes and a complaining woman were signs of lack of
control (Scott 1996:296), the worst of them, however, being female
adultery. One day I asked Jairo and some of his friends what would be
the worst thing in a man's life. All three, simultaneously, responded
"Traição!" (betrayal). One said, "I can bear everything from my wife,
bad moods, jealousy, and all the things she wants, but betrayal is more
difficult." "I agree" another continued, "the worst thing is betrayal.
You find your wife with another man, at home, out of home, no matter where, it is the worst thing that exists. We have to expect death
coming, even if we do not agree it will happen, but this...." And for a
while we discussed death and the pain of a loved person passing away,
until one said, "It is six years ago now that I lost my nephew and I keep
thinking, 'if I lose my daughter, what will happen to me?' But still,
I think the worst is betrayal. A man cannot allow losing his wife to
another man. It gives you that sense of incompetence, because to keep
a woman at your side is a question of competence. I was not capable of
keeping that woman at my side, so another man, maybe better than
me in some or other thing, stole her from me."

A favourite activity among the men was to catch birds by the river
and keep them in small cages, not for anything else than the sense of
graceful mastery, it seemed.[10] But wife and children were not birds; they
were more than symbols of control. Often one would see a man with
a small child on the arm and most men had strong sentiments around

the birth of their children. A young man who had recently become father of his firstborn, expressed it like this: "I think the best thing is to feel that he has that dependency on you. It is to feel that … I am his protector, you know. I give him safety." Procreation and protection were matters of virility. However, economic scarcity complicated these endeavours and when children and wife became too demanding, couples were often separated. That was a reason for women to stop childbearing – they did not want to be left alone with too many children – and why the men said they would never accept sterilisation themselves. They wanted to be able to have children with another woman, if needed. The pride of a man was very closely related to his capacity to provide life, food and safety (see also Nascimento 1999).

In between quarrels and worries football was always interesting and fulfilling. Hours were spent on discussions of football players and teams. To become a player oneself was a dream, a hope of one day being able to help one's mother, have a proper house, give everything one dreamed of to the children and be able to fully satisfy a woman. But as Jairo said:

> Today, you must have a sponsor for everything. Because for the one who comes from a cradle [from a good family] it is more easy to reach there [become a professional player], but when it is a person of the lower level, let us say poor, he does not have the conditions to pay bus tickets and all the other stuff, and then what happens is that he stays where he is. Like for instance Jefferson [his son], I have prayed so much to God every day that Jefferson should make it, his future, because he likes football, to become a player like I never became. It was what I wanted, my favourite profession, but I did not have the opportunity, and I try to pass it on to him….

The dream of becoming a professional player allowed Jefferson to skip school and not take other alternatives seriously. He used to give me his medals; when I met him on the road he carried my bag; and people said he already had a child in São Lourenço, which he, however, had not acknowledged. I wondered what would become of him.

A feminine domain par excellence
Living in the neighbourhood meant meeting each other in the semi-public space of the roads and lanes between the houses. There were several paved roads, each named after important men from Brazil's recent history such as Afonso Pena and Washington Luís, both presidents of Brazil. Between these roads there were lanes, muddy on rainy days, but useful for those who wanted to take a shortcut. Due to the open houses and often small individual plots of land co-residence also meant being aware of what took place in nearby houses, be it quarrels, music or cooking. Only in the best houses were the spaces between wall and roof closed; most houses were open for the fresh air, the geckos and the sounds to pass back and forth.

People knew a lot about each other which did not necessarily bring them closer together. Alliances and antagonisms crisscrossed the neighbourhood, along strange and often (to me) unexpected pathways. Relatives were sometimes close, sometimes remote, as persons from the same family often moved on very different social trajectories. Friendships could be unstable, but simultaneously also deep and long-lasting. And the relationship with close neighbours was often difficult due to the unavoidable knowledge about each other's lives. The women distinguished between *amigas* (intimate friends) and *colegas* (friends). *Amigas* were friends you could really trust and 'tell everything' to. They were rare; some women would say that they did not have any, others would mention their mother. *Colegas* could chat, share certain problems, help but never really trust each other. Neide had an *amiga*, Elizia, but when Neide's family was threatened by violence, Elizia disappeared. Sonia had an *amiga*, for whom she borrowed money from the bank, as the *amiga* could not do it herself but promised to pay the instalments every month. For a year Sonia had to pay 80 *reais* a month out of her widow's pension of 200 reais, because in the end the friend was not the *amiga* she had appeared to be, she never paid one single instalment. One thing was the money, Sonia said; another almost as serious as the first was that her friend did not tell her why she had cheated her. As Carmen said, one could easily be disillusioned with friends.

Gossiping was both a way of relating to each other and that which made relationships dangerous. Through gossip inclusion and exclusion of female networks were negotiated, and every word said could be turned against oneself. For me – the stranger – walking down the road returning smiles and greetings and knowing that people would discuss me afterwards was an experience I had to learn to live with. After some months I found that we had got used to each other, my surroundings and I, and I thought they had stopped commenting on me. It was Sonia who taught me that the commenting would never stop and that it included everybody. The more you became part of the daily routine of the place, the harsher the comments behind your back. Sonia said: "Here you find a lot of *olho grande* (big eyes).[11] You want to construct something, want to do something, and you tell somebody, like: 'Look, I want to do something – I will do this!' And immediately everything turns wrong. Immediately the criticism comes, you know. Nobody gives strength. They just want to step on you. I walk with one foot forward, the other behind. I am very suspicious, because when I hear the way people talk I want to know with whom I am living." When one day I felt uneasy and slightly depressed, Sonia was sure that *olho grande* had hit me.

The Brazilian anthropologist Claudia Fonseca has done research in two low income housing areas in Porto Alegre, Brazil, which in many ways resemble the neighbourhood I knew. One area was built on 'invaded' terrain and inhabited by what Fonseca calls the sub-proletariat: the section of the working class which does not match the available jobs or which constitutes an excess in relation to the demands of industrial production (Fonseca 2000:14). The other area had been divided into lots by the municipality. Family economies were neither low nor ascending (ibid.:89-90). 'My' neighbourhood paralleled both; it was partly lots, partly 'invasion', and the composition of family economies varied accordingly. In her study Fonseca describes life in the neighbourhoods as structured around notions of honour while I write of recognition, but these two concepts are not mutually exclusive. Rather on the contrary, honour understood as pride may be a result of recognition and honour as a code of social interaction could also be another word for what I observed as resistance towards feeling weak and defeated (see Chapter Two, 'Interviewing'). I have not, however, applied the notion of honour to my analysis, as it turns that which should rather be seen as a process on a more existential level into an established system of codes. Nevertheless, Fonseca's understanding of gossip as a forceful weapon in local negotiations of honour is revealing in relation to what took place in 'my' neighbourhood.

Gossip, Fonseca notes, is the feminine domain par excellence in which women actively create and manipulate their own and their families' reputation often by way of hints and insinuations (ibid.: 43). Surrounded by gossip the men are dependent on the women's negotiation of status. They may impose their will on their surroundings through violence or the threat of violence, but as gossip is hidden and indirect they are vulnerable to rumours and slander. Hence, gossip is a forceful tool for women to negotiate relationships with their husbands, as spreading hints about his incapacities as a man may pay him back for beatings or lack of attention towards wife and children. On a broader level, gossip works as a levelling force, a tool for the less powerful to improve their own status in the neighbourhood by lowering that of others (ibid.:49). However, Fonseca concludes, the self-respect achieved through such negotiations of status does not suspend the humiliation experienced in the wider society. It may, though, as in 'my' neighbourhood, be part of the sense of we-ness, as all are either actively or passively engaged in the negotiations, even a naïve anthropologist.

The family
Studies on family structures under conditions of urban poverty in Brazil show a marked tendency towards matrifocality (Leal and Fachel 1995; Leal and Fachel 1996; Scott 1996) defined as "a complex web of relations constructed around the domestic group in which, even with the presence of a man in the house, the woman's side of the group is favoured" (Scott 1996:287). In her study from Porto Alegre Fonseca found, though, that for both women and men consanguine ties were more important than the conjugal, they continued to have strong links with their family group, leading Fonseca to speculate whether the importance given to feminine alliances (to the exclusion of masculine alliances) in studies of matrifocality is not a consequence of methodology rather than a fact. Activities centred on mothers and homes are easily observed by the researcher, but that should not make us

overlook the ties between men and their parents (mainly mothers),[12] sisters and, in particular, brothers (Fonseca 2000:63).[13]

In the neighbourhood where I worked variations were so many that any systematic trend was hard to detect, except for the dominance of consanguine ties; the tendency towards matrifocality was visible but not unadulterated – women commonly had not only their kin living nearby, but often also their family-in-law. I was always asked about my mother. "How is she? Don't you miss her? Why don't you bring her, too?" people would say, making me aware that mothers were prominent figures in the world I had entered. Since this applied to men and women alike, it did at times create tense relations between women and their mothers-in law.

Neide's mother Dona Lívia lived just next door to her, her sister Gloria too lived near by (in a better part of the neighbourhood), another sister lived just a short walk away and a brother in the neighbour municipality São Lourenço. Neide's mother-in-law lived somewhere in Camaragibe, and on her rare visits she pestered Neide by insinuating that Neide was not good enough for her son, Airton, who should have married a 'proper' girl, and not just joined a woman like Neide. When Neide and Airton were passing through any serious disagreement he stayed overnight in his mother's house. Neide's father lived with Gloria; Dona Lívia had rejected him long time ago.

The families that settled here early had had the opportunity to buy much land which allowed family members to live next to each other. Gloria's husband had been successful; he had built houses for Gloria to rent out until the offspring needed a house of their own. Gloria's daughter and son, both married, lived in two of these houses. Another was ready for the youngest daughter, when she married. Sonia also belonged to one of the 'old' well-known families in the neighbourhood, and Sonia's mother owned a plot with four separate houses and a small yard in between. Sonia's mother, her sisters, her brother and her daughter, Anita, lived there. Sonia herself lived on 'invaded' terrain nearby. Her husband, Edilson, had his mother in a nearby neighbourhood and he often visited her with or without Sonia. A prosperous family like Neta's family-in-law had constructed a big house with several apartments for the parents and their sons' (they had no daughters) families to live. However, women who, like Carmen, lived on land belonging to their in-laws, could foresee difficulties in case of divorce. In general, if a marriage failed, wife and children commonly stayed on in the house while the husband left, perhaps returning to his mother's house. Living too close to one's in-laws meant having nowhere to live free from the ex-husband's control. In such cases, formal separation was a clear marker of independence.

To be formally separated, however, presupposed a formal marriage. In the neighbourhood being 'married' often meant living together rather than having entered marriage in legal terms. If a woman had been divorced she would often not marry again. Cohabitation was common, regarded as an 'as if' marriage (even though not as respectable) (see Rebhun 1999:138), and women generally referred to their live-in partner as *meu marido* (my husband). In contrast, the word *esposa* (wife) was mainly used when the couple were married. When living with a man without marriage, the woman would tend to say that she was *a mulher dele* (his woman). To have a formal marriage seemed more crucial for a woman's identity than for a man's. Weddings were therefore more important for the women, but due to the costs of a proper wedding or parents' disagreements, many a young couple just began, more or less dramatically, to live together.

Iara, a young woman of 17 years, eloped from her parents' house and went to live with her boyfriend in his parents' home. When her father fell ill, presumably due to a nervous reaction, she returned home with her new status as a woman and, it turned out, pregnant. When I visited her she lived in a room behind her parents' house with her newborn daughter and her 'husband'. Elopement and some kind of drama around a young woman's separation from her parents were not rare. It seemed to be a way of handling a situation in which the parents ideally should be in control, but either did not have the means or the interest. From their study in a low-income area in Porto Alegre, Ondina Leal and Jandyra Fachel write: "Apparently 'elopement' supposed the non acceptance by the girl's family of the union, but actually it is a culturally established pattern, a tacit strategy for legitimizing the new alliance" (Leal and Fachel 1996:10).

Less dramatically Anita, Sonia's daughter, had just got married when I met her, but only in the church, which is not legally binding. Anita was brought up by her grandmother and the grandmother's husband (Sonia's stepfather), who after their divorce paid Anita a monthly allowance as long as she was *de menor* (not yet legally responsible) and unmarried. Anita did not want to loose this economic support and she therefore did not marry fully. The halfway solution of marriage in church, however, guaranteed the respect she would not have had, if they had just begun to live together. She had got married in a borrowed, beautiful white dress, four months pregnant, and now had a photo album to show for it. Such albums were expensive, very formal in their mounting and central to the lives of the lucky owners, which were families rather than individuals. Marriage was the celebrated ideal; cohabitation the accepted norm.

Female-headed households are said to be increasingly frequent in low income areas of Brazil due to the tense economic situation of many families that undermines marital relationships (see also chapter 6 for a discussion of gender relationships). However, the existence of female headed households does not necessarily mean that these households are free from masculine control (Fonseca 2000: 61-65). In her study in Porto Alegre Fonseca found that all young women (below 45 years of age) 'belonged' to some man, for instance a father, brother, or even ex-husband, who would represent both the control and protection of their sexuality (ibid.:84). She also found that the composition of households was constantly changing and that the diverse categories of residence were complementary (ibid.:62). Rather than talking about a certain percentage of households being female-headed, it may thus seem more appropriate to think of units of 'mother alone with children' as transitory phases in-between conjugal unions (ibid.:62). Neide, Luzia, Irene and Sonia had all lived in other conjugal relationships than their present ones. Neide was still married to her former husband, who lived somewhere around Recife, as she did not want to loose the pension she was entitled to as his wife. Luzia had her first child, when she was 14, with a man who died soon after. She was later divorced from her second husband and was now living with Cleiton. Irene was divorced from the father of her two oldest daughters and now living with Jairo, the man with whom she had the rest of her children. Since her early youth Sonia lived with a man whom she had left and returned to, and who was later killed. She had then lived on her own, until Edilson joined her. These women were not older than me, but all of them had careers of motherhood and wifehood that deviated remarkably from mine.

In the life trajectory of a woman remarriage may be a more dramatic rupture than divorce because many leave their children with a mother or relative when beginning a life with a new husband (ibid.: 69). The reason, Fonseca writes, was commonly expressed as "men are not suckers – they don't bring up others' children" (ibid.). In her study she found that half of the women over 20 had already left at least one child in the care of others. Several of the women I met had done the same. Neide left three children with her mother when she began living with Airton. When her mother later threw them out Neide had to go to great lengths in order to feed and protect them. Sonia had left two daughters and a son with her mother; Luzia managed to keep her daughters when she 'married' her present husband and gave birth to his children but had, however, left a son with her first mother-in-law many years ago, when she married her second (and now former) husband. When I met her, he was 18 years old and Luzia kept talking about him. I think she would have liked to have had him around for extra protection, but she had no contact with him anymore and could not do much in order to get him back. And after all, he was now an adult and the neighbourhood was not safe for young men, she said.[14]

People rarely lived alone.[15] Men or women, who were unmarried, would live with their parents, brothers, sisters or other relatives. Old people, otherwise alone, would perhaps have a child in their house (grandchild or, less common, foster child) for company. In the neighbourhood only two people that I knew of lived alone: a sister of Sonia, who had chosen to stay on her own, and Josenita, who had inherited her father's house and after the death of her aunt owned it all by herself. Sonia's sister used to borrow Anita's daughters once in a while and have them sleep over at her home; Josenita's doors were open for strangers like me and acquaintances of hers who needed a temporary place to stay.

The larger world

Having returned to Brazil after several months in Denmark I came to see Josenita and discuss my plan of staying in her house for some weeks. We had a cup of coffee, exchanged news and Josenita told me about the recent death of her aunt who used to live with her. Josenita had witnessed the cheatings with the public burial assistance at the undertaker's and she was still furious, disillusioned and desperate, as she had not been able to give her aunt a proper burial while somebody else misused the system. However, without warning she changed subject and still with tears in her eyes she said: "Lini, I saw something very touching today!" She told me that she had been walking along the road back from the centre of Camaragibe when she saw a very big bird hanging from one of the impressive high voltage power pylons that had recently entered the landscape. When she got closer the bird turned out to be a human being: a worker fixing the power line to the pylon. She was still very emotional when she told me about this; I was mystified, associating her emotions to the previous story about her aunt, and not at all able to see the significance of the sight.

Much later I stood with my friend Alexandre, an industrious man in his late twenties, on a terrace with a fantastic view towards the skyline of Recife. Looking at the lights of the city he made a gesture and said "Isn't beautiful?" I could not see it; I loved the silence, the darkness and the stars over the neighbourhood. Alexandre continued, "I want to help bring progress to Camaragibe." It dawned on me that for both Josenita and Alexandre progress had a very specific significance charged with strong feelings. Both power pylons and city lights were loaded with promises of inclusion in the larger world and the changes had to come about through the work of simple people like Alexandre, Josenita or that man who at first sight had appeared to be a bird.

Politicians were of little use, people found, as they were generally occupied with their own economy more than people's needs. "There is too little love in Brazil," a taxi driver told me, "just look at the politicians, they don't care about people."[16] Corruption scandals haunt Brazil, but clear-sighted planning for the future also disappoints due to its lack of immediate results. People in the neighbourhood were used to operating within patron-client relationships and they somehow expected the politicians to provide immediate relief for pressing problems. Northeast Brazil has a history of exploitative patronage towards the poor going back to the sugar economy of the region's 'glorious past'.[17] The power of the plantation owners is now transferred to formal and informal employers, lawyers, doctors, and especially politicians, and the mechanism of this informal exchange of unequal resources is still in use. The protection provided by such a paternalistic system to some degree suspends legal rights and duties, but for those who know how to operate within it, it also provides opportunities (Rebhun 1999:51). Even the health worker Irene, who explained to me how a politician with all his promises and small gifts abandons the poor after the election – "he feels he owes nothing; he already gave, you see" – even Irene played the game. She was actually an expert in obtaining contraceptive pills, building materials, food and other necessities from politicians and people who were better off. However, politicians' talk about progress and development were mainly perceived as empty promises.

Images of the world beyond the neighbourhood entered people's lives through the ubiquitous television. Television itself was a marker of inclusion and since the 1980s more and more families had managed to buy one. In the houses I used to visit the television would often be on in the afternoons and nights. People would watch it, talk with each other if it was not the important *hora de novela* (the hour(s) of soap opera) and now and then catch up on news from the outside world. Strange occurrences in São Paulo would be commented upon as if they had happened nearby. Snow in Europe, the death of Princess Diana and the beheading of the Little Mermaid in Copenhagen were bits of news that people passed on to me, even though few of them would ever know whether Europe was located inside or outside Latin America.

The *globalização* was often mentioned as the reason for problems in Brazil, small and big, but I always found the word awkward in the mouths of people who rarely left the place they inhabited. They might have moved from the interior Pernambuco to the city, or they might even have lived for some time in São Paulo, but these moves were mo-mentous events, not part of daily life. The women would spend their lives in the neighbourhood, with just a few trips to an aunt or sister in another suburb or, as was most often the reason for leaving home, a visit to a hospital in the city. And yet, the larger world was full of significance. For Brazil in general the global economic and cultural fluctuations are of immediate importance. The price of the dollar and decisions taken in the economic centres of the world make a crucial difference to the prospects of the Brazilian national economy. Many people in the neighbourhood were aware of this vulnerability; they were also aware of their own similar situation vis-à-vis the Brazilian society.

The church
Other than television the church was a source of information about the world. Like everywhere in Brazil the neighbourhood was rich in churches. There was a Catholic Church centrally located, where two main lanes met, and there were the Pentecostal protestant churches to which the 'believers', *os crentes* as they were called, regularly flocked. Brazil is known as a Catholic country, but today protestant and especially Pentecostal protestant churches are growing rapidly. According to a survey carried out in 1992, a new Protestant church is opened every two days in the metropolitan area of Rio de Janeiro (Mariz 1994:1). The *Assembléia de Deus* (Assembly of God) is the largest Protestant denomination of them all (ibid.:26), and was certainly the most conspicuous religious community in the area where I worked, with approximately 100 persons attending the evening services.

Pentecostal churches are seen to attract more women than men among lower income Brazilians. In his book *Looking for God in Brazil* John Burdick (1993) proposes that women are especially attracted to the Pentecostal churches in spite of their emphasis on patriarchal norms (including male dominance in the home and a strict dress code for women), because these churches offer female followers support in dealing with their domestic problems. The women are indirectly empowered in relation to their families as the church offers them the acknowledgement they lack in most other relationships, and, as David Lehmann puts it, "even if the attraction of the Churches lies only in the chance of 'being somebody' outside the narrow confines of the household, it is a powerful one" (Lehmann 1996:133). In the neighbourhood I found a marked tendency towards more trustful relationships between husband and wife in families where both attended a Pentecostal church, and in line with Burdick's argument I found that women sought social support in the Pentecostal churches when facing difficult situations. Whether the women found recognition of their independent identity outside of family relations in these more than in other churches I did not reflect upon, but when recollecting the 'believers' among my informants it seems probable. The church seemed to be a source of structure and concentration, qualities that life in the neighbourhood generally did not encourage nor leave much room for.

Fatima, a mother of four children and pregnant with her fifth, used to attend the *Assembléia de Deus* at least twice a week. She and her husband had divided the days between them, and both went as often as possible. Partly due to her small children, partly because her husband did not allow it, Fatima very seldom left home for other reasons. Only Sunday afternoon and Tuesday evening would she leave the house, and walk to church with her hymn book and one or two of her children, tired but newly washed and well-dressed in her long skirt and her hair tightly put up. "I was 15 years old when I entered the church, and I will be 35 on Monday. I will never leave it for anything in this world," she said. I went with her one day. The church was full, people in their best clothes, whispering, singing and listening to the pastor's voice amplified by a microphone to almost unbearable heights. Seeing Fatima in this focused and animated world I believed her.

Others frequented different churches, as they went along with friends, or chose the church they found most profitable to attend for the moment. Luzia, for instance, decided to be *crente* (a believer) in the Adventist church, which she knew through her neighbours. She changed her way of dressing (as much as she could), stopped using make-up and gave up the little bit of beer she used to enjoy with her husband. As she wanted her daughter to have godparents, however, she decided to baptise her in the Catholic church as such a ritual did not exist among the Adventists. Like many others she had a background of Catholicism.

In my survey among the 192 women who had babies below two years of age, we found that almost 70 per cent of those who confirmed having a religion called themselves Catholics.[18] Among these 40 per cent visited the churches frequently, while the rest rarely or never went to church. Eleven women from the survey were traditional Protestants, while 25 frequented Pentecostal churches. Four were Jehovah's Witnesses, while 3 were spiritualists. More than half of the women had no frequent contact with a church.[19] My impression was, though, that like anything else in the area this was not a stable situation. There was a constant movement in and out of churches in a search for identity, affiliation and help. In a peculiar way God occupied the position of the ultimate protector, whose intervention could be sought when personal contacts proved to be of no use.[20]

The school

According to the municipality 73 percent of the population over 5 years of age in Camaragibe were registered as 'alphabetised' (or literate) in 1991 (FIDEM 1996). Public schooling for children is obligatory till grade eight in Brazil, but public schools are generally of low standard in marginal regions like Northeast Brazil, lacking supplies and inspiring teachers.[21] Grade repetition and dropouts are common. In the survey we found that 84 per cent of both men and women had completed grade four, while 35 per cent had reached grade eight, the last grade in primary school. Around 15 per cent of both sexes had finished secondary school and a few, more men than women, had a higher education.[22] However, many of the women with whom I talked would say that they read only slowly and with difficulty, and I often found that they were very slow at, for instance, reckoning the age of a child, as if numbers were difficult for them to handle. They had been to school, but that did not mean that their school knowledge was still in use.

Children went to school in shifts. Within the same family one child might study in the morning from 7 to 12, another in the afternoon from 1 to 4 and a third at night. Young people often preferred night courses which allowed them to escape home and be with their friends, chatting, or perhaps kissing in the corners of the school yard. Meeting friends was a major reason for going to school, but some boys would also go to school because their football club requested a certificate from the school in order for them to join the club. And then of course children went to school because schooling is necessary in modern Brazil. The parents often went to great lengths to have them enrolled in a good public school and worries were many if the children began to shirk. As one father said, "The most important thing is to study." However he continued, "The only thing in which you can be well educated today is, if you can work with a computer. I think that the computer will be very important. You find computers everywhere; in your country and anywhere else in the world." Where formerly literacy was the mark of a modern citizen,[23] the ability to use a computer seemed to have become the crucial distinction. Free or cheap computer courses were offered in Camaragibe and many, mainly young people, would attend them, but without cmputers at home they did not learn much on these short forays.

Integration into the world of computers created a need for English skills, a fact people were generally aware of, but English teaching in school was precarious. Some teachers did not pronounce the words in English, only in Portuguese. They would just write words on the blackboard and let the pupils copy them in their books. I remember one day when having found out that a certain young man had a computer with internet access I went to ask if I could send some e-mails and found him and his friend in front of series of pictures from the movie *Titanic*.[24] Each picture was accompanied by a simple text in English and they were happy when I translated the words, writing everything down so they could return to the pages and enjoy the story again. They had access, but were not fully integrated as users.

While young people were attracted by computer and English courses, some adults – mainly women – studied at night in order to improve or supplement their former school education. For many schooling was one long continuous process, slow, full of breaks and delays, but nevertheless continuous. Practiced in this way education was certainly for life, not something to be finished in one's younger years.

Living on a tightrope

My small rented house, or rather flat, near the health post was in a row of four flats owned by Dona Mónica, who ran a sweets and small ware shop down at the *avenida*. It had two small bedrooms, a living room with space enough for a small table, four chairs and a hammock, a small kitchen and a bathroom. We also had a small backyard with a concrete basin for washing clothes and some strings for drying them on. However, we never used that backyard very much. There were lots of rats and filthy washing water from the other three flats running by on washing days and rotting on the days in between. Like everybody else we only had water whenever the water company found it appropriate, and when no pipes were broken. Next to us lived old Dona Penha, her daughter and her two grandchildren. Dona Penha and the children were pale white. They almost never left home and were seldom out in the sun. Dina, the daughter, worked in Recife as a housemaid, and she returned late at night after a long day's work. I still remember the morning Dona Penha told me about Lady Diana's death. She was standing in the doorway when I passed, as if she wanted to share it with somebody: "What a pity! She was not part of my family, but one almost feels like that. She was so good, so young!"

The flat next to Dona Penha's was empty for quite a long time apparently because the rent was too high. Nobody wanted to live there if they had other options. Teresa, who lived in the last flat with her husband, Janio, and their small daughter hadn't. They had arrived from São Paulo with nothing in the hope of finding work for him and help from his family, who lived in the neighbourhood. Teresa had very little goods. They slept on the floor, had only one plate, and the old broom and the other few things she owned were gifts from Dona Mónica. Janio owned a television and an enormous music equipment which I never learned how he could afford. He used to turn the music on loud on Sundays, when he was at home, sitting in the shadow outside the house encapsulated in the sound, alone, or if some friends showed up with provisions, with a beer or a glass of rum, without talking to anybody. Teresa talked to everybody. She used to borrow small things from my kitchen. I also borrowed from her. I remember asking for a garlic press. She handed me an ordinary stone and told me how to use it. Thus we lived our lives as neighbours, helping each other with whatever we could. However, after a quarrel with Dona Mónica Teresa and Janio moved. The flat was later inhabited by another family, whom I never really got to know.

Running down the steep mud road along the wall of the concrete industry in front of Dona Mónica's house, passing by the house in front of which the girl with stunted legs used to sit, the balcony full of plastic flowers and the video game shop, one came to Nita's house.

It was not at all rich, nor nice. Sonia used to help her organise it a bit once in a while, but for some reason Nita could not make beautiful surroundings for herself. In an annex on her plot she had established a *biblioteca comunitária* (community library) with a lot of old books and pamphlets on sexual matters. Most visitors were children who needed information on one or another school subject.

Some streets away, uphill, lived Sonia with five of her seven children and Edilson, her husband. She always struggled to improve her house. The last time I saw it, she had painted the front light green. She had also got hold of an old washing machine and a pump for her well in order to earn money by washing clothes for people. She would use as little as possible and make the house even nicer. Sonia was a *lutadora* (a fighter). Her mother had been like that and her oldest daughter, Anita, certainly was. After the birth of her second child Anita opened a hairdressing salon and around Christmas and carnival time, when everybody wanted to look good, she worked so hard that her arms ached and she sometimes felt like fainting.

Sonia, her mother and her daughter were not the only fighters. In the neighbourhood individual initiative and persistence were respected individual virtues. But the individualisation of success blurred the structures that kept so many families in poverty, in the neighbourhood as in other similar neighbourhoods in Brazil. Josenita often complained about the lack of political engagement in the neighbourhood. She once said: "Today the struggle is to survive. There is the popular movement, there is the women's movement, many movements around here, but people on this place are more into that struggle of surviving. Like Anita. She learned to cut hair and is surviving, [it is] a way to have the things at home, with dignity. You see that in every corner here there is a stall, every house here has a small stall with popcorn, I don't know from where the clientele appears, but everybody makes a stall. And then it becomes that story about survival."

Fonseca calls it "life in a sandwich" – balancing on a tightrope between the fear of falling into marginality and the ambivalent hope of upward social mobility (Fonseca 2000:89 ff). In the neighbourhood the means of improvement were few, the risks of falling high, and the common struggle to cling on rife with tension and vulnerable to outer circumstances.

Chapter Four

Fertility and History

If one can apply the term bio-history to the pressures through which the movements of life and the processes of history interfere with one another, one would have to speak of bio-power to designate what brought life and its mechanisms into the realm of explicit calculations and made knowledge-power an agent of transformation of human life.

(Foucault in Rabinow 1984:265)

I talked with Ana one late afternoon soon after my arrival in the neighbourhood. I wanted to meet a woman who was sterilised, and for some reason Josenita picked out Ana. She was 50 years old:

I began to take the pill, but I couldn't use it. It got the nerves very agitated. I talked to the doctor and he said that if I got pregnant again, he could make a third caesarean and ligate. At that time I was 29 years old and I stopped [being fertile]. I got pregnant and made the ligation on November 9, and on December 9 I became 30, and there it stopped. [...] In the situation that we lived in I only wanted 2 children, because those were the conditions that we had in order to give them a better education, in order to make it easier for me to work. But I had to have the third, because I talked to the doctor about ligating in the second, and he said that he would not do it, because I was only 27 years old and I had to have the third. I had to accept. I foresaw some difficulties in my married life and because of that I did not want many children, and God saw it, and he who knows the future just gave me three.

Ana was a mother, a wife, and a very religious person. Besides that, she had been the patient of a doctor who had had the power to force her into a third pregnancy even though she found two children sufficient for her marriage. She might also have considered herself a proper Brazilian citizen being concerned and responsible for her children's education. And in that particular moment when she was talking with me, she presumably wanted – consciously or not – to be a particular person in my eyes. All these identities and possibly many others, temporal and fragmented, melted into one empirical being, Ana, when she presented her narrative to me.

In the complexity of life we constantly relate to other people and whether they are present or not, there are always some for whose recognition we yearn, often tailoring our behaviour in accordance with the image we imagine that these particular others have of us. However, "the individuals who carry the images fall naturally into classes" and we therefore have as many different social selves as there are "distinct *groups* of persons" about whose opinion we care (James 1950:294, his emphasis). This constant emerging in us of different, changing social selves is a result of a process of identification in which that which was once 'not-me' becomes 'me' in the undertaking of a given practice within a community of others. The many selves sometimes directly contradicting each other, are performances to be taken at face value; not abstract images created by a disengaged mind (Hastrup 1995:92).

When Ana was trying to decide if she really wanted a sterilisation, her identification with the images of a caring mother, a submissive wife, a faithful worshipper of God, a compliant patient, and a responsible citizen created a certain friction, a suffering, as these identities did not immediately overlap. Her joy in having children and her wish to follow God's will contradicted her sense of responsibility, the latter reinforced by the physician's double-edged proposal. In between these contradicting images was the fear of being the lone provider for the children. She might have feared that her independent decision would challenge her husband's sense of masculinity, but equally, she was aware of the risk she was already running due to "difficulties" in her marriage. In Ana's view, God saw her predicament and "he who knows the future" let things happen as they did; we may put it differently, saying that Ana managed to reconcile her contradicting emotions and images of what to do through a creative re-thinking of her God.[1]

Power over life

In quite another perspective, Ana was also sterilised because she was poor and female in a society that had changed from being mainly based on a rural economy, where people survived through work under slavery-like conditions, to become an urbanised and industrialised society based on consumption. In this society having many children no longer constituted a potential source of income to somebody; responsible individuals were needed instead of a mass of miserables; and health care became a mechanism of social control. Reduced fertility became crucial for parents as well as for the society in general, as life itself became a target of control.

According to Michel Foucault the modern power over life, "bio-power", has two aspects: one focused on the manipulation of individual bodies, another aimed at the control of populations, both conflating in the regulation of reproduction (Foucault 1994). Bio-power, Foucault argues, is the body politics that arose in Europe in the 18th century, characterised by the construction of the body as a bounded entity, made knowable and controllable by a system of experts and agencies with the welfare of the population in mind (Crossley 1996a:132). Medical health care is a central arena for the unfolding of bio-power and once taken charge of, life ceases to emerge accidentally "amid the randomness of death and its fatality" (Foucault 1980:265), that is, birth, mortality and health are no longer God-given, but matters of human control.

Foucault ascribes particular importance to the emerging role of the family as active provider of childcare and as subject to medical intervention and control (1980:166-82). In the development of bio-power new rules of behaviour are developed by experts; these codify relations within the family, obligating parents and children to physical contact, affective proximity, suckling of infants by their mother, hygiene, physical exercise and principally maintenance of the health of children and mothers (ibid.:173). Hence, "the family is assigned a linking role" between general objectives regarding the good health of the social body and the individuals' desire or need of care" (ibid.:174). In this process doctors are the advisors and experts, often replacing the authority of the priests.

A crucial point in Foucault's analysis is that bio-power does not prevent subjects from acting. Rather on the contrary, it addresses them as free agents capable of choosing in order to make them act in desirable, 'normal' ways. Power seeps into relations on all levels of society, links the mother who cares for her child to the needs of the macro-level of society, and little by little – through adjustments and invention – it penetrates even further into people's lives: "it was the taking charge of life, more than the threat of death, that gave power its access even to the body" (Foucault in Rabinow 1984:265).

The medicalisation that has taken place in Brazil in the second half of the 20th century resembles the European process described by Foucault in significant ways. Brazil has experienced an expansion of specialised and highly technical hospital-based medicine and a secularisation of norms in areas that gradually fell under medical authority (Faria 1997/1998:196). While curative care has grown, preventive health care has been limited (though increasing during recent years) and centred on the rhetoric of mother-infant care.

Among lower class people in Northeast Brazil this process has taken place only recently, since the late 1980s. When Nancy Scheper-Hughes arrived in Pernambuco for the first time in 1964 as a Peace Corps health worker she herself was "expected to try overcoming the 'resistance' of the poor to medical care," as she puts it (Scheper-Hughes 1992:197). But as Scheper-Hughes points out, the exposure of the Pernambucan population to clinical medicine has been phenomenal and exponential over the last four decades (ibid.:196). Statistics of infant mortality show the positive result of this development, though Northeast Brazil still ranks high in comparison with Brazil's other regions.

Table 1

Evolution of the infant mortality rate in Brazil and its regions

Year	Brazil	North	Northeast	Southeast	South	Mid-West
1940	164.0	-	-	-	-	-
1950	136.6	171.6	206.9	99.9	130.6	126.8
1960	105.2	122.0	183.6	67.7	107.7	104.1
1970	92.0	67.1	149.3	83.5	77.1	80.3
1980	87.3	100.0	130.0	67.0	55.0	85.0
1986-96*	48	43	76	33/42	25	34

Source: Martine and Camargo, Brazilian Journal of Population Studies, 1997/98 vol.1, p. 68

* Numbers for 1986-96 are from PNDS 1996. The Southeast Region is here divided into Rio/São Paulo

In Camaragibe a very recent emphasis on primary health care has led to a further decline in infant mortality reaching 23.2 per 1000 live births in 1996 (*Prefeitura de Camaragibe* 1999). Simultaneously, the number of children dying from diarrhoea has reached zero. Mothers have been educated in hygiene and the making of homemade rehydration solution, and the rate of breastfeeding has improved considerably due to a persistent campaign by the health care system. Today 50 per cent of all children are exclusively breastfed until four months of age (according to the municipality), while this rate for Pernambuco in general is only 30 per cent (*Secretaria de Imprensa* 1998:17). These changes have come about through an effective network of health workers, who like Nancy Scheper-Hughes in her young days, visit families, instruct mothers in particular and survey the population in general.

Life was similarly taken charge of in the neighbourhood. In the register at the health post families had become 'cases': they were "described, judged, measured, compared with others, in (their) very individuality" in order later to be "trained or corrected, classified, normalised, excluded, etc." (Foucault in Rabinow 1984:203). As the focus has been on maternal and infant health, women especially were targeted, requested to come for antenatal examinations, to bring their babies for check ups every month and to have regular gynaecological exams. They had learned to think actively about their own and their children's health in terms of medical treatment, and they generally assumed their responsibility as patients with serious commitment.

This chapter provides a description of controlled bodies – bodies subjected to medical authority – but also body-subjects who seek control in their own lives and therefore willingly grasp the means they are offered. I describe the social changes in Brazil since the 1960s with particular focus on expanding medical health care and the recent fertility decline. I then move to the section 'Tubal Ligation in Cama-ragibe', in which I turn towards sterilisation and fertility as I found these phenomena in the late 1990s in the neighbourhood where I did my fieldwork. Finally, I return to the initial discussion of medicalisa-tion and situate the presented data as elements in the process in which I see women as simultaneously controlled and empowered.

The Brazilian fertility decline

At the time I spoke with Ana she was 50 years old. It was thus 20 years ago that she had her third child in order to be sterilised. She was a small but strong woman, made of that leathery material that characterised so many of the older women. The long hair was rolled up in a firm knot. Sitting there with her on the terrace in front of her house I came to think that the old women appeared so much stronger than the younger ones. Was it just because they had had to fight much more in order to survive?

Dona Neuza, Dona Corina, Dona Beneditta – they all complained about the young women, who no longer knew how to work. "They have everything today, but they just throw it away!" Dona Neuza once told Josenita about a young woman, a neighbour, who came to her house one morning around ten o'clock. The young woman told the older that she had not yet had her morning coffee. Dona Neuza answered: "But girl, haven't you had any coffee at this time of the day!" Assuming that the young woman's house was without food, Dona Neuza took coffee, beans, manioc flour, rice and meat out of the cupboard and told her to take it home and cook a good lunch for her husband. But the young woman kept hanging around, and, as Dona Neuza said, "watched my face", and then finally it came out (the old

They had worked hard.

woman imitated the young woman's tone): "'Look, Dona Neuza, I will not take it with me, and you know why? I haven't got more gas!' I looked like this at her" Dona Neuza continued, "and then I said, 'Girl, stop for a while, you do not want to take this food, given to you, worked for, bought for sweat? You open your mouth and tell me that you do not take it, because you have no gas? Do you have a pan? Yes. Do you have water? Yes. Do you have salt? Yes. My girl, you live near a forest. You go and get some firewood and make a fire. Don't you see what I do? Take the food, make a fire, and at noon you will have food ready for your husband and your children.' Then she became like this [Dona Neuza made a gesture of refusal] and went away. What is that? It is laziness, *rapaz*!"

Listening to Josenita's description I could imagine Dona Neuza's competent movements in her kitchen while she described the idleness of the young woman. They seemed so full of pride, these old women; they had worked hard in order to feed their children. As Rute's mother told me: "I am not ashamed to say that I have cleaned sewers in order to make my children survive." And they apparently felt that the younger women did not appreciate toiling anymore. The meaning of life had changed and the young women seemed to expect a different, easier life from that of their mothers.

Changed living conditions
Everyday life in Northeast Brazil has changed over the last four decades. As in the rest of Brazil large numbers of people have moved from rural to urban areas, work has changed from subsistence to paid labour, health has been medicalised, television is widespread, and consumption an integral part of the 'good life'. Structural changes in the agricultural production in the mid-1960s forced small farmers and rural workers to move to urban areas. Almost 30 million Brazilians (more than one third of the population in 1970) migrated to the cities between 1960 and 1980 (Martine, Das Gupta and Chen 1998:198). Due to a sharp fall in real wages in the 1960s and 1970s combined with rising costs of living in the city, women had to contribute to the household economy for it to survive (Wood and Carvalho 1988:174). From 1960 to 1984 women's participation in the labour force increased from 12 to 36 per cent. However, as a consequence of the economic crisis in 1981-82 unemployment rose, especially in the Northeast, and left more women than men without jobs. This situation was particularly dire as societal changes had given rise to an increased number of female headed households. Living under conditions that left most other aspects of life in uncertainty (job, income, housing), the marital relationship was threatened by the husband's inability to fulfil his expected role as provider. Separations were therefore many. From 1960 to 1984 the number of female headed households in Brazil almost quadrupled peaking at 1 out of 5 households in 1984 (Goldani 1990).[2]

These changes led to an immense number of families living in slum-like conditions in the cities, dependent on the cash economy and without support from extended family networks. The so-called Economic Miracle[3] during 1968-1976 in Brazil only benefited a relatively small proportion of already better-off Brazilians, mainly in the urban South and Southeast, who increased their wealth due to the growing industrialisation (Skidmore 1999). In the Northeast most people just survived; as Scheper-Hughes writes, for them the miracle consisted in managing to stay alive (Scheper-Hughes 1992:32).

However, in spite of the misery people have experienced an improvement in living conditions. Health care facilities became more accessible, especially in the cities: for instance, the number of physicians per 10,000 inhabitants grew from around 5 in 1960 to a little more than 11 in 1980 (Faria 1997/1998:187);[4] under the INAPS, the public health insurance system, the number of hospitalisations per 100 inhabitants increased from 3.1 in 1970 to 10.0 in 1985 (ibid.:194). At another level credit policies designed to expand markets for the growing national industry integrated the lower economic strata of the population in consumption. Objectively, of course, these policies undermined family economies even further; subjectively, people felt enriched as it allowed them to purchase goods and services they could only have aspired to in the past culminating in the absurdity of consumer goods appearing in the middle of impoverished homes. For instance, in the neighbourhood where I lived almost everybody had a refrigerator. While television was the first crucial consumer good to enter people's life, refrigerators had been the second and almost equally important. Most women had acquired their *geladeiras* recently, within the last five or ten years. They were all very big refrigerators – used goods from wealthier families – and often just contained a plate with an onion, a green pepper and some used soft drink bottles filled with tap water. Drinking warm water was no longer appropriate for decent people.

Economic development made it possible for the elite to follow cultural developments in Europe and United States, while the majority of people were illiterate and subject to high mortality and morbidity, unemployment and general poverty. With the introduction of mass communication, especially television, new patterns of value orientation and behavioural norms diffused from better-off Brazilians to the rest of society. Television has existed in Brazil since 1950, but spread rapidly after 1964 when the military regime invested in the telecommunication system. In 1979 Brazil had the fifth-largest television audience in the world (Miranda and Pereira 1983 in Tauxe 1993:595), and by the end of the 1980s more than 75 per cent of all Brazilian households would have a television (Kottak 1990 in Tauxe 1993:595). The political agenda behind this development was national integration and the subsequent political and ideological control of the population (Tufte 1993:86) but television is now everywhere the most popular vehicle for entertainment and information. As Faria writes, "TV viewing has become the major means of relating to the world outside the narrow circle of the family, the local community, and the workplace" (1997/98:191).

However, Brazilian television is mainly tuned towards the audience of the South. Since the beginning of the 1970s the programmes with the highest audiences have been telejournalism and the renowned Brazilian *telenovelas* (Fadul, McAnany and Morales 1996:1),[5] produced in the South, representing upper or middle class people and constantly interrupted by advertisements directed towards better off consumers.

In between all these movements, one unexpected and initially unnoticed development has picked up speed: women have fewer children. In the late 1960s the Brazilian birth rate began a sudden and rapid decline. The average number of children per woman was 6.5 in 1940. This number remained fairly stable in the 1950s, but dropped to 5.8 in 1970. In the thirty years between 1940 and 1970, the level of fertility in Brazil thus declined about 11 per cent (Wood and Carvalho 1988:155). However, during this period the reduction was restricted to better off income groups and regions, and particularly to urban areas. The rest of the population experienced high and even increasing birth rates (Martine, Das Gupta and Chen 1998:170). From 1970, though, the decline spread to practically all regions and social strata. The poorest region, Northeast Brazil, underwent the fastest fertility decline in the subsequent twenty years, as here the fertility rate fell from around 7 in 1970 to 3.7 in 1990 (Martine 1998:171). In 1996 it was as low as 3.1 for the Northeast, 2.7 for Pernambuco in total and 2.1 for urban Pernambuco.[6] For Brazil in general the rate was 2.5 in the same period (PNDS 1996).

No public contraceptive services

As mentioned before, this decline happened even though Brazil never had any widespread public family planning programme. For many years the government's policy in relation to population was directly pronatalist, explicitly prohibiting dissemination of family planning information or devices, strongly influenced by the Catholic Church's traditional opposition to non-procreative sexual activity. Then, in 1974, at the Bucharest World Population Conference, a Brazilian governmental representative for the first time stated that couples were free to decide the size of their family and that provision of information on family planning should be the responsibility of the state. In 1979 the President Figueiredo announced this shift in policy in a talk to the Cabinet: "In present conditions in Brazil the success of social development programs depends in large measure on family planning, but with respect for the freedom of decision of each couple. While the principles and methods of responsible parenthood are well known to those of higher income, they are unknown to precisely those who are economically less fortunate. It behoves the state to make this knowledge available to all families" (Wood and Carvalho 1988:161).

This proved to be mere rhetoric. Strong forces within the government, the feminist organisations and the Church opposed the few timid attempts at effective action. The "freedom of decision" in practice meant that the majority of Brazilians, who could not afford private health care, had to rely on family planning services from private organisations or take recourse to induced abortion. Particularly in the beginning of the decline in the late 1960s and early 1970s the role of induced abortion in birth control seems to have been significant (Martine 1998:175)[7] (see footnote 10 here and Chapter One, 'Female sterilisation in Brazil', for a discussion on methods used).

Among other less dominant private organisations, the Civil Society for the Welfare of the Family (BEMFAM) actively promoted family planning in Brazil with financial support from the International Planned Parenthood Federation (IPPF) and other foreign sources (Wood and Carvalho 1988:162). This organisation was initiated at a meeting for Brazilian gynecologists and obstetricians in Rio de Janeiro in 1965 ostensibly motivated by the high number of induced abortions, the risks of health posed by a high parity, and the high child mortality rates (Serruya 1996:29). Since for many years the objective of this initiative was population control rather than assisting individuals to make the right family planning decisions, BEMFAM was criticised relentlessly by the ever stronger feminist movement.

Through agreements with municipalities, community associations and trade unions, BEMFAM created a wide net for distribution of contraception that has functioned through all the years without any state control (Ávila and Barbosa 1985:4). From 1973 the poor and child rich Northeast Brazil became BEMFAMs prime centre of action.[8] Here the organisation was criticised for merely distributing contraceptive technology, mainly the pill, with little information and no medical supervision (Ávila and Barbosa 1985:5). In the wake of this policy many women suffered serious side effects and unwanted pregnancies, which lead to high rejection and discontinuity rates and clandestine abortions (Martine 1998:177).

The history of feminism in Brazil is closely tied to the struggle against population control programmes like BEMFAMs (Pitanguy 1994:112). Taking an anti-governmental and anti-imperialist stance under the military dictatorship the feminist movement strongly opposed all abuses of women's integrity including organised population control efforts. Ironically feminists thereby contributed to the postponing of poor women's access to contraception (Martine 1998:182). However, in the early 1980s the feminist movement took the lead in the process towards a democratisation of family planning services within a framework of reproductive health.

As a result of a dialogue between the Ministry of Health, feminist women's health advocates and experts from the university, the Programme of Integrated Assistance to Woman's Health (PAISM) was launched in 1983 (Pitanguy 1994:114). This program included reproductive health care and contraceptive services and it constituted a very important achievement for the women's movement and confirmed its entrance into public policy making. However, subsequent political, administrative and financial problems undermined its efficiency and till today PAISM is not yet implemented throughout the country. Even in the late 1990s many health posts (including the one that became one of the foci of my study) did not distribute contraception or even information about family planning.[9]

In the vacuum created by unsatisfying and often irregularly distributed contraceptive pills and precarious and illegal induced abortions, women accepted sterilisation as a means of reducing family size. As Ana said, life did not offer them the conditions for big families, so the good God provided a way out.

The sterilisation-caesarean section circuit

According to the Brazilian National Survey on Demography and Health (PNDS), 40.1 per cent of formally and informally married women between 15 and 49 years old were sterilised in 1996; in the Northeast this number was 43.9 per cent. Simultaneously, Brazil has one of the world's highest caesarean section rates. In 1996 36.4 per cent of all deliveries were caesarean sections with the São Paulo region having the highest level at 52.1 per cent, while the Northeast rated relatively low at 20.4 per cent (counted alone Recife reached 42 per cent) (ibid).[11]

The high caesarean section rates are both a determinant and a consequence of the prevalent use of female sterilisation. As obstetricians in Brazil for many years adhered strictly to the dogma 'once caesarean always caesarean', women who once gave birth through a caesarean section would continue doing so for subsequent deliveries. Three caesareans have been a medically recommended indication for stopping childbearing due to a theoretical risk of complications in a subsequent pregnancy. In this situation sterilisation became a necessary intervention (Costa 1995:103). As the number of caesareans increased over the years, especially between 1970 and 1980,[12] the number of sterilisations equally escalated.

However, the caesarean section rate is also a consequence of the use of sterilisation as a means of birth control. Even though it is the most widely used form of contraception, sterilisation has until recently been left in a 'legal limbo' (Giffin 1994:357). The Federal Constitution states that every couple is free to choose how to regulate their fertility, while a paragraph in the Penal Code proscribes any kind of body lesion that includes loss of an organ or function. In this ambiguity the Brazilian Medical Council considered the tubal ligation illegal and not to be recommended from an ethical perspective (Vieira and Ford 1996:1428). All sterilisations have therefore been performed unofficially and often concealed by a caesarean section. The patient makes a private agreement with a particular obstetrician, who will sometimes do the surgery for free, but who may also charge a relatively high payment.

The advantage of this arrangement for individual physicians is obvious. At public hospitals the extra payment constitutes an economic incentive for the often underpaid public medical staff. In addition, as many public physicians have more than one job, less stressful conditions (such as sleep during night shifts) are preferable. For private obstetricians, who personally provide care for their clients, caesareans are a means to plan ahead in an otherwise uncontrolled work schedule. What counts for both groups is, as Molina da Costa writes, "no night work, no missed weekends, and no waiting" (Costa 1995:104). Physicians' preferences have, in this way, fuelled the development.

Another related factor is, as Cecilia de Mello e Souza points out, that the notion of high-risk pregnancies is being widened in today's obstetrics. In Brazil as in other countries an ever-growing list of medical indications for caesarean sections justifies more surgical deliveries than before. The technological development has made diagnosis more refined; 'foetal distress' for instance is more easily detectable (Mello e Souza 1994:360). However, as de Mello e Souza also indicates, the inclination for caesarean sections has lead many obstetricians to interpret dubious signals as justification for surgical intervention. 'Absence of sufficient dilation' is often used to justify surgery even after very short labour (ibid.). And 'foetal distress' can be used as justification for caesareans performed hours after the diagnosis (Carranza 1994: 147). In my material many women, according to their own explanation, had unplanned caesarean sections either due to *falta de dilatação* (failed dilation), *neném sentado* (sitting baby [breech presentation]) or *neném colado* (stuck baby).

Legalised sterilisation
In an attempt to regulate the prevalent but hitherto uncontrolled use of sterilisation the paragraph in the Federal Constitution considering family planning was finally amplified in November 1997 in order explicitly to include sterilisation as a fully legal procedure for both men and women above 25 years of age or with a minimum of 2 living children.[13] The intervention can be performed with a period of 60 days between request and surgery, however, not during abortion or child birth (except in case of a series of caesarean sections) (Rocha 1998:46). Within this period counselling including information about reversible

methods and the irreversibility of sterilisation must be provided. Yet the question is whether this law will make any noticeable difference; at the very least, a very consistent public intervention along with financial backing is needed, if change is wanted.

In December 1998, a year after the legalisation of sterilisation, I interviewed Dr. Olímpio from CISAM, which is one of the clinics now authorised to provide sterilisations in Recife. He said: "It has not been implemented yet, which means that the hospital does not receive any money, but we have already changed our procedures. Thus, today we follow the law, or *norma tecnica*, because some just call it a *norma tecnica*. A law is something heavy like 'in all maternities it has to be done like this,' while *norma tecnica* is an orientation to be followed. You don't need to, if you disagree, for instance at a private clinic. I do not know for sure how it is, but we have already changed and follow the prescriptions exactly. [...] We spread the information that it has changed, that women now have the right to sterilisation, but very limited and not in the newspaper, the television or the radio, because if we did that we would not have the conditions to receive such quantities of people."

Dr. Olímpio then told me that women who visited the clinic would first be offered an IUD. After having tried it for a while they could return and have it removed, if they still preferred a sterilisation. In itself it sounded reasonable to me, as I knew that today too many women are sterilised too young and may later regret it. However, when I learned that the woman would have to return to have the IUD inserted during her menstrual cycle, and that the doctor would be accompanied by several medical students, I doubted whether any of the women I knew would ever appreciate such an offer. They all considered menstruation very dirty and shameful, and having to expose their genitals in such a humiliating condition would certainly not be attractive, as long as alternatives existed. It seemed almost calculated to fail, pushing women even further towards the private sector and uncontrolled sterilisations rather than reinforcing the public, state regulated system.

Anyway, in Camaragibe nobody seemed to know the law. Not even the health care providers with whom I talked knew the exact content a year after its passage. Everything continued as before.

Tubal ligation in Camaragibe

We had only been in the neighbourhood for a short time, when I sat with my husband and our two timid children on a bench in front of Dona Mónica's house enjoying the quick sunset and the sounds of the falling darkness with some of our new neighbours. Ricardo, the father of two boys who persistently tried to engage our children in play, asked me if I had only two children. I said yes. "Ligou?" he asked me straight away. Did I get sterilised? I told him slightly embarrassed that I had never considered sterilisation an option and that I had an IUD. The last information was provoked by his confusion, when I neglected the obvious fact: a woman with two children, educated and apparently well-off, how could she not be sterilised? I later returned to that situation in my reflections on the status of sterilisation in the neighbourhood. Female sterilisation was something to discuss with new acquaintances apparently free of the privacy and sexual connotations that we apply to contraception in Denmark. Neighbours usually knew who was sterilised in the houses around, and word of new achievements was often spread just like other prestige giving news in the neighbourhood. Sterilisation had become part of public discourse and was perceived as a natural aspiration for any woman. I had entered a field where women talked about 'my ligation' as a step in the female life course almost as obvious as 'my menstruation'. With the difference that menstruation was only mentioned with shame and in oblique terms.

Local patterns of sterilisation

Statistics for Brazil in general (Table 2) show that the percentage of sterilised women among all married women using contraception increased from 7.1 per cent in 1975 to 44.4 per cent in 1986 (Berquó 1989 cited in Costa 1995:13).

Table 2
Sterilisation trends among all currently married women using contraception
Brazil 1975-1986

Year	%
1975	7.1
1977	9.0
1980	18.1
1984	31.5
1986	44.4

Source: E. Berquo. 1989 in da Costa 1995: 13

According to the National Survey of Demography and Health (PNDS 1996) this proportion has further increased; Brazil in general shows a rate of sterilisation of 52 per cent of all married women using contraception, in Northeast Brazil the proportion reaches 65 per cent, in Pernambuco 69 per cent. That is, seven out of ten women using contraception in Pernambuco are sterilised. Among Pernambucan women the use of other methods of modern contraception is limited: 15.5 per cent of all married users age 15 to 49 use the pill, a little less than 10 per cent use the 'other methods' (distributed equally on condom and IUD's/injections).[14] The remaining users rely on so-called traditional methods (withdrawal and rhythm). Use of male sterilisation, vasectomy, is rare; very few cases were mentioned in the neighbourhood, generally as something nobody else would ever do. Both women and men seemed to agree on loss of potency as a risk related to vasectomy.

In the survey that we conducted among all women within the area covered by the ACSs, 1762 women over 15 years of age were visited. Out of these, 623 women were sterilised, that is, 35 per cent. If we isolate the age group from 15 to 49 the percentage reaches 37 per cent. We did not ask about marital status or use of other forms of contraception and therefore we cannot isolate either 'married women' or 'contraceptive users'. However, in Brazil in general 27.3 per cent of all women between 15 and 49 years old are sterilised (PNDS 1996). This means that the area in which we worked ranked high compared to the national level in the use of sterilisation as a contraceptive method.

Our material does not show the changing percentage of women sterilised over time. However, the distribution of sterilisations in the neighbourhood suggests that the main proportion of women were sterilised after 1980 (Table 3). We found that till the beginning of the 1980s the number of children per sterilised woman was relatively stable at 5.28. However, a significant drop (P 0.01%) in the average number of children starts in 1980 and reaches a new level just above 3 children per sterilised woman in 1985 (also Table 3). The variation from year to year in the number of children is very low after 1985, suggesting that when sterilisation became a significant method of contraception, the number of children per woman simultaneously settled at 3.

Table 3
Distribution of sterilisations and number of children at sterilisation over time
January 1999 (n = 623 sterilised women)

Year of sterilisation	No. of sterilisations	Mean no. of children
before 1965	3	—
1965-69	8	7.00
1970-74	28	5.04
1975-79	67	5.69
1980-84	105	5.01
1985-89	148	3.31
1990-94	146	3.11
1995-99	118	3.04

In addition, we looked for data on age at sterilisation. We found a small, but statistically significant drop (P 0.2) in the mean age at sterilisation after 1985. From approximately 29 years the mean age fell to just above 27 years of age at the time of sterilisation.[15] This mean age is lower than the mean age of 29 found in the National Survey of Demography and Health 1996; however, compared to 1986 the survey also registered a decline of two and a half years in age at sterilisation (PNDS 1996:60). Bearing in mind that the average number of children per sterilised woman has decreased from 5 to 3, this rather stable mean age indicates that women after 1985 have given birth to fewer children over a longer time period. Data from the qualitative interviews suggest that this may be due to the use of contraceptive pills for spacing between births.

The distribution over time of sterilisations organised by age (at sterilisation) shows the decline in mean age as a clear trend towards sterilisation of women in their twenties. We thus found that 64 per cent of sterilised women were sterilised before the age of 30 (Table 4).

Table 4
Distribution (in percentage) of sterilised women
according to age at sterilisation against years elapsed since the surgery
January 1999 (n = 623 sterilised women)

Years since	Sterilisations (% of all sterilisations within the period) according to age at sterilisation								total	number
	-19	20-24	25-29	30-34	35-39	40-44	45-49	50-		
0-4	1.3	30	39.3	15.3	8.7	4.7	0.7	—	100	150
5-9	6.3	26.6	33.5	25.9	5.6	1.4	—	0.7	100	143
10-14	8.1	36	25.7	22.1	3.7	4.4	—	—	100	136
15-19	3.8	23.6	24.5	21.7	15.1	4.7	4.7	1.9	100	106
20-24	1.8	13	31.5	35.2	16.7	—	1.8	—	100	54
25-30	—	28	40	20	—	12	—	—	100	25
30-	—	33.3	22.2	44.5	—	—	—	—	100	9
Total no.	27	174	197	141	51	23	7	3	—	623

It is important also to note that 32 per cent of the all sterilised women in the survey obtained a sterilisation at less than 25 years of age – the minimum age according to regulations of the 1997 law from the Secretary of Health in Pernambuco. In comparison, for Brazil in general, the proportion of women sterilised under the age of 25 is 'only' 21 per cent (PNDS 1996). Forty-six women (7.4 per cent) in my study reported that they were sterilised before or at the age of 20 (Table 5). This percentage is remarkably high as sterilisation at an early age is considered a significant factor in risk of regret (Machado 1998). However, according to our findings sterilisation among very young women has decreased recently, perhaps due to the public debate and attempts at regulation.

Table 5
Distribution of sterilised women under age 25 by age at sterilisation
against years elapsed since surgery
January 1999 (n = 201)

Years since	Age at sterilisa-tion	14	15	16	17	18	19	20	21	22	23	24	total
						(numbers of women)							
0-4		1	—	—	—	—	1	4	4	18	8	11	47
5-9		—	—	1	—	2	6	6	7	9	7	9	47
10-14		—	—	1	—	2	8	4	6	17	8	14	60
15-19		—	—	2	—	1	1	4	3	3	7	8	29
20-24		—	—	—	—	—	1	—	3	1	1	2	8
25-29		—	—	—	—	—	—	1	1	1	2	2	7
30-		—	—	—	—	—	—	—	2	1	—	—	3
Total		1	—	4	—	5	17	19	26	50	33	46	201

I was interested in the use of caesarean sections as a means to obtain sterilisation. Initially, we found the rate of caesarean sections to be 33 per cent of all deliveries (n = 210) within the two year period 1995-1997. Later, we asked sterilised women (n = 610) about their last delivery.[16] The frequency of caesarean sections as opposed to vaginal births as last delivery before sterilisation appeared to be remarkably stable over the years. The overall frequencies were 69 per cent caesareans and 31 per cent vaginal births. A caesarean section as last delivery does not necessarily indicate that the sterilisation was performed at the same time. It is, however, probable that the caesarean section in most cases was either conditioned by a wish for sterilisation or became the opportunity to have the wished for operation performed. In the five year period preceding the 1996 National Survey of Demography and Health 59 per cent of all sterilisations in Brazil in general were performed in combination with a caesarean section (PNDS 1996). In Northeast Brazil this percentage was 43.2, while for urban Pernambuco it reached 53. Hence, the estimated proportion of sterilisations performed during a caesarean section in our study is near the pattern for Brazil in general, but exceeds that for both the Northeast and Pernambuco.

The area thus represented a high level of sterilisation of women at a relatively low median age, a high percentage of women sterilised under the age of 25, and an estimated prevalence of sterilisations performed during a caesarean section that passed the present level found for both the Northeast and Pernambuco.

Methods of sterilisation

In the world in general the most common technique of female sterilisation is tubal ligation, accomplished by occlusion of the tubes with ligatures, clips, bands, rings or electro coagulation. The tubes are most often reached through the abdomen, either by use of laparotomy, mini-laparotomy or laparoscopy (Costa 1995:3). Laparotomy is the medical term for the approach through an abdominal incision of more than 5 centimetres and this method usually requires hospitalisation, the use of general or local anaesthesia, and a relatively long recovery period. This approach poses a greater risk of complication than other methods. In the mini-laparotomy a small incision of 3-4 centimetres is made and this method can be used as an outpatient procedure. For both methods, the surgeon lifts the tubes out of the abdomen to ligate them and divide them with a cut, whereupon in some cases a piece of the tube is removed. In laparoscopy an optical instrument is inserted in the abdomen, whereby occlusion is performed within the abdomen with clips or bands without removal of tissue (WHO 1992: 16). The latter is the most easily reversible as it does not involve cutting of the tube; studies of reversal surgery suggest that the degree of damage to the tubes when sterilisation is performed influences the success of a reversal, that is, the chance of a pregnancy located in the womb (ibid.:127).

Women I met during fieldwork insisted on having a piece of tube cut out – some even wanted to see it afterwards – and doctors generally seemed to be ready to meet this demand. The only sterilisation I observed was made with the so-called 'Irving' method in which a section of both tubes is removed, whereupon the tube attached to the womb is folded in and sewn over. This method is only suitable for big incisions as in caesarean sections. It is very effective and hard to reverse (WHO 1992:127).

Sterilisation can be performed throughout most of a woman's reproductive life. It can be done postpartum, either in combination with a caesarean section or shortly after a vaginal delivery (most often within 48 hours), in the interval period, that is, 42 days or more after last delivery or post abortion which means immediately after an induced or spontaneous abortion (ibid.). However, for the women in the neighbourhood 'all at the same time' (*todo em uma vez*) was much coveted. 'All' meant a caesarean section, a sterilisation plus a perineum plastic insert to lift the bladder and tighten the vagina (a procedure which they referred to simply as 'the perineum').[17] The women did not see any use in being cut twice as they said, first the episiotomy[18] and next the sterilisation. Most of them assumed the intervention of the mini-laparotomy to be as comprehensive as the caesarean section, and besides, they found it difficult to leave home twice and to go through two periods of recovery. In addition, being hospitalised was a big change from the daily routine, and one had to bring a proper nightgown and preferably new plastic slippers. It was better to 'take advantage' (*aproveitar*) when having to go to hospital anyway. In addition, both a caesarean and 'the perineum' were status giving in the daily relationships of the neighbourhood.

Sources of sterilisation
Sterilisations can be obtained at private hospitals, where caesarean section rates are high, if the woman or her husband has a private health care plan or is insured through her or his employment. At the local hospital's private section a health care plan including antenatal care, a caesarean section and a sterilisation was sold for 625 *reais* (at that time around 500 US dollars) paid, if necessary, over several months. Public hospitals deliver sterilisations in case of 'risk to health', that is, after a series of caesarean sections or in particular cases of hypertension or other serious health problems.[19] Besides, women with many children were in some cases allowed sterilisations at the public hospital in Recife to which 'high risk cases' from the local health post were transferred. Those women who had neither of these characteristics had to search for a willing provider. Most sterilisations at public hospitals were obtained through agreements mediated by a third person (somebody who worked at a hospital or knew a doctor) as an act of beneficence.[20] Politicians were also good sources; some of them were doctors themselves, others had 'friends' at hospitals.[21]

The local vice-mayor and gynaecologist Dr. Nadegi was known to provide sterilisations. Besides her job at the municipality she ran a small private gynaecological clinic in Camaragibe. On days where she was expected to be present the waiting room was full of women who hoped for her assistance. Most of them would not be able to pay. As Dr. Nadegi said, "The money comes from my pocket." I asked her about the sterilisations and she answered, "Some of the women are not so sure, some even regret it later, but the majority really needs [to do the sterilisation] as they do not have the conditions [to take care of more children]. If I could decide, I would do them all. I do not think that tubal ligation is good, but I think it is bad to suffer from hunger. At times I send food because they are dying from hunger, they bring the small children and I give cans of milk, because the small children are dying from hunger and they have nothing at home, and I feel sorry for them. To ligate the tubes isn't good, but they do not know how to avoid more children. Isn't it better to ligate than abort, suffer from hunger, and bring up *marginais*?[22] Those who do not agree with me will have to excuse me, because I think so." Dr. Nadegi had certainly positioned herself as the saving angel. Everybody liked her and told me that she was the right kind of politician: a person that looked you in the eyes and listened seriously to your sorrows and complaints.

However, everybody knew that she did it for votes. Carmen was opting for a sterilisation, but came too late. She had to wait till after the election, and as Dr. Nadegi did not win Carmen presumed she had lost her chance. Another woman told me that Dr. Nadegi had refused to sterilise her as she was not allowed to vote in the municipality but somewhere else. However, for Dr. Nadegi there seemed to be no discrepancy. She had worked in the municipality as a gynaecologist for 18 years and she had initiated a career as politician because she felt compelled: "As a doctor you become a psychologist, a politician, a social assistant, you do everything. Because you stop looking just at the belly of the mother and you see the child in the street, where she lives, the street full of holes, and then you get involved [...] You stop seeing that person as a patient and start seeing her as a citizen, and then you begin to see the conditions of that person."

Dr. Nadegi's slogan: *Agora eu tenho escolha* – Now I have a choice.

Just like Dr. Nadegi old Dona Severina employed the image of the starving mother with many children when she helped her neighbours to get a sterilisation. Dona Severina worked as a cleaner at a hospital in the neighbouring town but had, she claimed, many other responsibilities at the hospital. That particular hospital was known to be dirty and poorly managed. Dona Severina seemed to be on friendly terms with the physicians, and apparently she obtained the sterilisations without any obligations on behalf of the women. "These girls ask me because they want to do the ligation," Dona Severina told me and continued to describe the procedure: "Then I say: 'How many children do you have?' And then [imitating her approach to the doctor], '*Doctora*, for the love of God, this poor woman, the *Senhora* just needs to see the situation of this girl, a horrible situation.' Then the *doctora* says, 'Very well, Severina, give these papers to her and make her do the examinations.' It is a lot of surgery that I have arranged. I don't even know the number. There are two up there, two down there, there on the corner are two, well, I don't know the number."

After Dona Severina died, the women had to find other strings to pull. Some would still procure their operation at the hospital where she had worked, as the ACSs passed the news around that for 50 *reais* (around US$ 30) the hospital still performed sterilisations. Others would find someone or other who knew a physician, worked for a hospital director, or who in some other way was affiliated to a beneficent patron. The image of the poor starving mother opened many doors, but as the following passage from an interview with Christina may illustrate, the women saw themselves as agents, not passive victims of hunger to be saved.

Christina was 25 years old, had three daughters with two different men, but lived alone with the girls. During the last pregnancy she had contacted a political candidate, and this is what she told us:

Christina: I went there to get bricks, sand, to build my house of bricks.[23] When I arrived there, a girl said: "Look, he is giving ligations"…. I was with a big belly. Then she said, "Look, that man is giving ligations, too, why don't you talk with him?" Then I left bricks for later, sand for later, cement also, and went to talk to him, and he said, "We give ligations, do you want?" I said, "I want!"

Line: Was it at the time of elections for the town hall (1996)?

Christina: Yes, it was.

Line: That doctor…

Christina: No, it wasn't a doctor, it was a *doctora*, her name was Ana Claudia.

Line: Was it the candidate who recommended her?

Christina: Yes, it was the candidate who recommended her to me.

Line: Do you think that she is a friend of his? Did he pay her?

Christina: Yes. He paid her. For all the women who went there, he paid. He paid with a little card, I don't know where, if it was in the bank, but she received on that little card.

Line: Did you speak with other women, who also…?

Christina: If I did? Yes, I spoke with the women, all the women in the room; they were operated, all of them. One said: "My friend was operated, that went well and her boy is already 15 years old, and she has no more children, and her sterilisation is good." And the girls said like this: "I hope that mine will work out well, too." One has to do a ligation. To suffer [give birth] and then not achieve it – isn't that careless. Afterwards giving birth again…?

Out of the 28 recently done sterilisations we found in the survey, nine were paid for by politicians. Five women had paid for a combined caesarean section and sterilisation (respectively 150, 200, 200, 420 and 630 *reais*) at private clinics. Most of the women who paid were relatively better off. When paying they not only achieved an immediate result; they also demonstrated their economic capacity, or rather their husband's. Four other women delivered and were subsequently sterilised at private clinics, because they or their husbands had private health insurance as part of their employment. Obstetricians at private clinics are known to be more than willing to perform caesarean sections due to their 'commitment' to each individual patient. As Taciana recalled the conversations with 'her' doctor at the time of her first pregnancy: "I talked with her about the two, normal and caesarean, and she always said, 'Look, it depends on the circumstances when you are closer to give birth, because something unforeseen can happen and we will have to take the baby out, but at present it can be normal.' And she always said, 'I tell you that if it becomes a difficult birth I make a caesarean. And if you ask me to do it, I will make it, too. It is enough that you tell me.' She always said so. But I had it in my head that I wanted a normal birth." Not surprisingly Taciana had to go through surgery due to 'unexpected' complications. And in spite of her disappointment she would opt for a second caesarean, when the time would come, she told me. In order to *aproveitar* (take advantage).

Understandings of sterilisation
People generally called a sterilisation *ligação* (from *ligação tubária*, that is, tubal ligation) instead of using the word *esterilização*. Josenita was the first person to advise me to use this expression, as she thought nobody would consider themselves *esterilizadas*. I found that interesting. *Ligação* means something beyond the English word 'ligation', 'something that binds' – a telephone call, a relationship between two persons or the binding together of the tubes. The women were very aware of this binding, as they all preferred being cut rather than just bound. "I asked him to do the cut instead of the knot," they could say, indicating that doctors performed both methods of sterilisation, but that they themselves only trusted the cut. Everybody knew that after a knot, the tying together of the tubes, a woman could be pregnant again,

according to some after seven years. Some women directly asked the doctor to show them the pieces cut out. And according to the women some doctors emphasised that a cut was performed, even though the woman did not ask. One woman brought part of her tubes home in a glass, Carmen told me, when I asked her how she knew with such certainty that a tube looked like the gut of a hen.

From her study among lower income women in São Paulo (1996) Vieira also reports about this cutting or tying of the tubes.[24] She categorises the importance that women place on this distinction as a misunderstanding. Rumours of sterilisation failures create uncertainty among the women, she writes, as do some doctors' apparent assurance of the reversibility of the operation, be it due to communication failure or pecuniary interest. In this uncertainty women in Vieira's study believed that two different kinds of methods were in use (Vieira and Ford 1996:1430). However, there seems to be some reason for this distinction. Molina da Costa mentions one method, the Madlener, which is not as effective as other methods, because the tube is not cut, but just crushed after having being tied up in a loop. This method has a high failure rate; however, it is seldom used nowadays (Costa 1995:4). My guess is, though, that failures have occurred, and that some of these failures have been explained as results of a non-efficient method. Women had integrated this uncertainty in their perception of sterilisation, which meant that they could never be sure about its effect, but equally that a sterilisation was not necessarily the end of their fertility. At least this was the ambiguity we found in the neighbourhood.

Josenita asked some women about the word *esterilização*:

Josenita: Do you think that you are a sterilised woman?
Maria: No, by no means. I already had my children.
Josenita: Then for you what is a sterilised woman?
Maria: One who never had children. I think... because doesn't the doctor call it sterility...sterilisation? That is for a woman who never had children and wants to be pregnant. That is what I know.

———

Josenita: Do you consider yourself a sterilised woman?
Jacione: I never paused to think, but I suppose so.
Josenita: You think that you are sterilised?
Jacione: I am afraid of reverting…
Josenita: But you are conscious about being sterilised?
Jacione: I am conscious.

———

Josenita: Sterilised? Do you know what that is?
Maria: That is a woman that has hygiene…

———

Josenita: Do you think that you are a sterilised woman?
Lili: I think so, because it is already three years ago and I haven't caught another pregnancy. And we haven't stopped having sex, by no means.

———

Edilene: I was ligated when I was 32.
Josenita: And about the freedom to sterilisation, what is your opinion?
Edilene: Masculine or feminine?
Josenita: Both, because today people know more about vasectomy. No, in the case of the woman, sterilisation for women?
Edilene: I would not do it.
Josenita: What?
Edilene: The sterilisation?
Josenita: What is your opinion about the freedom to sterilisation? Formerly it was more difficult, wasn't it?
Edilene: It was. For the woman to be sterile? I do not know much about that subject. I am not very good at this subject.
Josenita: This expression: "That woman is a sterilised woman." What do you understand by a sterilised woman?
Edilene: I do not understand anything.

———

Josenita: Do you think that you are a sterilised woman?

Anelita: I think that I am not, because even though I made the ligation, it is, as I said, not for sure that I am free from this... from pregnancies. Because it may be that I become pregnant again, as I do not know how my ligation was made. If it was well made. Everybody is subject to this, everybody runs the risk. I myself run the risk. I cannot confirm that I will not have one (pregnancy). I am sure that I am ligated, but if I later will have ... that I already doubt.

Josenita: But do you think that you are a sterilised woman?

Anelita: Yes. As long as a new pregnancy does not show up, I am.

––––––––––

Josenita: Do you consider yourself a sterilised woman?

Josefa: What is that?

Josenita: Do you see yourself as a sterilised woman?

Josefa: Sterilised in which way?

Josenita: Sterilisation... Do you know what sterilisation is?

Josefa: Sterilisation is when we sterilise a thing at the hospital, what I know is this, that clean thing...

Josenita: And a sterilised woman is what for you?

Josefa: I don't know! (she laughs heartily)

––––––––––

A husband: A sterilised woman... I think like this, she is a woman that was never ligated, but is sterile, who does not have children. That is it. And she who was operated, who made a ligation, she is a de-ligated woman... ligated woman... I do not know how they say it...

Thus there were certainly some women who immediately recognised the word *esterilizada* correctly as designating a sterilised woman. When asked if they themselves were *esterilizada*, their doubt was related to the efficiency of the surgery; was it well done or would it later show inefficient? Other informants were not accustomed to the use of the word. They either associated *esterilizada* with hygiene or with sterility. The husband quoted above revealed the extent of the confusion about the terms and the procedures, with ligation seen as a process that had a simple and opposite relation to 'deligation'. The practical consequence of this investigation was to stick to the words *ligada* and *ligação*, but the use of this word was also telling in itself. Understanding and naming are intertwined processes, "the sense being held within the word, and the word being the external existence of the sense" (Merleau-Ponty 1962:182), and the use of different words therefore also revealed women's perceptions of their state of fertility. All the women used the word *ligação* in daily speech when referring to a sterilisation, apparently a word with a much more positive connotation than *esterilização*. *Ligação* designated a dynamic situation: something was bound and could get unbound if badly done, underneath the preliminary intervention the woman was still fertile. That seemed to be important even though also a threat. I will later return to the significance of fertility in both male and female identity (see Chapter Six); here it will suffice to say that the ability to procreate was essential for a woman's relation to her husband, mother and female network.

The linking to sterility embedded in the word *esterilização* seemed less important in the women's perception of the surgery; for some sterility was even totally unrelated to their present status. However, emphasising their underlying fertile status the women seemed to neglect the irreversibility of the operation. Or rather, being so used to uncertainty and arbitrary vicissitudes they valued the finality of the surgery, but, (for the same reason), did not trust it, and continually striving for the 'final finality' they seemed not to have realised that they had actually reached it. Everything in their lives may still change, but it is unlikely that any of them will have more children.[25] The use of the word *ligação* seemed to blur this reality especially for those whom it hit hardest: the youngest women, who had grown up in a world where sterilisation was taken for granted. Only a few young women talked about the irreversibility in a serious tone of voice. Among those was Suely, a 34 year old mother of two children:

Josenita: And for how long time do you think that this ligation will last?

Suely: Mine? I think for the rest of my life. At times I become sad, because I will get no more children. Because it is closed. When one thinks rightly, it is a cruel thing, a ligation.

Early sterilisation

Among the very young sterilised women we found, for instance, Dona Severina's daughter-in-law, Rosilene. She was 11 when she arrived in Dona Severina's house, having eloped from her parent's house to live with Dona Severina's son, who was 8 years older than her. When she was 12, she had her first child. Severina then obliged her to use contraceptive pills, but after some time Rosilene was disgusted by the smell of beans, and Severina realised that she was pregnant again. The young couple had nothing to eat, no bed, and no milk for the children. Dona Severina found the situation too uncertain, and she asked the girl if she would like to have a ligation. She accepted and Severina made the arrangements with a physician at the hospital where she worked. He agreed to do the surgery even though the girl was only 16 years old. "She did not have the living conditions for more children, and the pill spoils a woman's health," Severina said when justifying her initiative. Rosilene was 19 when I met her on one of my walks with the ACSs. Her scar was very fine, almost non-existent.

On the same walk we visited Iris who had her sterilisation at the age of 21, after having 3 children. Everything around her had been miserable: she could not use contraceptive pills due to their side effects, she easily got pregnant, and her husband earned very little and irregularly. Dona Severina had helped her, too. We later visited Daina, who lived nearby but under much better conditions. She was sterilised at the age of 19, helped by the director of a local hospital for whom her husband worked. She now had two girls at 10 and 7, and wanted a son for her husband. He always wanted a son, and when the second daughter was born, the obstetrician asked her if she was still sure that she wanted him to ligate her tubes, before he sutured the incision. Apparently he foresaw the problem. However, tired of everything, Daina had asked him to go ahead. Now she hoped that he had just tied her tubes, which would leave some possibility for a third pregnancy, a first son.

Rute, whom I knew better, was also among the relatively young sterilised women. She had her first child when she was 17 years old. At that time she had lived with her husband in his parents' home for one and a half years as his woman. They never married. She was using contraceptive pills. However, she stopped without his acceptance in order to become pregnant. In between the first and the second child she used the pill again, but the side effects made her decide to stop.

Immediately she became pregnant. When the second son was 3 months old, she became pregnant again. Her husband wanted a girl, and they both hoped for a girl in the third pregnancy. During this pregnancy they decided to stop having more children and after giving birth she obtained a sterilisation from a physician, who had already sterilised her sisters and a neighbour of hers, who lived in the neighbouring town, São Lourenço. She was 22 when she was operated on after having given birth to yet another son. Rute said, "I wasn't forced. It was because of our economic situation. But it wasn't from the heart either, because I wanted a girl. I thought a lot. I already had three very small [children], I lived in the house of my mother-in-law, not in my own, and all this I found a bit too inconvenient."

Rute loved to make Neide's small daughter Nila look beautiful – give her a bath, set her hair, and spray her with perfume. And like every other woman she loved to talk about pregnancies and preparations for the new family member about to arrive, make *chá de bebê* (baby tea), where everybody would bring small presents for the coming baby. Just as she would have loved talking about preparations for children's birthday parties, if her husband had let her buy the things needed for such a party. But in between these joys there were days full of troubles: no food, noisy children, a man who came home late, quarrels and worries. Children were a joy, occasions for many small feasts, but they were also part of a too trivial life. Rute was not going to have more.

Spacing between births
Most women in the neighbourhood had tried to use the pill for some time – perhaps for just a month or two, perhaps for years. It was used as a temporary method, mainly for spacing between children. When I told women that in Denmark we often use contraceptive pills or IUDs instead of sterilisation after completed childbearing, women would say, "Taking the pill for the rest of your life? God save me!"

In the neighbourhood IUDs were seldom discussed. Only one woman out of the many I met used an IUD. She was later hospitalised as the IUD had "disappeared in her body", thereby corroborating what everybody already knew: IUDs are dangerous. Condoms are expensive and the men did not want to use them. Some condoms were of poor quality, rupturing too easily. A few women used contraceptive injections and were satisfied, but most women did not consider this method as a possibility due to its relatively high price or because they were not accustomed to it. Nobody knew about the diaphragm. The rhythm method, called the *tabela*, was used periodically mainly by *crente* (women attending Pentecostal churches), but women got pregnant while practising it. Interrupted coitus, 'to throw outside', was equally used temporarily by many, but men were considered to be weakened by this method and, besides, they did not like it. Therefore, in most cases the pill was seen to be the only efficient method to be used until a sterilisation was reached.

Contraceptive pills are sold without prescription at any local pharmacy in Brazil and at a relatively low price, around one and a half real for a month's supply of the most commonly used brand, which amounted to a little more than one per cent of a minimum salary in 1997. I found the expense for pills quite heavy for a family economy like Neide's, for instance, whose husband earned between two and five *reais* a day. But Neide said, "No, it is cheap; it is only one real and eighty. For twenty-one days, and then comes the menstruation. But it isn't good; it disturbs the mind of the person. One becomes nervous. It is twenty-one days that you have to eat it. And three children, I caught a belly three times, while taking the pill. I did it right. And with the others I thought: 'No, I will not take more pills.' I stopped, and then I caught yet another belly." We continued talking about Neide's pregnancies, and I asked: How many times were you pregnant?

Neide: Twelve.
Line: And how many abortions?
Neide: Seven. And five alive.
Line: These abortions, did you want them? Or did you want to have all the children?
Neide: No, I did not want any of them. But... I became pregnant, and if I could choose between abortion or alive, I would prefer alive because I suffered a lot with the abortions. I aborted with eight months, seven months, four months, because I could not secure the child.
Line: Eight months, that is a living child, isn't it?

Neide: It was a girl. She was born dead. I had many abortions, more than I wanted. It is worse than a normal birth, because a living child helps the mother, it has strength, and when it is dead the mother is alone. It is very bad to have a dead child, you see?
Line: Do you like to give birth?
Neide: No, I don't like to give birth and I don't like children very much. They annoy too much. I am full of white hair because of my children. They annoy in the belly. They annoy when you are going to have them. They annoy afterwards. They annoy in every manner and I do not like it. But I had a lot by accident.

Aborto means both induced abortion and miscarriage; here I have translated the word as 'abortion', even though I do not know if Neide ever ended any of these pregnancies by choice. Miscarriages were common and explained as due to poor health, bad nutrition or *susto* (sudden fright). I know, however, that after this conversation, when I had returned to Denmark, Neide became pregnant again and she had done much in order to end this pregnancy, or as she would have said, "to make the menstruation come". Her husband had been furious with the pregnancy, scolded her as he said that they could not afford yet another child. "But God wanted it so, I became pregnant while I took the pills," she wrote to me. And I knew she was right; she had been taking pills. She had been responsible.

Yet I also knew that the pills she had taken were given to her by a neighbour. This neighbour had received two packages from her *patroa* (the woman in whose house she was working). She had then given one package to Neide, and Neide had made use of it in order to save money. But she bled three times in a month, and as she knew that she had to stop when menstruating, she stopped each time. "I think I did not do very well with those pills," she said when telling me about them.

Neide was not the only one to take pills irregularly, often changing brands. The discipline of taking pills just did not fit into the daily struggling along of many of the women. And then there were the 'false pills'. I first heard about these false pills during my first stay. Carmen got pregnant due to a false pill, and Luzia and Neide figured out together that this was also the case of Luzia. I found it a very interesting way of explaining failures, calling upon some native superstition. However, when I returned the following year I heard that false pills made of flour had actually been found among the pills called Microvilar, the most widely used brand in the neighbourhood.[26] Carmen had gained some moral satisfaction. "You see," she said, "everybody thought that I had just been careless!" My embarrassment when remembering my response to the 'superstition' that I found the year before taught me at least one thing: contraceptive side effects are difficult to assess. It is easy to see all failures as results of either users' ignorance or supply of poor contraception to poor women. However, reality seems to be found somewhere in-between, as ideas, practices and the quality of remedies interact. As Tine Gammeltoft points out in her study on the use of IUDs in Vietnam, "The reactions of a woman's body to a contraceptive device seem to involve much more than just 'raw' physiology'" (1999:248). In life, physiology merges with social stress, hopes and longings and it seems futile to try to define where nature ends and culture takes over.

In the neighbourhood women perceived the pills as causing nausea, headache, nervousness, tiredness, depression and last but not least, unwanted pregnancies. And women often got either fat or thin during use. Besides, pills were perceived as piling up in the womb creating a mass that had to be removed by surgery. Several times I heard about this mass, but I was surprised when Gleisse too, who was so young and clever, told me in passing: "You know, I don't want to go on with it for long – it creates that mass inside." Carmen said the same when I pressed her to tell me how pills function: "Pills create a kind of wall in the womb. And a big part of the mass stays in one's body".[27] And thinking in terms of a growing mass I perfectly understood Carmen, when she said, "Really, having to swallow a pill every day ... it is horrible!"

To conclude, women did not find any reversible method satisfactory. The reasons why were many: lack of availability, the unreliability and uneven quality of pills and condoms, lack of knowledge about alternatives, lack of power to negotiate in sexual relations, and in the end, disgust with the only 'choice' they were left with.

A young mother.

Some ordinary stories

Many studies in Brazil point towards the same conclusion: Dissatisfaction with pills (sometimes due to wrong use) and lack of alternatives press women into sterilisation (Ávila and Barbosa 1985; Berquó 1998; Berquo and Arilha 1992; Diniz, de Mello e Souza and Portella 1998; Giffin 1994; Kaufmann 1998; Serruya 1996; Vieira 1994; Vieira and Ford 1996). The following are thus very ordinary reproductive stories in which pills were used on the way to sterilisation. Simone represents the woman who can control herself. She was a virgin when she got married, had two children and a sterilisation without any unexpected 'accidents'. In contrast, Luzinete's turbulent life was full of accidents as she moved towards her sterilisation. And then there was Maria José, who "never cared". At least, so people said.

Simone

Simone was 23 when I met her on a visit with the ACS. She lived with her husband in a separate section of her parents-in-law's home. It was a family striving upwards, working hard to earn money and educate their children. Simone had just given birth to her first child, a son, through caesarean section. Her husband was a mechanic and he had a private health insurance through his employment. Simone therefore gave birth at a private clinic. She had entered the clinic with three centimetres of dilation. However, after 24 hours she had not progressed. Meanwhile, a woman had aborted twins in Simone's presence, and she had become scared. When the doctor told her that she could either wait for her delivery to progress or have a caesarean immediately, she accepted the caesarean. She was happy with her firstborn, her marriage and her caesarean, when I interviewed her.

When I visited Simone the following year she was close to giving birth again, this time with a scheduled caesarean. The doctor had assumed that she wanted a sterilisation, and Simone never contradicted it. She said to me, "Sometimes I think that perhaps when I am around thirty, I would like to have another…but then I return: two is enough for me. If I had only one…but two is fine. And then I conform. Because at times… it happens that one gets pregnant immediately… think about that, one after the other!"

Simone had used the rhythm method between her wedding and her first pregnancy a year later. Between her first and her second pregnancy she had used contraceptive injections and pills. However, these caused loss of appetite and pre-menstrual symptoms. She feared using an IUD, which she had considered an alternative, because IUDs caused cancer, she said. She never discussed these considerations with her doctor, though, and when giving birth to her daughter Simone was sterilised at the age of 25.

Luzinete

Luzinete was 27 when Josenita and I visited her in her kitchen as one of the 28 sterilised women from the survey. She was a widow, but now she lived with a new man. She had had four children and two abortions, at least one of them deliberately induced by the use of medicine. Her last child was one year old, and Luzinete had delivered with a caesarean section, the first she had ever had. She had been informed that a sterilisation could be performed independently of the delivery, but she preferred both in one in order not to go through two pains, as she said. Luzinete had made the agreement with a physician at the local public hospital for 150 *reais*. However, on the day she arrived already in pain, he was not present. She was put in a room with a woman who gave birth without any attendance, and she ended up scared that with the normal delivery progressing she would not get her sterilisation. She went home in a taxi to get her card for the bank in order to pay the full price for a caesarean section at the private clinic of the same local hospital. She paid 630 *reais*; money she had received when her husband died.

Luzinete had used contraceptive pills periodically since the birth of her first child when she was 18 years old, but never for very long as she did not feel well when taking them. She had used a condom once, but it stayed inside her for three days, and she would rather die from AIDS than use one again, she said. She used to wash herself with salted water and herbs after sex, but she doubted the efficacy of this procedure. She told us that she only wanted her first child, at that time she was "crazy about getting children". The rest just appeared.

Maria José
Maria José was 33 years old. I heard about her from Tereza, my neighbour, who though poor as the poorest herself, tried to help Maria with some used clothes. Maria had six living children, three other children had died: one in birth, another at the age of eight months due to heart problems, and a girl of six had died due to an electric shock. Her man, to whom she was not formally married, was in prison. She lived from the money and food that her two oldest sons at twelve and eleven received from their small services here and there. She had been sterilised with a laparoscopy two years ago, because, she said, she had "a whole lot of children", words others used in describing her. She had always liked having her many children, just because "it is good to have one's children", but now she had stopped, she told me, apparently proud of her decision. A neighbour woman had helped Maria

to obtain the sterilisation. It was during election time and Maria was sterilised by Dr. Nadegi. Meanwhile, Maria discovered that she was pregnant. Apparently she had been newly pregnant when operated, and as Dr. Nadegi did not ask for pregnancy tests, this had not been detected. Maria, however, was left in doubt. Was she really sterilised or had Dr. Nadegi fooled her?

She had tried contraceptive pills once, but did not do well with them. "I got full of anguish and I broke everything in the house," she said. Her house was very small, just one room and made of mud, plastic and branches, and it did not contain very much to break, so I supposed she just used a manner of speaking that circulated among the women. However, I did not investigate further into Maria's letting things drift. I just concluded that she simply never had the resources to think ahead.

The control of bodies

Let me once more return to Ana. At the time Ana was sterilised – twenty years ago – having only three children was still rare, as was a caesarean section. At that time many women still gave birth at home[28] with a *parteira*, a local traditional midwife, like Dona Laurinha who at the time I was around was still alive and active but no longer helped women in childbirth. When Ana had her caesarean sections, the neighbourhood was still a wilderness. Very few families lived there, water had to be brought from far away, and transportation to Recife was difficult. Ana found it difficult to cope with her daily work after the operation.

A caesarean can be a life saving procedure for the poor as well as the rich, but the question was whether Ana really needed her caesarean sections. She explained to me that she had no dilation after three days with pains, so they had had to do the surgery. She had naturally been relieved when her firstborn was saved, even though the convalescence was hard to go through. However, I thought of all the women whom I had already met, who had no dilation and therefore had to undergo caesarean sections; were the obstetricians at that time already quick to declare 'failed progress'? Ana at least did not want the surgery. The first caesarean led to the subsequent two, and she came to feel that she had missed something. "At times I thought that I wasn't a mother, because I hadn't had a normal birth," she said. "I wanted to feel the pain of being a mother, to know what a mother goes through in order to put a child into the world without it being a caesarean. I had this curiosity. I suffered. I passed three days in pain, but to put a child into the world normally by my own strength, I couldn't. But so it is," she concluded, *"É assim mesmo!"*

Listening to Ana I remembered Eliane, who had almost the same considerations in relation to her caesarean sections eleven and ten years ago. She related that her sister-in-law used to tease her by saying, "You are not a mother; you are just an incubator." And I came to think that none of the younger women who recently had undergone caesarean deliveries had mentioned this lack of 'maternal pain'. Even though unpractical due to the prolonged recuperation they all seemed to accept the caesarean sections they underwent.[29] Submission to medical authority was no longer a foreign element in women's lives.

Medicalisation

Within the growing field of modern medicine women in the neighbourhood had found not only an end to childbearing but also a space for expression of personal worries and ill health. Hypertension for instance was central to the women's experience of their bodies as blood pressure was constantly checked at prenatal examinations and as it constituted a way to sterilisation. However, it had also become an idiom for expression of female distress.[30] The women had the impression that few men suffered from hypertension, and they presumed this difference to be related to a difference in life circumstances. Fat, salted food and distress were seen as causes of hypertension particular to women's life.[31] As one of the ACSs explained it to me: "Women are generally more worried. They do not have leisure, do not have amusement. That makes a difference – and then the food itself. I think men get better food as they often eat at the job, and their alimentation is healthier." Suffering from hypertension thus signalled emotional and economic pressure as well as confinement to the house. As husbands were supposed to provide economically for the household, worries about economy might also be felt as lack of attentive care. Suffering from hypertension communicated all this to a woman's surroundings.

Sonia was sure that her hypertension stemmed from her many worries: "My blood pressure is emotional. It rises when I am nervous; when I am angry...then it passes the limit." She was treated for hypertension as nobody could help her with her worries.

In *Death without Weeping* Scheper-Hughes defines medicalisation as "the process whereby more and more forms of human discontent are filtered through ever-expanding categories of sickness, which are then treated, if not 'cured', pharmaceutically" (Scheper-Hughes 1992: 196). Seen from one perspective, the women's use of medical explanations for their distress confirmed the relevance of this definition as it undoubtedly constituted a redefinition of such unmet and basic human needs (Scheper-Hughes 1992:199). Side effects of contraceptive pills were used among the women in the neighbourhood as explanations for sudden outbursts of despair. One day as I talked with Luzia about her wish for a sterilisation, she told me that she could not use contraceptive pills. She got nervous, broke everything in the house, shouted at children and husband, and felt nauseous every time he came near. I asked her if she was sure that these effects were caused by the pills. She was, everybody knew that these were side effects of pills. However, later she told me that during the period when she used the pills, she had recently been divorced, her ex-husband's new woman threatened Luzia and her daughters with a knife, she did not know how to make ends meet, and her relationship with Cleiton, her new man, was not yet stable. I asked her if this turmoil could not be the reason for bad nerves. Her surprise seemed genuine, when she said, "Do you think so?"

Medicalisation is a double-edged sword, both allowing (agency and expression) and alienating, as the active subject willingly entering the medical discourse is simultaneously made subject to the same discourse. Both younger and older women in the neighbourhood perceived women today as physically much weaker and less healthy than before. Thus, Dona Neuza who was 59, proclaimed: "Today one sees a young woman with a pain here and there, I do not know what, all ill. But look at the old one! Thank God, if it wasn't for my spine, my back and this problem of sinusitis in my head... Thank God, beneath I have nothing. That thing of uterus, of ovary, that it is with discharge...this or that! Thank God, I do not have it." Ivanice, who was in her twenties and a mother of two, agreed that younger women were weak as she told me why she was sterilised: "She [her mother] had thirteen children. You see, it is always like that with our mothers but with me it is different. I cannot. Not everybody is equal, and I did not have the health that she had. I could not have more children." The increased supervision of women's health implied an acceptance of feminine weakness in need of medical control: once this was accepted, the women's role was defined as that of the compliant patient.

Responsible behaviour
Women's and children's health had become a matter of responsibility in the neighbourhood. Children were expected to be taken by their mothers[32] for monthly examinations at the health post during their first two years. And families were visited once a month by an ACS who would make sure that child vaccinations were done on time and pregnant women came for antenatal examinations. In addition, the women were generally very aware of gynaecological diseases and their duty to have them examined and controlled. Neide thus told me that women often came to her to get advice about a tea or herbal bath for a gynaecological problem. "And then they go to the health post to know what it is," she said. A recent campaign for screening of cervical cancer had reinforced the emphasis on women's duty to have their health checked, as it had been effectively promoted in the media.

The women had incorporated into their experience of their own body the notion that they themselves did not know the truth about it.[33] Examinations of blood (used to test pregnancy), regular examinations of faeces (tests for parasites), ultra sound screenings (to know the exact age of a foetus) and various other examinations had entered their world and changed it. The fear of the uncertainty of life was now directed into the medical realm in a hope for some safety, just as it had already been for long for better off Brazilians. And compliance with medical authority seemed to give some sense of self-respect as, faced with one's weakness, one had at least done something. Accordingly, Serruya proposes that one reason for preferring caesarean sections and sterilisations might be the degree of medical involvement in these procedures and the corresponding decrease of responsibility put upon the women themselves. In search of control of their own bodies the women opted, ironically, for a method in which their participation was entirely passive (Serruya 1996:155).

People, and especially women, had entered the realm of "health consumption" as Lefevre puts it, where "the only way of being healthy is consuming health. This means consuming medicines, consultations, exams, and a wide range of other merchandise that symbolise health" (cited in Rozemberg and Manderson 1998). As doctors in Brazil, like in many other places, seldom explain the reasons for one or another procedure, patients are obliged to submit unconditionally to medical authority once enrolled in the health care system (Rozemberg and Manderson 1998:178). When, in addition, submission is perceived as conveying the status of the rich, the willingness with which people seek medical assistance is understandable.

In Foucauldian terms, the women had incorporated their ascribed role as responsible citizens and, simultaneously, docile bodies, through their identification with the role of compliant patient. Indeed, life was taken charge of in the neighbourhood. With the awareness that children should no longer just survive, but become proper citizens, and with the desire not only to be a fertile body but a regulated fertile body, women had incorporated the idea of responsible behaviour. As Nations and Rebhun state: "When new technology becomes available, the poor expand their system to incorporate it" (1988:156). In a situation of social and economic constraints any means to control (real or imagined) is welcomed.

Responsibility meant submission but also a sense of control in one's own life, and rather than seeing women's compliance as a matter of false consciousness I found that they employed the means at hand provided by the health care system to reach a feeling of competency and choice. Seen from a distance they were being controlled; seen from their own point of view they had gained control; as Margaret Lock and Patricia Kaufert write, "At the site of the individual body [...]bio-power may be experienced as enabling, or as providing a resource which can be used as a defence against other forms of power" (1998:7). However, one aspect still needs emphasis: the gendered approach to health care. As childbearing, childcare and contraception were women's responsibilities, men were less involved in these changes. Bio-power engages the family as a link between general objectives and individual desire,

Foucault writes, but most of the families that I describe were torn by women's perception of urgency and men's exclusion from means to act. Through the medicalisation of health women had acquired a resource to think about and act upon their lives in ways that men did not share. This difference left its mark on men and women's attitudes to life.

Chapter Five

Fertility and Recognition

If no one turned round when we entered, answered when we spoke, or minded what we did, but if every person we met 'cut us dead', and acted as if we were non-existing things, a kind of rage and impotent despair would ere long well up in us, from which the cruellest bodily tortures would be a relief; for these would make us feel that, however bad might be our plight, we had not sunk to such a depth as to be unworthy of attention at all.

(James 1950:293)

I could not but associate the passage cited above with all the stories I had heard about neglect in public hospitals in Recife – about people who, because they were poor, were left unattended in pain for hours, as if they did not exist. The women in my study directly or indirectly mentioned the 'ignorance'[1] with which the health care personnel treated them as one reason for wanting a caesarean section.[2] With all the apparatus in place, arms strapped and no sense of their legs, they knew that they would be attended. Some even mentioned as particularly enjoyable the anaesthetist who would chat along with them, as if they were not aware that he did it just in order to know that they were still alive. It was part of his job. In order to be treated 'properly' the women had to reduce themselves to props in the medical game.

This chapter is about the human need for recognition. It is also about the shame and unworthiness experienced by people in my study when in contact with better off Brazilians. And it is about the wish for control over one's own life that in a consumer society like the Brazilian translates into the desire to buy and be happy in consumption. All this relates to sterilisation: their lack of recognition and care and their impotence as consumers, motivate women to improve their social position and one way of doing so is sterilisation. It promises repositioning as it is, in itself, a consumer good and the resultant reduced fertility is associated in different ways with social acknowledgement.

However, let me begin with a discussion of recognition. It will move the focus away from Brazil for a while, but later serve to illuminate women's motivations for sterilisation.

A need for recognition

Can we assume that all human beings possess a need for recognition from other human beings? That we all have a desire to be desired and a fundamental fear of passing through life with nobody noticing us and acknowledging our particularity? William James did, but in this argument for the accuracy of his insights I will choose Hegel's notion of recognition as my starting point.[3]

Hegel identified mutual recognition between human beings as a prerequisite for the emerging of self-consciousness. Consciousness becomes aware of itself, according to Hegel, when it becomes aware of other consciousnesses and its own individuality. In his own words: "Self-consciousness exists only in and for itself when, and only by the fact that, it so exists for another; that is, it exists only in being acknowledged" (Hegel 1979:11). Only through the mediation of the other do people experience themselves. Human beings share with animals the desire for natural objects such as food. However, the 'I' created through the desire for natural objects is "a merely living I" in Hegel's view, revealed to itself and to others only as a "sentiment of self" (Kojève 1969:5). Only in the "desire to be desired", that is, the wish to substitute for oneself the value acknowledged by others, do human beings obtain self-consciousness and thereby differ from animals. Because "I want him to 'recognise' my value as his value" (Kojève 1969:7) others possess a certain power over our lives: we are willing to go to considerable lengths in order to be of value in their eyes, and we are "influenced by others because others matter to us and we are, in a sense, incomplete without them. We can be controlled because we do not want to have their recognition withdrawn, or again because we do not want to be seen in particular ways" (Crossley 1996a:141).

Although an important point of reference, Hegel's notion of recognition is not unique in Western philosophy and psychology.[4] James enters the discussion with his definition of "man's social selves" based on the recognition he gets from his mates (James 1950:293). A man identifies his self with the images that others have of him, James writes, and "to wound any one of these his images is to wound him" (ibid.: 294). Hence, self-consciousness is not consistent over time. The need for recognition creates a number of constantly changing, mutually overlapping and probably contesting identities for the individual, which he or she will be strongly motivated to maintain as long as significant others are presumed to value them.

Without focusing on these our many selves, but adding a temporal aspect to the emergence of self-consciousness, George Herbert Mead proposes two concepts, the 'I' and the 'me'. The 'I' is the 'me' a moment ago, since the 'me' arises as an objectification or recollection of experience (Mead 1965:174). The 'I' consists of the "possibilities in our nature [...] that lie beyond our own immediate presentation" (ibid.:204), and Crossley suggests that we understand it as the 'Merleau-Pontyian body-subject': perceiving and active, but not yet reflectively aware of itself (1996a:55). This conceptualisation establishes the understanding of self-consciousness as inherently 'delayed', and, simultaneously, acknowledges an unknown individuality that strives to be realised through the recognition of others.

Merleau-Ponty describes this 'imaginary me' arising out of human interaction as an inevitable step in a child's development and the origin of a fundamental split in its self-perception, which occurs during the 'mirror stage' that a child passes through before the age of two. The mirror serves to illustrate the alienating element of the emerging 'me' as the mirror image is a public 'me', perceived as capable of being experienced by others, and thereby self-alienating, as it pulls the subject out of itself and separates it from the immediacy of its experiencing being (Crossley 1996a:61). In Merleau-Ponty's words, "In this sense I am torn from myself, and the image in the mirror prepares me for another still more serious alienation, which will be the alienation by others" (1968:136). This alienation need not necessarily be negatively experienced, as it may result in pride, self-esteem and dignity, feelings that we can usually have in relation to others. It does, however, constitute a threat as the subject may experience itself as "captured in the experience of the other", unable to control its exterior image and define the meaning of its own actions (Crossley 1996a:61).

Being able to interact and not just being controlled by others is, however, a prerequisite for being a self for oneself. An experience of nothingness, explains Michael Jackson, arises out of "being reduced to passivity, of not being able to do or say anything that has any effect on others" (Jackson 1998:17). In his view, being is choosing, while, consequently, nothingness is the dispossession of choice. In this sense every human encounter involves a risk of being reduced to nothingness by the other.[5] However, what is at stake is a balancing movement rather than a choice of one over the other (ibid.:18); that is, a striving to be in the world of others, but equally, a striving to define what one wants to be in the world of others, thereby resisting the dependency or threat implicit in one's need for recognition.[6]

We seek this balance through different means. Basically, we act upon the world through physical movement, speech and emotional expressions. Whether we listen attentively, turn our back, cry or laugh, we work upon the intersubjectively negotiated interpretation of events by adding our own evaluation of the situation. Not that we intentionally put on a 'face'; we *are* different faces according to the situations we are in, believing in our sadness when we mime grief.[7] Objects and artefacts may work as mediators between the desiring and the desired, that is, between the subject and the recognition he or she longs for (Crossley 1996a:19). Wealth, albeit in something as mundane as a pair of high-heeled shoes, may be collectively valued and bring recognition to its owner.

Being a pé de chinelo

One day I sat with Sonia on the cool floor in Josenita's house. I was there waiting for Josenita; Sonia had just been passing by. She apparently wanted to get out of her house, away from dish washing, dirty clothes and the demands of children and husband. As we seemed to have plenty of time, we went along with our ongoing conversation about women, poverty, Sonia's interest in spiritualism and so on. Sonia lit a cigarette from the packet she used to keep under the elastic band of her shorts. It was a lazy and warm midday. I suddenly remembered that I wanted to ask her about the meaning of being a *pé de chinelo*. I had heard people in the neighbourhood describe themselves in these terms. As usual I asked Sonia when I needed explanations. I liked the way she looked at things, pragmatic, serious and deeply involved as she was. After taking some drags on her cigarette Sonia began her explanation with a description of everyday situations of neglect:

Sonia: If we go to town, we do not enter just any place. Not all the shops. Because if one enters, people will look at you, because you could be a person who was going to steal. But sometimes you go there just because you find it beautiful and want to look... I went into a shop, and it was very beautiful. So many beautiful things! But those who are in there, they are already against you, because you are poor, a *pé de chinelo,* and afraid. Because in there only the society[8] enters, the *granfinos,* and even the *granfinos* become like that. They do not feel well, because a poor person entered the shop. At the hospital it is the same. When a well-dressed person enters, he is treated well. The nurses, the doctors, they all treat him with more affection. But when a poor person enters, it is shouting. He is there dying from lack of care, until they have got time, until they like to attend. Sometimes they are chatting in the kitchen, sometimes they are chatting in the room where that dying person arrives, but as it is a *pé de chinelo* they do not care.

Line: What is a *pé de chinelo*?

Sonia: Me, the illiterate (she laughs).

Line: *Pé* is foot, but what is *chinelo*?

Sonia: The slipper. But when the heels arrive, *né*? The *pé de chinelo* is the poor, the society is the heels, and when the heels arrive everybody is running, they are all treated well, received well, it is only nice talk. But with the *pé de chinelo* they say, "When I have time, I'll go there!"

Being a *pé de chinelo* in Sonia's experience thus meant being subjected to a gaze from a superior position in a hierarchy and, by definition, found lacking. As Crossley puts it, objectified by the gaze of the other the subject constitutes an image to the other, which does not necessarily have anything to do with the subject's own self-understanding, and on which she may not have any influence (1996a:61). In this objectification the subject is made passive; in order to recover subjectivity she has to act, transgress the passivity. Acting is to deny being labelled by others. It is to fight for the right to control the intersubjectively negotiated image of oneself.

No wonder Sonia one day succumbed to temptation and bought herself a pair of high-heeled shoes for a party. In order to save the money for the bus ticket she bought them from a vendor who came to her door, at a price more than twice as high as the prices in town. They were cheap plastic shoes unbearable for broad feet such as hers, accustomed to the freedom of the *chinelo*. I saw the bitterness in her eyes, when she told me all this – proud Sonia who always struggled to preserve her dignity. She could not admit that she had been fooled, but I think she knew it. Fooled by her dream of being respectable. She had had to take off the shoes even before reaching the bus stop the day they went to the party.

Low status lives

Although, as mentioned, the alienation inherent in self-consciousness may lead to self-esteem and dignity it may also result in shame, such as when disrespected or neglected by another. According to Sonia, being a *pé de chinelo* was tied to certain spheres of daily life; she mentioned shops and hospitals, which was not at all accidental. Besides service jobs in private homes, shopping and clinical health care were the main activities of daily life that brought poor women out of their own domestic spheres and in direct contact with upper and middle class values.

There were other conversations with Sonia in which she told me of the humiliation related to working as an *empregada* in richer people's houses. Of the constant mistrust, and her pride that made her quit a job once, when the *patroa* denied her milk in the coffee and insisted on deciding how much food Sonia was allowed to eat. "I had my own plate and cup, that was okay with me; I ate separately and this I always prefer. But I wanted to decide for myself how much food I wanted to eat. And even though I do not drink milk at home, I always have a spoonfull of powdered milk in my coffee, when I work in a family home."[9]

When working in such a house Sonia inhabited, by definition, the position of a servant, which was associated with certain rights but also with rules of separation, dictated by the role rather than by her as a person. Being a customer or a patient, on the contrary, held out prospects of equal rights to all participants, and the experience of being treated as inferior in these situations therefore hit that much harder. The feelings of shame that sprang from such moments of neglect were perceptible in people's narratives, though sometimes hidden behind indignation and self-justification.

Meetings with schoolteachers, and talks with priests or politicians were moments of interaction with middle class people that could also have been studied further here. However, schoolteachers, like the nurse and the doctor at the health post, had become part of the familiar milieu of the neighbourhood and were perceived more as individuals than as typified 'middle class' persons. The politician often had a local, well known mediator, and the priest would sometimes be poor himself; in fact, pastors in the Pentecostal churches were often as impoverished as the congregation.[10] Hence, only when people left the neighbourhood did they feel objectified as low status persons. In this chapter I will therefore focus on the experience of being, respectively, a consumer and a patient.

There are, however, some status markers that I will not touch upon, namely, literacy and race. Until 1988 illiterate persons were not allowed to vote; they were as Scheper-Hughes writes 'nonentities'(Scheper-Hughes 1992:84) and today literacy is still somehow tied to the notion of being somebody in a societal perspective. To be dark-skinned is another aspect of inferiority, even though skin colour was seldom mentioned directly in the neighbourhood. To be dark-skinned is another aspect of inferiority, even though skin colour was seldom mentioned directly in the neighbourhood. People I talked to generally cast social inequality in terms of economy rather than race. This was probably partly due to "cultural censorship" (Sheriff 2001)[11], partly due to historical circumstances blurring the racism inherent to Brazilian social structure. Blacks and browns have historically been excluded from competing with whites on the labour market and today this is manifested as a class difference rather than racial inequality (Telles 1995: 397). Hence, while colour may be at the root of the disrespect shown poor people in Brazil and should be seen as an ever present undercurrent, I did not single it out for further investigation and will therefore not discuss it here. Let me turn to consumption and hospitalisation.

Being a consumer

Since the mid-1950s and especially during the military regime (1964–85) the Brazilian state actively promoted consumption in order to increase the growth of national industry (Faria 1997/98; Martine, Das Gupta and Chen 1998). Liberal public credit policies and state supported promotion of unified national consumption tastes through Brazilian television networks were part of the economic modernisation explicitly impelled by the military government (Tauxe 1993:596).

However, public policies did not balance the appetite for consumption with the means to participate. The credit policies only allowed lower-income groups access to consumer goods through huge indebtedness. In the neighbourhood where I lived, collectors regularly came to collect debts. Loans were only reluctantly paid back and many families owed more than they could pay, each month being fined with higher interest. Most people in the neighbourhood were not at all free to buy what they wanted. In fact, most of them just had enough for bare survival. My impression was that they found their incapacity as consumers profoundly dull and unsatisfying.

According to Zygmunt Bauman an ideal consumer society is characterised by "the absence of routine and the state of constant choice that are the virtues (indeed, the 'role prerequisites') of a consumer" (1998: 25). In the consumer society buying is valued as the quintessence of action, of being part of the world of others and having an impact in this world. Consequently, being poor is unworthy. Not because one may be unemployed and idleness is worthless but because lack of purchasing power excludes one from the recognition associated with consumption. Hence, being poor in the consumer society has implications beyond material deprivation and bodily distress. It represents exclusion from whatever passes as 'normal life' and may lead to "a fall of self-esteem, feelings of shame or feelings of guilt" (ibid.:37).

In Brazil consumption is certainly marketed as 'normal life'. Brazilian television is full of commercials promoting this or that product, with exciting views from shopping malls and amusement parks; desire is constantly evoked.[12] However, the desire to buy and the wish for excitement ran counter to the slow and monotonous life in the neighbourhood, where I lived. Most days were just like the day before and the day after. I remember meeting Sonia in the street one evening; I was tired and on my way home, she excited, with a box of domino pieces and a packet of cigarettes. "Where are you going?" I asked. She said: "To Maria"s house. Domino! In order not to feel the time pass." So it was. Life was full of company, of play, of peaceful conversations. A commonly heard remark was: "As long as everybody is healthy we are fine." However, there was a worm gnawing at the apple of the 'humble' life.[13] It seemed to have lost its taste, and everybody had aspirations for something 'happier'.[14] As Carmen's aim in life revealed: "To be able to amuse myself and my children a little, to be able to go out, to be able to feel more..." I asked, "More what, Carmen?" And she answered, "More happy! It is exactly what I want."

The daily food was in many families a clear sign of lack of capacity to buy. Tânia, Irene's daughter, once did a survey for me of the meals in a few families during one week. One of the families was, as Tânia said, "structured". They would have good, varied food thrice a day. The rest, however, ate the common meals of white and weightless bread, cuscuz made of corn, or spaghetti and some kind of biscuits, with eggs, beans, small salted fish or chicken on special occasions. And then oil and sugar to make it more filling. Thin coffee and cigarettes would constitute the luxury of the everyday. In Tânia's own house food was really monotonous and bad, she told me. Most days they had bread, margarine and sweet coffee morning and evening, sometimes with eggs and powdered milk, and for lunch a very thin bean stew made of beans, water, onion, oil and a stock cube served with spaghetti or rice with oil and tomato paste. Only on rare occasions was there some meat or fish. Everybody complained. Tânia's father quarrelled about his wife's failing care of him. That she never 'made his plate', that is, served his food. Irene replied: "Why should I? It is not really food. If I had a real meal to serve you, then I would make you a plate."

Sudden purchases of telephones, clothes or kitchen utensils were temporary distractions from this boredom, as was the ongoing buying and selling in the neighbourhood, from sweets and clothes to used items. Everywhere something was sold. To me it appeared to be a constant circulation of the same few *reais*, as nobody had money but everybody bought. Women were very active in these efforts. Nails were painted, hair cut, ice cream, cakes and sweets sold. Some women went to the market town Caruaru to buy clothes for further sale back home. Others sold jewellery on commission for professional sellers, who came once in a while to collect the money. And others again sold kitchenware, cosmetics, toys and other knick-knacks from catalogues. Tupperware was at a premium.

People did not always pay immediately. Debts were accumulated which, if repaid, took the form of cash or kind, including favours. In this way the women managed to cook a meal on days when there was no money, as they borrowed or bought on credit. The constant exchange was primarily a way of surviving, but the logic of the system seemed based on the play with choice rather than the need to survive. At least, this interpretation gave meaning to the fact that relatively few people grew some kind of vegetables or kept animals, even though they could.[15]

It gave meaning to the phenomenon of biscuits, too. Children were often fed with sweet biscuits in between meals. The supermarket was filled with biscuits of different flavours, according to my taste all extremely artificial. I never really understood this obsession with biscuits, until I saw it within the larger consumerist puzzle and realised that it was not merely an obsession with biscuits, but with consumption in general. Neide once said something astonishing that later filled a gap in that puzzle. We were talking about food and I used the word *jantar* (having dinner). She said: "No, we do not have dinner, we just have coffee. You see, I cannot even buy *lanches* for my children." I found it strange that lack of money for *lanches* (snacks), which I saw as extras, indicated that she could not afford dinner. As if *lanches* had higher priority than dinner. Another day I met one of the smaller girls, who used to chat with me. She asked: "Lini, do you prefer *danone* [yoghurt] or biscuits?" I understood that these were the only choices she had, and even more, what was important to her was perhaps the choice itself. I remembered all the commercials for yoghurt, biscuits, chocolate, different kinds of sweet drinks and other inventions for children that were shown on the television. And I understood Neide's pain in not being able to buy. To buy even biscuits was to enter the world of consumption in which choice is essential for happiness. And who would not want to make her children happy?

The wish to be part of the happy, exciting life was realised on the day of a *picnic* (pronounced *pikiniki*) at the beach. Preparations were many, as the women had to collect bathing clothes for everybody and preferably also sunglasses and sun oil. Food had to be brought, since it was too expensive to buy it all at the beach. The day I joined Neide and her family was one with big expectations, as Neide had not been at the beach for ages. Her children and her old mother, Dona Lívia, who offered me her company, had never been to the beach, even though the nearest beach could be reached on a local bus within three-quarters of an hour.

In the early morning families and a group of young men on their own met in front of Manuel's small shop to wait for the rented bus to come. Manuel had sold homemade tickets during the last weeks and made sure that more than enough people would participate. 'Picnics' had become a way of earning a little extra money for the person in charge of the arrangements, so naturally he overloaded the bus, but nobody complained. The beach we were heading for was known as *the* beach, and everybody was excited when we left the neighbour-hood. We drove for hours and passed or were passed by several other busses, old and slow like ours, apparently also on their way to the beach, and each time people would shout out of the open windows to each other. The music was terribly loud and the sun started to heat up the air in the bus. Dona Lívia sat seriously worried at my side in the middle of everything looking forward to meeting the unknown and never experienced.

When we arrived at the beach at least fifty buses had arrived before us, all shabby old vehicles that usually served as local public buses. The rest of the day was one big feast smelling of barbecue, sun oil and decomposing rubbish. Everybody swam in the same small corner of the beach and the water was completely churned up and full of sand. The men got drunk; old people slept in the shade; a man died as he had stumbled on the beach and fell asleep in the hot sun; the one and only transvestite titillated everybody with his demonstrative sexuality; and the women had to divide their attention between playful children wanting ice creams and excited men wanting female attention. We returned at night, everybody satisfied, sun burned and tired to the bone. We had participated in the happy life and such a day lasted for some time.

However, over and over again the monotony of everyday life returned and with it the feeling of lack of worth. Thus, one late afternoon I sat and talked with Neide, when she said: "I am 37 years old. If I had taken care of myself, if I had had money, I would not be as I am, Lini. If my house had been plastered I would not have had this dirty skin. Look, when I do like this [she scrapes her skin with a nail and some white dust comes off]. The whole body is full of dust because of the house. If I had a plastered house, some money, and a job so that I could fix myself up, I would not be what I am. I would be something else. I would have value. I would be more beautiful as I could use cream for the skin, cream for the arms to remove this grey stuff. If I had money to take care of myself, had money to have a comfortable house, I would have been different. I could have been an interesting woman. But as I am....?"

Neide did not only feel her inferiority under the gaze of better off people. She had so internalised her want of worth as a consumer as to make it part of the experience of her own body. In the words of Drew Leder: "My awareness of my body is a profoundly social thing, arising out of experiences of the corporeality of other people and of their gaze directed back upon me" (1990:92). Once incorporated, the gaze of the other starts an inner evaluation no longer dependent on the actual other. Seeing the dust on the skin, or the *chinelo* on the (unfashionably) broad foot, reaffirmed one's lower status. Over and over again.

The fact that everybody in the neighbourhood was more or less in the same situation was no relief: "There is nothing ... that one can do to resist the stigma and shame of being an inadequate consumer, even within the ghetto of similarly deficient consumers. Keeping up the standards of the people around you will not do, since the standards of propriety are set, and constantly raised, far away from the area under the neighbourhood watch, by daily papers and the televised glossy twenty-four-hours-a-day commercials for consumer bliss. None of the substitutes that the local neighbourhood's ingenuity could invent are likely to withstand the competition, warrant self-satisfaction and assuage the pain of glaring inferiority" (Bauman 1998:40).

Being a patient
Nowhere did people feel their bodies as devalued as within the medical sector.[16] A small act like the shaving of pubic hair made it clear to me how women experienced the degrading gaze of hospital staff on their bodies. All pregnant women that I met shaved their genital hair before giving birth. I heard about the practice by accident and wondered how it was possible to shave anything underneath a pregnant belly. Knowing that the women usually avoided being naked in front of anybody, I could not imagine that they received any help. I learned that women always shaved their genital hair or cut it very short in order to feel clean. It was thus not an act restricted to pregnancy or medical examination. However, what they told me about the reactions of the medical staff if they arrived unshaved revealed the dynamics of unequal power relations, which can lead to shame because "when confronting another who has potential power over one's life and projects ... there is a tendency on the part of the powerless to a heightened self-awareness" (Leder 1990:98). I talked it over with Carmen:

Line: When you went to the hospital did you shave?
Carmen: I was already shaved. Since I discovered that I was pregnant I did the 'cleanliness' regularly.[17] Because many don't like it. There was one there, who ... when she arrived it was the nurse who did it, and the nurses don't like it.
Line: Why don't they like it?

Carmen: Because they think it should be done at home.
Line: Did you like to do it?
Carmen: No, I had a huge difficulty, because it was impossible to
           see, because the belly was very big. But I had to do it.
Line: Why?
Carmen: In order not to get a telling-off when arriving at the hos-
           pital. They call everybody's attention to you and it is very
           bad to be called attention to.

Compared to so much else, shaving was just a practical detail, but I
found it telling in all its littleness. I spoke with the nurse at the health
post about it:

Line: Do the hospitals prefer that the women shave their genital
           hair at home before arriving at the hospital?
Nurse: Trichotomia? We call it trichotomia. No, they think it is
           better at the hospital, because there the staff is trained
           to do it. At home they can cut themselves with the razor
           blade. A woman with a huge belly who has to do it? No.
Line: But the women with whom I already talked told me that
           the hospitals don't want to do it?
Nurse: In that case it isn't the hospital, but the medical assistants
           themselves who will not do it. At times it is the staff that
           says that it has to be done before, because they do not want
           to do it. The right thing is that the hospital does it.

However, the right thing was not practised. Like Carmen, others told
me how they feared being "called attention to". The nurses would
say "Don't you have *Gillette* at home?" insinuating that one was
either poor or sluttish. Having heard many such remarks at different
hospitals I knew they were not as harmless as they sounded. Nurses
or doctors often talked patronisingly about a woman in her presence
as if she did not exist. For instance, while Luzia was having intense
contractions and was almost in despair, two staff members stood near
her bed saying, "She will never make it. She is doing it all wrong. If
she had just done it properly, we would have been down for lunch.
Oh, I need my lunch now!" Or, as I observed a vaginal delivery, the

well-intentioned physician wanted me to understand the situation, and told me that the woman was very ignorant, apparently illiterate, as she had not been coming for her antenatal examinations. The woman was there, hearing it all and struggling to keep her mouth closed, so that we would not see her missing teeth. When she spoke, she covered the embarrassing fact with her hand.[18]

At all three hospitals that I visited, women in childbirth had to take out their false teeth, when entering the maternity ward. And they had to dress in a kind of smock, often ragged and sometimes impossible to hold together. One day when I sat in the examination room where women arrived, a beautiful and very neat young woman came in. She stayed near the door waiting for someone to attend her. I saw that she was in pain. Suddenly water ran out between her legs and she looked utterly embarrassed. Still nobody paid her any attention. The female medical student in charge had just finished a private telephone call on her mobile phone and was writing something in the big book in front of her. I left the room before the young girl was taken care of. Later, in the labour hall where the beds stood in rows beside each other, I saw her again. She was trying to keep her terrible smock together and even though in pain she was once again waiting politely for further instructions. Nobody was around and I went over to talk to her. Later I found somebody who could show her to her bed. I felt awkward; she must have felt worse.

I had just observed another delivery, when, on coming out from the delivery room into the hall, I saw a male nurse dragging the young woman to the delivery room. "No, no, let me pause for a second, please!" she said, apparently having a forceful contraction. But she had to proceed. She looked terrible now, her hair in disorder, the smock still untied, and her face out of control. I saw what for some reason I had not noticed before, that many of her teeth were missing. They put her on the delivery table, and the medical student from the admission and one of her mates entered the room. It turned out to be one of those deliveries that I could hardly bear to observe. The students complained a lot about her not being able to press properly. In their opinion everything was wrong. The only help they gave her was to say "press downwards, press downwards" with no further explanation. They sounded as if they had already given up. The male nurse entered the room.[19] Violently but effectively he gave the young woman a hard pressure over the belly in the next contraction and the baby came out. The woman screamed: "No, no, not like that, for God's sake not like that" before she just screamed in pain. I had to leave the room when the medical students began to sew her wounded genitals without effective anaesthesia. As I went out I heard the medical student answering her mobile phone, once again, it seemed, initiating a private conversation: "Yes, yes, I am. Just delivered, yes, I am here with blood on my hands! (giggling)" The once neat and polite young woman was reduced to nothing, bereft of the possibility of doing or saying anything that would have any effect on others.

I saw several violent deliveries more or less like this one. Delivery practices are currently under intense criticism in Brazil.[20] Procedures known to be harmful or inefficient such as routine use of intravenous infusions,[21] expulsive efforts early in labour,[22] or the painful 'Kristeller manoeuvre'[23] are used in daily practice at most hospitals. In addition, repeated vaginal examinations and the use of episiotomies are considered a routine part of the violent Brazilian obstetrical practice (Diniz and d'Oliveira 1998:39).[24]

However, what still made the strongest impression on me was the humiliation within small acts and utterances. Knowing how people in 'my' neighbourhood worked hard to look respectable, in ironed clothes, nice-smelling and almost shining with cleanliness, I found the ragged smocks, dirty sheets and missing teeth a sharp contrast. The staff would often be in 'civilian' white clothes and wearing jewellery, expensive watches and make-up. Under caring circumstances it might have been perceived differently, but even though nobody told me this directly, these contrasts must have been felt as humiliating in the violent atmosphere in which it all occurred. When a doctor was more occupied with a few drops of blood on his white trousers than with the woman giving birth, or when the same doctor charmed all the nurses and students in the room with ironic remarks on women's worries about their *chinelos*,[25] these were clear signs of disrespect and negation of the women's worth as equals to the staff, though some of the staff, at least all the nurse assistants, might not be of a higher economic status than most of the women.

In her study of humorous remarks in Italian maternity wards,

Franca Pizzini emphasises the way power relations are strengthened and situations defined by use of humour. First of all, she argues that when humorous statements are played out within an institutional hierarchy they have to be initiated by the 'status-superior': "Witticism released downward supports the status structure, whereas it can be jeopardized by witticism aimed in the opposite direction [...] A person low down the hierarchical ladder 'may' make a joke if he or she uses him- or herself or someone below as target" (Pizzini 1991: 484). Moreover, group identity is marked by jokes, since "smiling or laughing in response to humour [...] means that those present underline their acceptance of [the] moment" (ibid.:478).

Pizzini's study from Italy proposes a rather harsh interpretation of the joking atmosphere that I met on my short visits at the public hospitals in Recife. "You did not complain when you got it in, why do you complain now that it has to get out?" was a standard joke. And there was the humorous remark about the need for episiotomies: "We have to cut it, you know. It is a very small hole. How should the baby get out if we did not? You have never seen it, nê, then go home and see yourself in a mirror!" If they did not stay very silent, the women giving birth often laughed at such remarks. However, seeing their laughter in the light proposed by Pizzini, the women took part in a common sharing of their irresponsibility (having sex for pleasure without considering the consequences), their ignorance (not knowing anything about their own body) and, in conclusion, their inferiority.

At the hospital no resistance seemed possible, but at home the women complained about doctors being inattentive and nurses being rude. Voices were raised in indignation.[26] Anita thus told me the following about the birth of her daughter: "There was nobody around. Just one. I said to her, 'I cannot stand it any longer, I cannot' and she came to do the 'touch'.[27] And it was with 6 centimetres, and she said, 'You will not have it now' and then pronto [she went away]. Later I called, but they are very rude. They do not care about you, they do not talk with you, you see? If I had not had any information from the health post about how a birth is, I would have...I would have suffered even more. They leave you there and they just come, when the child is already being born. Really, if she had not pulled me in a hurry to the delivery room, the girl would have been born in the bed."

Luzia told me that she suffered during the birth of her oldest daughter (her third child) due to an ignorant doctor, who did not take her weakness into account: "The Brazilian doctor is rather ignorant. Because when it was that doctor... when I had Milena, and he did not have patience to wait, to see that this was weakness ... [he should have understood:] 'this is a moment of weakness, she did not eat well during the nine months.' But he was not interested ... he should not have done that with such ignorance – just put his arms and pushed. When he did that I screamed. I went to the other world and returned. I passed the nine months with hunger, Lini."

When Luzia was to give birth to her fourth child, their economic situation had improved and her husband had paid for the anaesthesia. At the time I met her she was pregnant with her fifth child, a boy. Her new man, Cleiton, could pay for neither anaesthesia nor a caesarean section; they had almost no money. Luzia tried to get a combined caesarean section and sterilisation through some of their personal contacts, but failed. As she later said: "It is money that gives orders. But as I did not have any, I had to accept the pain until the very end." When she gave birth at the local hospital I was with her and during intense pain she whispered to me: "If he had seen me like this, how I suffer... he should have paid. How can he let me suffer like that?" Being poor, being female, being a patient; for Luzia it all blended into the feeling of not being treated with the care she felt she deserved.

As the prevalent use of caesarean sections spread from better off women in the South to poor women in the North and Northeast of Brazil, surgical deliveries became associated with high status.[28] Cecilia de Mello e Souza writes: "because these changes in obstetrical practice begin at the top of the social hierarchy, they become associated with culturally positive representations of the dominant classes. In other words, the socio-economic status of these patients who request and receive C-sections also contributes to this procedure's legitimacy" (Mello e Souza 1994:365).

During my last fieldwork, the famous Brazilian television star, Xuxa, had recently delivered through a caesarean section. Xuxa is one of Brazil's symbols of beauty, blond, blue eyed and extremely rich. During the last ten years she has hosted the most popular children's show in Brazil (Goldstein 1999:571). Xuxa announced that she would give birth to her daughter in the way that would be best for the baby, without revealing beforehand whether that would involve surgery. The suspense attracted a lot of attention to the fact that, eventually, she was delivered with a caesarean section. The national news at the Globo network transmitted for ten minutes from the expensive private hospital in Rio, showing Xuxa, beautiful as ever, sending messages to fans before entering the elevator to the surgery room. Another television star, the actress Cláudia Raia, declared without hesitation that she would have a caesarean section.[29]

Logically, the women in the neighbourhood perceived birth pain as being a result of poverty. Teresa, who worked in the only local crèche, put it this way: "The number of caesareans increases with the social class. The high social class does not want to feel pain, they have persons who care for them, and then they opt for a caesarean. [...] But today, Lini, the doctors resist to do caesareans. They do not make caesareans with the same frequency as before. At my time there were more people having caesareans, but today the doctors wait and wait and cut a lot in order to have normal deliveries. Not for those who have money to pay, but for us, who do not have money... they wait till the very end."[30]

Thus everybody knew why doctors were brutal, but the consequences went beyond the physical, since "the forms of practical maltreatment in which a person is forcibly deprived of any opportunity freely to dispose over his or her body represents the most fundamental sort of personal degradation" (Honneth 1995:132). The pain blends with the feeling of being defenceless at another's mercy, in this case because one is poor. It is the very body that is regarded without value – a low status life. No wonder that women wanted to change their bodies.

The embodiment of change

As I have shown, with reference to theories of selfhood, self-esteem and recognition, we want to have value in others' eyes; we want to be desired, not neglected and maltreated. However, value is never objective, but socially and culturally defined according to dominant truths shared by the community we are part of. Our need for recognition makes us susceptible to the anonymous, omnipresent and truth-pro-

ducing power of modern society. According to Foucault it is our sus-
ceptibility that turns this power into a productive force (Heede 1997:
42). It unfolds in the endless networks of relations in which value is
negotiated (ibid.: 39), and is positive in its effects as it produces socially
desired states of normality rather than merely suppressing undesirable
attitudes (Crossley 1996a:132).

Nothing was more evident in the neighbourhood where I lived
than this productive effect of power. People struggled and struggled
to improve their lives. Houses were built, clothes were bought, and
some women even started a gymnastic team in Anita's yard. In the hot
evenings we would jump and stretch drenched in sweat and covered
in dust, in order to trim our bodies. Individual bodies were reshaped
in order to change social selves in accordance with the desired norms
of respectability.

The following passage about Neide's house has nothing directly
to do with sterilisation, which I will return to later. It has, however,
everything to do with this Foucauldian mechanism of power. I will
describe Neide's efforts to improve her house and the sense of self-
worth that she seemed to derive from her success, as I want to argue
that social worth is at once publicly performed and inwardly felt. There
is an immediate (that is, without medium) relation between inner and
outer worth, and the most intimate sense of self-worth can be acquired
through a reshaping of one's physical manifestation, be it one's house,
clothes or body. I wrote the narrative just after having arrived home
from my second fieldwork. By that time Neide's son, Fernando, had just
died and she had moved out of the neighbourhood. However, on this
particular day she was still happy with her self, her life and her house.

Neide's house

At that time Neide worked at her lottery stand – *jogo de bicho* – down
at the road in front of Manuel's little shop, where one could buy everything for the house. She took care of it every day from early morning to
sunset at 6 o'clock. At lunchtime she went home to get the meal ready
for the children and herself: beans and rice, often chicken or perhaps
chicken feet. She also prepared the bean dough for the *acarajés* (bean
balls) that she would later sell to people passing by or to the men who
always hung around near Manuel's shop.

How she could take that particular day off I did not know. When I arrived towards nightfall with my tape recorder everything was ready. She had spent the whole day cooking and cleaning, and decorated the house with a Christmas tree with small twinkling lights. The children too were freshly washed and Airton, her husband, had arrived from work and went around with Luzia's son on his arm. Neide and Airton were his godparents, but even so I was puzzled by the boy's presence. Did he often stay in their house? Altogether I was puzzled. Everything was so neat?

Had I not been there before, I would perhaps have accepted it: a staged family idyll to present to the stranger. But I had been in and out of that house since the beginning of my fieldwork, and just the day before I had sat in the kitchen between piles of dirty plates filled with flies, with the smell coming in from the toilet that, like everything else, stayed dirty until the water came. Neide had been tired. Worried about something, she had just pecked at some beans, but soon preferred a cigarette instead. Not until later did I begin to understand: on this particular day I was there to interview her, and it was therefore not just any usual kitchen talk that we were entering into. I had not interviewed her since the year before and much had changed. The house had, first of all, been improved.

Neide's house lay in the 'invasion,' the area once occupied by squatters. The owner had thrown people out, but they had returned and slowly occupied more and more land. Family and friends moved in, and lots were sold at increasingly high prices. As in any other place of this kind – some called it a *favela* – the houses were placed just anyhow. There were no roads, just more or less passable paths. Somewhere soil steps leading from one level to another, somewhere else a rotten board over a drain. Some houses had with time become very comfortable, plastered, with a wall in the front and grates on windows and doors. Some even had two floors. Others were really poor, made of combinations of wood, plastic or branches and mud.

People used to talk about the 'invasion' as 'in there' as if it was an indistinguishable mass of houses. And in a certain way it was. Houses in the 'invasion' did not have proper addresses. As there were no roads, there were no road names nor house numbers. People living 'in there' would therefore use the address of somebody living on a proper road outside the invasion, if, for instance, they were expecting mail. Nobody had sewers, and electricity was illegally connected. The water only ran sparsely, because the pipe system was fragile and complicated, made piecemeal as needed, and because the area was located on a hill. The dustcart never entered the area and people threw their rubbish at the corner, the place where one climbs the muddy hillside to get to the 'invasion'. Later, dogs or humans would search it for usable bits leaving it spread over an even bigger area than before.

Neide's house lay near that corner. It was made of simple bricks. The previous year it only had three rooms: a bedroom, a kitchen and a sitting room with a television, a stereo, a worn out table with a plastic lace cloth and a couple of chairs. At that time there was no entrance door, just a grate to be locked with a padlock at night or when the family went out. Neide had been afraid of sleeping alone in the house when Airton worked overnight. "So many bad people live in this area," she said, "people who want to disturb and make trouble." Neide, like many of the other women, was not satisfied with her house. They all wanted a better one. One which would, as an extension of themselves, raise their status, outwardly, and give them value, inwardly. But at that time I thought that Neide would never get any closer to her dream. Like everybody else she was waiting for assistance, fantasising about all the things she wanted to do. She would go to the mayor and ask if he would give her some bricks. "But why should he, Neide?" I asked. "To get votes!" she replied. Fighting for ones own life, everybody depended on others, it seemed. I had listened to so many dreams built on illusions about help. 'Don Sebastismo' my friend Nathan called it – the saviour on the white horse.

Anyhow, when I returned after a year the house was both bigger and better. The walls in some of the rooms had been plastered, there were two more bedrooms, a big kitchen with washing area and a real toilet with a cesspool. Neide had struggled. *Uma lutadora* – a fighter! Before she opened the lottery stand near Manuel's shop she had sold bean balls and different types of corn food down at the *avenida* and she had earned well. The money had been used to buy the materials for construction, and Airton had built everything. There seemed to be different explanations to why she stopped working at the *avenida*: Pedro Nascimento, my field assistant, thought that she had earned more than Airton down at the *avenida* and that this had created problems between the two; Neide told me that it had been too far to carry all the things to and fro; and others told me that the men had gathered around Neide's booth at the *avenida* which may have made Airton jealous. Whatever the reason, the fact was that she had shifted to the lottery stand near her home and now earned less. But she was still able to buy things with her own money, like the dress she bought for New Year's eve from one of the other women in the neighbourhood. It was white, tight and with a small basque around the hips. She looked good to me, and to Airton too, it seemed. He was, in general, very satisfied with his work. The year before she had complained endlessly because he never made that door, never cared for her. Now he had built her the house she wanted and showed himself to be a real man. Almost – nobody mentioned where the money came from.

However, it was not only the house that had changed. Neide herself seemed to feel much better now that she had money. She could buy things for the house and for herself. To me it seemed that she felt her own value to have improved. The year before when I asked her if she enjoyed sex, she had told me that she did not. "Sometimes when he seeks me I do it for his sake but not for my own. I would rather be without," she said. "It is good to have a man to live with. He brings food for the house [...] It is good in one way, bad in another. It is bad only in relation to sex ... that is bad and I don't like it." In the same breath she also told me that she considered having her perineum tightened, as she felt she was too loose down there. Not that Airton had complained, but she felt it was so, and he might keep silent in order not to hurt her. Like everybody else, she knew that if a man were unsatisfied, he would find other women. Airton had, in fact, had another woman recently, but she thought it had stopped. She had not wanted to ask. I asked her if other women felt like her about sex: "Most of the others say that they like it; few say they don't. When I sit and chat with some women, most say they like it [...] Then they turn around and say 'And you, Neide?' and I say, 'Well, I don"t know...' But to tell the truth, I don't like it."

Now that I had returned I saw her several times tittering with Elizia, her friend and neighbour, over matters related to sex. Elizia's sexy panties, or, as on the day where we discussed the shaving of genital hair, my lack of cleanliness. "Doesn't the hair then get long and flow-ing? (titter, titter)." As if she had gained the right she lacked before to be heard on such subjects. I knew, of course, that her earlier statement about not enjoying sex was put forward especially for me, when with friends everything was different. I had seen that often before: with me they said one thing, with friends, another.

Nevertheless, I felt that Neide had changed, and Airton with her. As a good provider he came home every night with some nice food. Always something delicious in the bag – often fish – and bread. When he came, Neide used to rush out into the kitchen to unpack and make coffee for him and us. I really enjoyed those nights on Neide's terrace with the view of all the houses in the 'invasion', each with a lit bulb swinging over the front door. There were no streetlights, just crickets and a mild wind. Only after some time and in relation to something else did Neide tell me that the money for food came from her. Airton was supposed to pay for the stereo and the shelves bought on credit, which, however, he did not. Now they had been fined due to the delayed payment. That was the difference between Neide's former husband and Airton. "The other was good, he bought me everything," Neide said, "a watch, jewellery, everything that I wanted, but he hit me. I married him when I was 14. Oh, Lini, everyone has his faults and his advan-tages. This man is good, but he cannot give what the other gave. This man gives very little." But with Neide's contribution to the household they had found a way of living that made both of them happier. The debt, rapidly growing, was forgotten on happy days.

This was what Neide wanted me to see when I came to interview her. The house was as nice as possible, Airton was the caring husband with a baby on his arm – the protector of the family – and the food was good. The children were clean and on the way to bed. All was well.

The house and the self
Having a good house was important on many practical levels for people in the neighbourhood. As Neide told me, a house with a proper door naturally provides more security in an area with criminal violence. 'They' would sometimes enter ordinary people's houses and steal what-ever they needed, people said. As when my friend Irene organised the campaign for a politician and was to pay her helpers in the afternoon.

Three men held her and her husband Jairo at gunpoint and she had to give them all the money. Afraid of reprisals she never informed the police about the robbery. Nobody really felt safe, and everybody did as much as possible in order to provide the house with some security.

A big house with several bedrooms was also a protection in a different way. It protected against uncontrolled sex. Boys and girls should not sleep in the same bedroom, I was told, even though for practical reasons most of them did. And parents should sleep in a separate room in order not to expose children to their sex life. In one of the families that I came to know, a father had just raped his adult daughter, who lived with her parents after a separation from her husband. This was the kind of thing that could happen when precautions were not taken.

And of course a proper house was also a matter of hygiene. In houses without toilets people had to urinate and defecate somewhere on the ground, but even when having a toilet, hygiene was problematic. Where I lived people mainly coped with the irregular public water provision by using well water. However, many houses were not connected to the sewerage system, and people had to channel their sewage into the ground. As the water level at least in some areas was fairly high and as most wells were constructed without adequate inner cover, this practice made the use of well water rather perilous.

Having plastered walls inside the house was attractive mainly because the house was easier to keep clean. However, Sonia was also decided on plastering her walls as the open bricks full of holes attracted vermin. Several times she had had snakes in her house, and they were difficult to get rid of as they hid in the holes of the wall. But more than anything else having a proper house was a question of respectability. William James proposes that, next after clothes and close family members, our homes are part of our material selves. "We all have a blind impulse to watch over our body, to deck it with clothing of an ornamental sort, to cherish parents, wife and babes, and to find for ourselves a home of our own which we may live in and 'improve'" (James 1950:293), indicating that our materiality does not end with the skin but is manifested in an 'extended body' as well. Similarly, Drew Leder writes: "I live in bodies beyond bodies, clothes, furniture, room, house, city, recapitulating in ever expanding circles aspects of

Mother and daughters sharing housework.

my corporeality" (Leder 1990:35). The extended body in which we dwell in intimacy can, however, also be thematised in the objectifying gaze of the other. When others look at our clothing critically, we suddenly become aware of its shortcomings. We become self-conscious, identifying our self with the clothes we are wearing. Similarly, the house we know 'as our own pocket', as the saying goes, may turn into our social self, when objectified by actual or imaginary others.

In the neighbourhood, houses certainly represented both men and women's social selves, they were a means of self-expression, though in different ways. *Bargunza* (mess) was the sign of the unfit housewife. Pots and pans hanging in the kitchen should shine brilliantly, as they did in Anita's house; I never saw them darkened by the gas like mine were. And when Luzia once wanted to cause a rift between Neide and me and turn my attention towards her, she made insinuating remarks about the mess in Neide's house. Men, on the other hand, were responsible for providing a safe house for the family to live in, thus fulfilling the role of the true patriarch. Children and women were supposed to stay at home, and a wall in front of the house signified the ultimate protection against the dangers of the street. Hence, when I went to see Luzia and she could not let me in because her husband had locked both doors before leaving, I heard pride and tenderness in her voice.

However, living in the 'invasion' was not a good starting point for social acknowledgement. For people who lived outside, the area 'in there' constituted both a threat and a point of reference ('they' are what 'we' are not or no longer). The 'invasion' represented disorder, and even though living under disorderly conditions was a shared experience, it was important for those who could, to mark a distance. For instance, Neide's wealthier and more respectable sister visited neither Neide nor their mother, who lived near Neide, as she did not want to enter the 'invasion'. Living on 'invaded' terrain was to live too near the margin. 'In there' lived the criminals, the paupers and those who could not afford to buy a proper piece of land. And even though some of the houses in the 'invasion' were really comfortable, they would bear the stigma of marginality until the day – during a time of elections – when the land would be bought by the municipality and given to the users to give political mileage. Both the owner and the users apparently waited for such an initiative to come. Till then people would have to justify their habitation in the area as a practical choice in a general strategy towards improvement. As Sonia said,[31] "there are many who say: 'I would never live in an invasion.' But at times it is much better if you are within the invasion, not paying rent, than outside and paying rent. Those who have to give rent will never climb up, never. It is paying… paying today, tomorrow already owing another payment, then paying, owing another."

The laborious transformation of shacks into dream houses has been termed the process of "autoconstruction" (Holston 1991). Autoconstruction refers to the phenomenal house-building activity among lower income people in urban peripheries of Brazil. According to James Holston, the term was originally used to distinguish property owners from squatters, as property ownership was supposed to engender a commitment, an incitement to build up a future, which had no place in the squatters' mindset. However, this distinction is no longer relevant, Holston points out, as squatter settlements often become legitimised and are made into privately owned lots, while sold land may turn out to be illegally purchased (ibid.:451). Holston therefore bases the definition of autoconstruction on two features independent of ownership status: first, the conditions of urban peripheral poverty; second, the dream represented by the house of a life quite different from those conditions. "It is about the future, about the possibility of someday having a house of one's own with the security and sense of accomplishment that people believe it entails" (Holston 1991:448). In line with Holston's argument, I did not find any difference between squatters' and owners' obsession with house improvement in 'my' area despite the formers' often fragile economy. Everybody struggled on their level of possibility towards an imagined future, where individual worth and particularity would be manifested by choices – of tiles, colours and furniture.

Carmen, for instance, had *her* dreams. She lived in a small, but separate part of the house of her parents-in-law. While I was there her husband added a terrace to the house. But Carmen wanted more. "I want to change everything," she said, "I want to change my house and myself. I want to lift the front, so that when you come you will be better received. Make a veranda with a hammock and a lot of space. I want the kitchen here where it is, but much more beautiful. With cupboards on the wall, you know? A stove with six jets, and a rather nice sink, you see? I want everything new. Not this floor, I want a floor of tiles. And cement in front of the house, and a new door. There are much better doors than this one. One day when it is possible I will buy little by little, a door for my room [the bedroom], for the room of Milena [her daughter], and for the room of Emerson [her son]. A nice sofa and a better table to put in the sitting room, because I like having a table in the sitting room. Just to receive guests, you see? This house I have planned in my mind, you see, and I will get it one day... I don't know how, but I will get it one day." I asked Carmen if she had ever seen a house like that, and she said: "Lini, I see it more in the television, mainly in the foreign films. And if not, I see it in the shops, when I go ... when I go to the city I look like this in the shops, I stop and look ... and they even have a washing machine, which is another of my dreams. Then I look like this and say, 'Oh, my God, is it so that one day I will have all this?' Because I think it is nice, Lini. A cupboard on the wall – that is more practical in relation to space. It does not need to be many things, it is just some simple things that I want, but at the moment the capital is lacking."

People struggled and I learned by experience not to underestimate their agency. However, as Holston writes, their struggle could not be understood independently of political intentions to control the home sphere of their lives (1991:456). Since the 1930s the Brazilian state has expanded its interest in and capacity to influence issues clustered around the home and the personal. Home ownership is a central means in this process, as is the medicalisation of health. The overlapping development ideologies of the elites and the government have used the creation of demand in these areas as a means to discipline workers and create a mass consumer market for building and household commodities (ibid.:449). Consumer credits have played the major role; real estate speculators and big warehouses for building materials, all sell on instalment plans. Through home ownership lower income Brazilians have acquired a heightened political awareness of rights (to sewage lines, water, pavements and so on), engaging themselves as citizens with rights in the Brazilian state, but they have also become involved in obligations that submit them to the norms of the officially defined 'proper life'; this is consumption through indebtedness (ibid.:456). In this process, they are not just "transforming themselves as citizens but they are also changing the images of disrespect that bind them to a denigrated sense of their own persons" (ibid.:462). That was precisely what Carmen said: "I want to change my house and myself."

Houses had become metaphors of selves in the neighbourhood – metaphors in the sense proposed by Jackson: not as linguistic means to indicate the "thisness of that", but as manifestations of an actual experience of unity, the experience that "this *is* that" (Jackson 1989: 142). Metaphors merge social, personal and natural aspects of being and facilitate the coping with stressful aspects of life by transference to neutral, but corresponding areas (ibid.:149). Thus, houses in the neighbourhood mediated between ideas about structure and control and the actual individuals who lived in them. They were "good to think with"... "because [houses] channel personal experience into a public idiom, architecture, which enables people to evaluate that experience through a precise vocabulary" (Holston 1991:456). Tiles on the floor, plastered walls, separate bedrooms, doors with locks, verandas with lots of space to receive guests, they all manifested socially accepted ideas about the proper life.

Autoconstruction of bodies

In her work on body images in a Brazilian shanty town and in British working and middle class urban dwellings, Ceres Victora points out how embodied notions of time and the spatial organisation of house and neighbourhood shape people's experiences of their bodies (Victora 1996). She builds her analysis – inspired mainly by Pierre Bourdieu – on the notion of the domestic environment as both embodying the social order and shaping the perception of the individual body (Victora 1996:35). In the British case she found that regular and rigid time and space structures and the possibility of making long term plans were reflected in perceptions of the body as stable and bounded by rigid boundaries. In the Brazilian case, on the other hand, flexibility in time and fluidity in the physical environment were integral parts of people's lives and thereby central to their perception of their own bodies. Victora's characterisation of life in the shanty town resembles life in the neighbourhood where I worked in many ways.[32]

However, self-conscious of the shortcomings of their lives, people in the neighbourhood had turned the metaphorical relationship between body and social order upside down. They wanted to structure and bound their bodies and houses in order to give structure to their entire lives. The fluid milieu of the houses and the neighbourhood found in the 'invasion' represented the fluidity of life that people wanted to control. Fluidity and marginality were too closely related; uncontrolled fertility was part of it. As one woman put it: "there are so many single mothers who are carelessly having children, and the children suffer. I think it is better to be ligated. They have children, give them away, or even throw them in the rubbish, maltreat them. I think that ligation should be made free so that they can all be ligated."

What they strived for was control and structure, characteristics that poor people were not expected to have, but which seemed to be the only way out of disrespect. Like another woman said: "I ligated because I did not want many children; it has no future." They knew that it was too difficult to bring up many children; that they would be worn out by many childbirths and sole responsibility; that a proper life was a life with consumer goods; and that control and planning was essential for the ability to consume, particularly because economic means were few and should be invested with care. "No future" meant marginality: throwing newborn babies in the rubbish, having one's sons killed as teenagers, or perhaps just having to live in a shack unsuitable for 'proper' people. The day we went on the picnic, we passed an area full of shacks, apparently inhabited by newcomers to the city. "Look, a *favela!*" people shouted. Dona Lívia nudged me with her elbow: "Look, a *favela*", she said. I knew she had lived like that most of her life and answered, "Yes, a *favela*, but it works as a place for living." "Yes, it works," she quietly affirmed. In fact most of the people in the bus lived in the 'invasion', by others called the *favela*. The margin was always threateningly near, and one's distance from it had to be repeatedly constructed, established and reiterated. One way of doing it was to make female bodies less betraying, less unpredictable, and less permeable to external influences.

Neither contraceptive pills nor IUDs were the right solution; they both represented too much of the uncertainty, fluidity and movement that people were striving to leave behind. The IUD might move uncontrolled in the body, and get lost in the unknown space inside. It was even said to cause cancer, an uncontrolled growing threat to the life one wanted to secure. And the passage of pills through the body did not feel right, it was nauseating, the women felt like vomiting, as if the mass growing inside had to come out. The pills made the body swell up or get dry and thin and these fluctuations were out of the individual woman's control. Besides, pills were not safe enough: failures were too common.

> Take the case of my sister-in-law. When she got married she was very thin, her trousers were size 38! And you see her body today ... that is the pill. She had how many children? Four, five, six, yes, because one was an abortion, and she has four alive ... and the first died. It died after the birth. Look at the body of that woman! Fat!

Why I stopped using the pill? Because it gave me a strong wish to throw up.

I did not do well with the pills. I got too thin, I felt really bad. I was totally without appetite when I took the pills.

I became afraid because many women, thick or normal, immediately become thin, dry, without appetite, it gives that agony of no appetite. A woman becomes weak if she has no appetite. Because a person who does not eat is nothing.

As in the case of Sonia's shoes or Neide's house, inside and outside merged in women's perception of the pill. Bodily reactions and physical appearance melted into one experience of being out of control and worth "nothing". In addition, the pill was too closely associated with poverty. It had to be bought over and over again, reminding women of their lack of economic power. In contrast, sterilisation was often directly related to caesarean sections and thereby with purchasing power and access to private hospitals. Therefore, the need to use the pill indicated exclusion from the 'real thing.' The women felt they were given something that they deserved to get in a better form. Although nobody said this explicitly, there was no other way of understanding their attitude to sterilisation:

> I do not feel nor want to feel any wish for more children. Because everything I wanted was to do my ligation. I really wanted it.
>
>   (24 year old woman, sterilised at the age of 23)

> I always thought that one day I would ligate… in my mind I always had this, I always thought so.
>
>   (37 years old woman, sterilised at the age of 34)

This thing of regret I will never have. It was the best thing I did in my life until today. I should have done it much earlier.

(29 years old woman, sterilised at the age of 28)

Sterilisation had come to symbolise structure as opposed to fluidity, social inclusion as opposed to exclusion, and potency as opposed to impotence. The women wanted to change their selves and their lives through the sterilisation. They wanted to be recognised as worthy members of the society in which they lived, and pills were simply not appropriate building materials in this autoconstruction of bodies.

Chapter Six

Fertility and Home

The life-world is the quintessence of a reality that is lived, experienced, and endured. It is, however, also a reality that is mastered by action and the reality in which — and on which — our action fails. Especially for the everyday life-world, it holds good that we engage in it by acting and change it by our actions. Everyday life is that province of reality in which we encounter directly, as the condition of our life, natural and social givens as pregiven realities with which we must try to cope. We must act in the everyday life-world, if we wish to keep ourselves alive.[1]

(Schutz and Luckmann 1983:1)

To understand why some women in the neighbourhood ended up sterilised, while others did not, it does not suffice to situate sterilisation within economic capacity, or contacts to willing providers and persuasive doctors. Neither was an achieved sterilisation only the result of individuals' striving to be recognised as good citizens. To understand why one or another decision was taken and what the final outcome was, we have to examine the pushes and pulls of daily relations and interactions and the field of emotional attachment within which women moved. A pair of high-heeled shoes was not important as a symbol of mastery in itself, but as a symbol of mastery *for somebody in particular.* In order to understand why Sonia bought the shoes, we thus have to ask whom she wanted to impress, or rather, which relationship(s) did she want to work upon? Likewise, when Neide wanted to be an interesting woman, she might have had in her mind the beauty and attraction of women in telenovelas or advertisements, but the need she felt of being like them was generated in her daily relationships. Knowing that one is poor and powerless is not the same as feeling it in relation to the people whom one cares for. In this chapter I will argue that it was within the daily co-existence with husband, children and other women that sterilisation gained or lost its motivating importance in the midst of other concerns.

Multiple concerns

As my analytical starting point in this work I have taken the human need for recognition and the motivating force integral to the desire to satisfy this need. It is a need to exist and be acknowledged in the world of others and, consequently, a desire to be identified by others with values that these others appreciate. This need is nothing but a condition in itself. It can be likened to an empty frame, which must be filled in order to exist. For Hegel, man is undetermined as a species. "[I]t is human nature to have no fixed nature," as Francis Fukuyama paraphrases Hegel (Fukuyama 1992:64), and it is the movement out towards recognition by others that engages the individual in history and turns her undifferentiated need into a need for something in particular.

In the search for recognition the relationship between self and other is thus mediated by a third element, which may be a thing (shoes, skin lotion, houses), an emotional attitude (mother love), an action (obtaining a sterilisation), or a moral stance (responsibility) – anything that represents the desire of others. This, in turn, implies that relations to others are based upon a transposition of one's thoughts and feelings to others (Crossley 1996a:68). If not, how should we know what others value?

Through his discussion of the child's engagement in play and games George Herbert Mead illustrates how the individual learns to assume the attitude of the other (1965:152-164). Through the role play the child learns to assume the viewpoint of specific others; through the game it enters into a shared world, a common activity, and takes on the values and goals that belong to the 'generalised other' of this world (ibid.: 219). Mead proposes that the identification with specific others, their attitudes towards the individual itself and towards each other, is not enough for an individual to develop a full sense of self. According to Mead, it is in the engagement with a common undertaking, the phases and goals within it, that a full social self emerges (ibid.:154-55). It arises by 'doing' and gains its importance for the individual through a gradual process of imaginative identification (Crossley 1996a:63); one has to feel for the game in order to be part of it. Through identification with the 'generalised other' of a given community the self enters a world outside itself with norms, values, rights and duties, with which it can reflect upon itself and act according to shared projects.

In Chapter Five I described the women's identification with the 'generalised other' of the consumer society and the negative evaluation of themselves that the assumption of this viewpoint lead to. In this chapter I want to employ the notion of the 'generalised other' to investigate shared norms and values within the community of 'mothers' and within the more problematic, but equally engaging game of 'wives'.[2] Relations to children, husbands, mothers and friends (often neighbour women) carried particular weight – socially, materially as well as affectively – for the women. They achieved their importance through the daily, trivial co-existence; the sharing of meals, sorrows and joys. Despite being the essential elements of 'home' these relationships did not achieve their motivating force independently of the 'outer' non-domestic world. Ideas about structure, autonomy and responsibility penetrated women's evaluation of their home world, as we have already seen in the previous chapter, and the inferiority felt in public life, found an echo in the inability to perform as a caring mother or an interesting wife, as we will soon see.

However, in the domestic sphere interests were many and diverse. Strategies to construct a better life through sterilisation, house building, health care and children's education had to be pursued in contest with other goals, some of which pulled in opposite directions. Choices had to be pondered and possible futures compared, always with the consideration of an actual or generalised other in mind, or as Alfred Schutz expresses it, always with a particular interest.

"The life-world is something to be mastered according to my particular interests," Schutz writes (1973:15).[3] In *The Structures of the Life-World* he develops a framework for analysis of action consisting of hierarchies of projects within levels of urgency and importance. On each level of a project there are "in-order-to motives"[4] which become chains of motivations leading backwards from 'later' to 'earlier', that is, from the goal of an act through the intermediate stages of the project back to the beginning (ibid.:212). Applying this to the quest for sterilisation, several minor goals lead towards the final goal and vice versa: obtaining a sterilisation can itself be an "in-order-to motive" in a major project. Schutz also points out that several projects may co-exist and either be interrelated or mutually exclusive.

In the women's life some projects were related, as when one goal (sterilisation) was just an intermediate step towards the next (recognition), while other goals were mutually exclusive, as it was with the urge to be sterilised and the competing wish for yet another baby. However, as Schutz writes, "I project my own plans into the life-world, and it resists the realization of my goals, in terms of which some things become feasible for me and others do not" (ibid.:15). Decisions in the neighbourhood were often a matter of immediate relevance and practicality. In the unpredictability of daily life, the constant emergence of hindrances and changes, one often had to accept what was possible.

I have described the search for control in one's life as an ongoing negotiation of selves, in which the alienation and complete objectification by the other is a constant threat. In this chapter I continue to focus on this working upon one's surroundings through acts, emotions and attitudes in order to achieve a sense of control. As said before, within the world of close relationships in the neighbourhood the search for control was not just a matter of survival as a member of a group but of survival in its very material, most literal sense.

To be recognised by other women as a loyal and generous neighbour gave access to small loans of food, money or other necessities, which made the vicissitudes of life bearable. To be recognised by one's husband gave access to the needed economic means of survival and, perhaps, his care and attention instead of his neglect and violence. Despite the emotional tensions that particularly characterised marital relationships these shared worlds were based on expectations of mutual recognition, and the struggle to remain part of them was an ongoing project for the people involved. Even Carmen struggled to love her husband, though she explained to me how she saw her husband having sex with her as on a television, that is, truly alienated from him and the woman she represented to him. As Mead writes, "It is that self which is able to maintain itself in the community, that is recognized in the community in so far as it recognizes the others" (1965:196), and Carmen had to join the game, if she did not want to be excluded from the recognition it implied (see this chapter p. 240ff).

What follows is a look into the dependency and recognition imbedded in the relationships which constituted the prime concerns of the women. I will situate fertility and sterilisation within the shared worlds of motherhood and wifehood, in which sterilisation proved to be empowering for the individual women, even though it was often just a pragmatic solution to a situation with contradictory concerns and demands.

Being a mother among mothers

After my first fieldwork I was left with several unanswered questions; one of them concerned Luzia. The day before I left the neighbourhood Luzia finally gave birth and I was with her during the last three or four hours at the hospital. She really suffered. She was treated without respect by nurses and nurse assistants, who complained about her failure to press properly. The knuckles of her hands became white as she squeezed the iron bar of the bed. In Brazil women are often told to press during the first stage of labour,[5] and Luzia pressed and pressed though she was already exhausted. Among the women at home she had always wanted to present herself as a misplaced princess, who had lived a much better life in São Paulo, but under these conditions I saw her as the illiterate girl from the *sitio* (small farm), who had to work hard in order to compensate for the burden she represented to her adoptive parents – the girl that she had told me she once was.

However, the following day she arrived home in a taxi, more the princess than ever. She wore a white lace nightgown from São Paulo and new *chinelos*, bought especially for the occasion. At home the women had cleaned her house and prepared lunch, and the cradle was ready for the baby. As I was leaving for Denmark the same afternoon, I had promised to pass by to take a photo before leaving. Luzia was in her usual clothes, lying on the sofa, while the neighbour women sat around her. We chatted a bit before I took my photos and left.

Later, at a seminar for colleagues in Denmark, I showed some slides, and Luzia appeared, lying on the sofa. "Look at her," I said "look at her dark and wounded eyes." I was telling my colleagues about the disrespect at public hospitals, and I found Luzia's case a good example to draw from. "She looks very satisfied and happy to me," somebody remarked. I could not see it. I only saw the pain that I had observed at the hospital. However, recalling the situation in Luzia's house I had to admit that the atmosphere was relaxed and satiated with a sense of fulfilment.

Mutual recognition
Lying on the sofa surrounded by women Luzia was at home, and she could relax. To be at home is the comfort of familiarity, of being at ease. "Things flow. There seems to be no resistance between oneself and the world. The *relationship* is all" (Jackson 1995:111, his emphasis). For the women in the neighbourhood 'home' was primarily the house in which they lived, inseparable from marriage and family.[6] In the Brazilian gender hierarchy a woman's world is categorised as the 'home' and includes the children, the cleaning, the food, the neighbour women and the relatives, and within this world she organises her time and tasks according to her own wants and her husband's needs. The men for their part are expected to stay in the 'street';[7] the jobs, the bars, the football fields are the sites of masculinity.[8] As one man said to me during an interview: "I prefer just to be at home to sleep and watch football [on TV]." Adhering more or less to these cultural prescriptions women in the neighbourhood stayed near their homes all day long; only a few had jobs outside the neighbourhood, and visits to family members or the hospital and rare shopping trips to Recife were the only reasons for the rest of the women to leave the area.

Within the neighbourhood there were, however, degrees of familiarity that the women had to consider when leaving their house. They needed to dress properly before going to the local health post, even though it was near and everything was familiar. To go shopping at the *avenida* implied moderate dressing up, as did the hanging around Neide's lottery stand in the afternoons. Showing oneself in public meant taking care of one's reputation, as Elizia told me; one had to dress as a married woman. But in the shadow in front of Elizia's house where Neide, Rute, Fátima, Elizia herself and sometimes Luzia used to sit in the hot noon, nobody thought about appearance. The women just sat, chatting, going through magazines advertising things to buy, complaining about laziness and uneasiness, or commenting on this or that person passing by. "Who is that?" one would say. "Isn't it Rinaldo's girlfriend?" "That black woman? No, I think he has a girlfriend in Bairro Novo..." "Oh, I feel so listless!" And so on. Everything was really 'laid back', subtly familiar.

The sense of familiarity sprang from the incorporation of the way of life that the women shared. "Over time, that which is acted out, rehearsed, and repeated seeps into one's organismic ground" (Leder 1990: 32), and becomes part of one's habitual universe. For instance, the experience of time as flexible was familiar to the women I knew, but a constant source of wonder to me. Time was not a rigid structure, as few things had to be done at a fixed hour.[9] The women who stayed at home all day long had a lot of housework to do – *serviço* they would say – washing clothes and dishes, cleaning the house, cooking. However, there was often plenty of time in excess. The public water supply was irregular and on days without water the piles of dirty things just grew, while the women hung around. When the water finally came, everybody would abandon other activities and rush to fill up barrels and buckets. When playing domino at night was interesting, families would sleep longer the next morning. When there was food in the house one would eat, when there was none, everyone would find his or her own way of filling the stomach. Scheper-Hughes' comment from her Alto do Cruzeiro certainly matched my experience: "One is immediately plunged into (...) another tempo, another chronicity altogether" (Scheper-Hughes 1992:88). For whoever stayed in the neighbourhood time was rather fleeting. As Elizia said, "He leaves for work at ten, and then at times I do the housework, and I sometimes sleep in the afternoon because I have nothing else to do."[10]

Within this shared universe life was not without conflicts, but the necessity of staying where 'home' was implied commitment and a constant search for some sort of reconciliation. Rebhun writes that due to economic crisis and deteriorating living conditions social networks have become increasingly important to the economic survival of the Brazilian working class. Therefore, the pressure to conform to "norms of co-operative friendliness" has increased (Rebhun 1999: 56). In her article 'The Self in a World of Urgency and Necessity' Unni Wikan generalises this need to conform and proposes that the more a person is constrained by necessity, the more he or she has to fight for social worth, since change or escape from sociality is impossible (1995:275). Among the women that I came to know endurance, self-management and the ability to keep relations going were indeed crucial and implicated skills in the orchestration of what Erving Goffman calls "face".[11]

The women were impelled to behave in ways that were acceptable to others as they depended on them for the intimacy, the food, the chatter or whatever else was important in their lives. They were bitterly aware that their security and pleasure were on loan from their surroundings. Everybody had to be on guard in order not to have this loan withdrawn. Scheper-Hughes writes that people were "continually 'checking' themselves and each other" on the Alto (1992:390), but I would call what happened in the neighbourhood more than 'checking'. Possessing very few resources to act independently of others' help (be it money, childcare, or other prerequisites for action) the women were experts in impacting on others and manipulating the image they projected to others.[12] While an immediate need of money, sugar or company might prompt a discrete action, one's positioning in relation to others would be decisive for the outcome of any initiative. As Goffman puts it: "Ordinarily, maintenance of face is a condition of interaction, not its objective" (1995:226).

In spite of the mutual recognition in this shared habitual universe, the women always ran the risk of typification and exclusion from 'we-relations'.[13] That happened to Neide in the moment her sons were typified as criminals. It also happened to Luzia when she turned out to be 'different'. As Neide said, "When you tell her something she spreads it to everybody else. That creates fear. Every woman needs somebody to talk with, but not somebody like her [a nod in direction of Luzia's house]. She is different." Luzia was for a while thoroughly excluded from the *mulherada* (group of women) around Neide. She struggled hard to regain respect, but the women were relentless. "She is very shameless," Neide said, "because if I went to your house, and you had that *cara feia* [ugly face] I would not come again. But she comes. One can put on *cara feia*, put on anything, she comes. If you came here and I closed my face for you, treated you badly, would you return? If I did not treat you well, because I did not want you here? Every woman understands that, but she doesn't. She just lives smiling."

Living close together as Luzia and Neide did, it was a hard time for Luzia to go through. With tears in her eyes she told me that she wanted to leave, "get out of here". She planned to go to São Paulo, she said. However, as things turned out she found it impossible to sell her house and had to stay. And in the end, Luzia got the best of it. Neide was suddenly alone due to the threat of violence; only Luzia was ready to support her. When Neide had to move, Luzia for a while defended Neide's interests, but she had to be pragmatic and care for herself. In a letter I received from Neide recently she wrote: "I don't know what I did in my life to suffer so much because of my children. My family has left me. Even Gleisse [her daughter] who lived with mum was sent back to me. Rute, Elizia, Ceça and Luzia distanced themselves from me." Neide had to bear the burden of social exclusion now that she was no longer of any use.

Mutual recognition as well as mutual dependence were the conditions that the women had to cope with and actively foster in their daily interactions in the neighbourhood. Having children both intensified dependence and reinforced the need for recognition that would counterbalance the surrender of control to others.

Being a mother: A shared burden

Being a mother among mothers was the main project in most women's lives and the ability to procreate was perceived as essential for a woman in the neighbourhood. A *menina* was a female human being who had not yet entered the field of reproduction; a *moça* was one who had had her first menstruation; a *mulher* was a one who had had sex; and finally, a woman after menopause was considered of less value and subject to disease. Semantically the different stages of the female life course were clearly distinguished by her relation to reproduction and everybody followed these rules in daily speech. "When I became *moça*" thus meant "when I had my first menstruation". However, as many young women today have sex before marriage, that is, while they still live at home, they may in practice continue to be called *moça* as a way of respecting the family. At least, so I was told, when I asked about something as obvious as the difference between a *moça* and a *mulher*. A *mulher* was by definition a sexual being.

For the women living was synonymous with having children. Some young women became pregnant while still living with their parents, and if possible marriage was then hastily arranged. Others were married or had eloped with a man in order to 'become a woman' and have children.[14] In general they all expected to have children soon after establishing their own household. "I do not have children, but as soon as I find someone to marry, I will have some. It must be beautiful to have children. I have always thought so. But I will only have two." The woman who said this was around 20 years old. I met her in a minibus, where we sat squeezed together in the late afternoon both on our way home. However, any young woman could have said exactly the same. Becoming a mother was often referred to as a 'dream' and a 'happiness' as it promised the fulfilment of one's life in the venerated role of the loving, dedicated mother.[15] As a young woman said about the birth of her firstborn: "It was great, because the most beautiful thing in life was born. He opened my heart. It is the most beautiful thing in the world, when a person becomes a mother for the first time."

Initiating married life with a man meant, for most of the women, being confined to the home. As the man would seldom be at home except for meals, sex and sleep, the woman would be very alone in her new role as housewife, until a child was born. If a woman did not become pregnant soon after *casamento* (marriage), she would start to worry and become depressed. Nalva, a young woman full of initiative and always very direct in her approach to life, referred to the painful time before the birth of her son, once when we were talking about me living alone in my small house. She said: "How horrible! I have been alone once, right after my wedding, but now thank God things are better. I have got my little *companheiro* (companion, that is, her son)." Nalva's experience of loneliness resonated with Elizia's ideas about married life:

Elizia: I think that the liveliness of a home is the children, because a couple alone within a house has no charm. He leaves for work and she stays alone.

Line: But she could leave for work, too?

Elizia: She could. But most women... The desire of all women is to have a child, because they feel alone...

Line: Do you know a woman who has no children?

Elizia: No. I know one from sight, but I have no intimacy with her. I think it must be very bad.

Line: Why bad?

Elizia: Because being alone in the house is too bad. One has to have something to do, somebody to play and to talk with. I think a child is important in the life of a couple.

It seemed difficult to think differently. With an arm around his wife's shoulder one man characterised a woman's life project like this: "A fulfilled woman is a woman who fulfilled her dreams; the children that she wanted, everything that she has, husband, children, home, everything!" A woman was not expected to wish for more; in practice she might even have less as husbands were not to be counted on. "Children bring joy to a house", "a woman's only joy is her children", "everything I have in my life is my children". The sayings were many, but they expressed the same bittersweet truth; children were the only people a woman could depend on, for good and for bad, at least till they had grown up. The joy of having children was evident. When I asked old Dona Lívia, a mother of 16 children, what was the best part of her long life, she said without hesitation," *Meus filhos!*" with a sudden very big smile. And Carmen always told me how happy she was with her children, especially the youngest. "He is a joy!" she proclaimed, "but both are very affectionate. I think that helps me a lot."

Yet having children was also difficult, as I have already described (see Prologue). Food was often scarce, clothes were expensive, and childcare was not publicly available. Besides, education was difficult and children more and more demanding. As Dona Benedita said: "Before it was bad; now it is worse, because before nobody had luxury. The children walked barefooted, naked." She explained that today they demand clothes, sweets, all the good things in life. Carmen already talked about the day when she would need to buy a computer for her children. The mothers seemed to feel guilty when they were unable to fulfil a demand. Ana thus said to me: "It is difficult to be a mother, the most difficult thing in life. You have to divide, if you give to one or the other there is jealousy, you have to please your children. It is like being a tightrope walker in a circus." To be a good mother meant to be able to fulfil the needs of each child, and the women's incapacity hollowed out their sense of self-worth.

They helped each other with food and small loans of money. Children's clothes circulated, and exchange of childcare was part of everyday life. If a woman were found unable to bring up her offspring, family members or perhaps neighbours would often intervene. Sonia related to me how she once helped a neighbour woman with a child: "She told me that she had not slept all night because of the girl. I said, 'She is like that because she is hungry.' And then I took the girl, put her in my arm and brought her here. When I arrived I made a little milk, gave her a bath, and the girl ate. I put her on the children's bed and she slept all day. I said to myself, 'She will never wake up again!' I looked at her … could it be that she had died? But she breathed. From moment to moment I looked at her, and she slept till five o'clock in the afternoon. Then I said to myself 'My God in Heaven, what a hunger this girl had!' And I took a bottle of milk and gave to the mother." The young mother did not give all the milk to the baby; she was forced to share it with other people in her house and Sonia then decided to bring the baby home twice a day to feed her. Later, when Sonia went to hospital to give birth, the young woman took care of Sonia's house and children, and so one favour was exchanged for another.

Childcare was thus a shared burden and a woman was expected to engage in this common undertaking. Not wanting to have children was often cast in terms of selfishness. A young mother, Anita, put it like this: "I always wanted to become a mother. But some women are bad, they don't want children, they just think of themselves." However, while motherhood was perceived as a submission to some natural, God given order, wanting to have many children was also perceived as self- ish. A woman could not go on satisfying her wish for lovely babies; she had to consider the burden she constituted to others and the life she could offer her children. Being poor, a woman simply could not 'afford' to have many children, even if she wanted to. "If I had the economic conditions," one woman said, "I would have more children, because I love children." Put this way fertility control became an additional submission to the self-abnegation inherent to motherhood. As Serruya writes in her study: "In this way, the women consented to a solely numerical transformation of maternity, all the time diminishing the number of children, while fundamentally remaining mothers, if only to one child, continuing to consider the maternal sentiment holy and untouchable" (1996:165, my translation). Indeed, in the community of mothers in the neighbourhood responsible reproductive behaviour was the admirable act of a dedicated mother.

A woman's responsibility
In practice, though, sterilisation was also a way to diminish a shared economic burden, an act in which certain others had a considerable interest, namely the woman's mother or mother-in-law. In the neighbourhood contraception was women's responsibility. Even though some couples agreed on the need of birth control, women were the ones to undergo sterilisation and often also the ones to obtain the operation through agreements and negotiations with physicians or politicians. They often had an ally in their mother or mother-in-law though these relationships were not unproblematic. In the interviews we found that remarkably many women had been strongly motivated by their mothers. Utterances like "my mother gave me the greatest support" were common.

Mothers were significant figures in the women's lives. Setting up one's own separate household was a fundamental part of female identity (see also Scott 1996:292), but the women preferred living next to their mothers to receive her help when needed. It was often the mother who accompanied her daughter to hospital to give birth, and the mother who helped during *resguardo* (confinement) after childbirth. And if a woman was left by her husband, she would probably return to her mother's house like Neide did when her first husband left her: "I gave Gleisse to my mother, when she was four days old. Because when I got her, the father left me, so I left her with my mother, and went out to work." Gleisse and her brothers stayed with Dona Lívia all day long, while Neide worked at the bakery in order to provide for the children. When she met Airton, she started a new family and she left the children from her former marriage with her mother. As did Sonia, when her husband was shot. She went to São Paulo to work, and her two daughters learned to call their grandmother "mum", and their mother "Sonia".

However, tensions between mothers and daughters were common. Mothers expected daughters to care for them. When still young, daughters helped with the housework but as the daughters grew older and set up their own households, mothers' and daughters' interests parted. The mothers' expectations and their daughters' aspirations for life did not always conflate and the daughters' fertility became a threat to the elder women's hopes. The mothers complained about their daughters using them while giving nothing in return. Tereza, my neighbour, who lived with two daughters, their three children, and a son of a third daughter, one day burst out with all her complaints. Full of self-pity she cried that nobody took care of her though she had worked like a beast in order to provide for her children all their lives. Dona Maria, Sonia's mother, expected to be cared for, too. She said: "I have always dedicated myself to my children, and I hope that when I reach the point of failing, they take care of me with the same patience. That is what I want. It cannot be possible that in the middle of.... Because there is Sonia, Anita, Jane, Renata, Leonora, five women...I want to see if not one of them will have patience to struggle with me. There has to be!"

In his examination of structural factors pushing Brazilian women into fertility control George Martine mentions changes in the social security system (1998:196). He points out that the burden of responsibility for old age security has shifted from the family sphere to that of the state and that most old people therefore no longer depend on family networks for survival. Rather on the contrary, as the social security assistance is relatively small, older people may be interested in sharing it with as few as possible. This was the case with Neide's mother, Dona Lívia, who received 120 *reais* per month, which was very little, but still more than Neide would often have for her family. Out of this money Dona Lívia provided for Neide's three older children. If she had had only Gleisse, the girl, she would be much better off, she told me. Grandmothers had no interest in having too many grandchildren to bring up. They were the ones who needed to be cared for, they felt, and they wanted what little they had for themselves.

Therefore, as marriages were unstable, and as women expected men to be unwilling to adopt children from former marriages, grandmothers had a certain interest in their daughters' sterilisation. Regina, who was sterilised at the age of 24, had a mother who, according to Regina, carried through her own project:

> I had my first child when I was 18. It wasn't a planned pregnancy, and the father did not accept the boy. My mother did. I went to Rio and got married and had my second child. That did not work either. In no way did it work, and I preferred not to have more children. I preferred to make the ligation [when giving birth]. It was my mother who obtained it for me. She worked with some relations of the mayor there in Rio de Janeiro, and she talked with them.... I was very ill, too ill, and my mother once came to her *patroa* and told her that I was ill, that I was losing a lot of blood with this second child, and then she indicated a doctor for my mother. An excellent doctor. My mother went there and told him my story, that I had married two times and that it did not work out well. And my mother told him she preferred that I ligated. And then he said ... he asked my mother if she really wanted it, and my mother said she did. In the surgery room he talked with me, told me that I could marry again, but even so I said 'No, no!' I did not want more children. I did not know if afterwards I would arrange to get another man, if I would have luck, but I had no luck the first time, neither the second time, so why should I have luck the third?

However, mothers also helped their daughters to obtain sterilisation as they knew what life with too many children was like. The reality that Scheper-Hughes met 20 years ago was still very present in these women's life experiences: endless pregnancies with very uncertain outcomes and hard work in order to survive with as many children as possible. In the structured interviews we conducted among 28 newly sterilised mothers, the average number of children at sterilisation was 3, while the number of children born alive by their mothers was 8 per woman, on average. However, these mothers had lost several children before the age of 14, which diminished the number to 6 per woman.

Dona Corina could have been one of these mothers. She lost three out of ten children, and when we asked her why, she said:

> At that time the children often died because when they began the nourishment that was very weak there was no.... Medicine one could not buy, food one could not buy, neither a glass of vitamins, because when you bought for one you lacked for another. Then you either saved one or another. I think like this, that in former times more children died because of this. The parents could not give their children what they needed, because what did they have? Sugar cane for the person to work. At that time there was no work to get. Just that same thing, the sugar cane and the washing of clothes. To walk almost two leagues to wash a bundle of clothes, in order to buy what? For four or five children at home? A sardine, a handful of *farinha* [manioc flour], in order to eat what? *Farinha* and water? With food like that the children already were born skinny, very dehydrated, weak. Only if God wanted to bring them up, they survived.

Dona Severina who had helped provide so many sterilisations for younger women, had been even harder hit. She lost 12 out of 16 live born children.

Severina: I worked a lot to give food, to pay rent, to take care of the children, to bury children...
Line: Did you bury many?
Severina: A lot.
Line: At which age did they die?
Severina: Things like two or three months, four months, five months. When I thought it would grow up, there was the setback and it died. Then came the funeral. I just bought the coffin at the undertakers on credit. They were all born alive and normally and of nine months, they just had the problem that after some months there was this problem that is with children.
Line: Which problem?
Severina: High fever.
Line: Did they also have diarrhoea?
Severina: Yes.

The stories were many and more than once did I recall the despairing resignation described by Scheper-Hughes. As when a young woman echoed the voices from the Alto do Cruzeiro by saying: "My mother had 18 children, 4 are alive. She did not cry when they died. She used to say, 'Why cry? Crying does not bring a child back into the world!'" In the world of motherhood that these older women knew, being a mother was an endless struggle, and it was in this context that they acted when they sought sterilisations for their daughters. As Schutz says, interest in a particular future motivates action, but always against a background of personal incorporated history and sometimes this history has particular force: "[S]ome projects are triggered by specific sediments of encounters and lived experiences" (1983:19). Jacione's mother had such a project, which, however, failed.

Jacione's concerns

Jacione was 24, when I first met her. She was pregnant and she wanted to ligate. I asked her why. "High blood pressure," she answered. "Many problems. I really become ill. I feel a lot of pain. Many problems. My pregnancy is really risky, of high risk." The day before I had been to the health post with Luzia, who had done her best to persuade the nurse into declaring her of 'high risk' as she too wanted a caesarean. Taking advantage of the blood pressure apparatus being in disorder, Luzia had talked a lot about her dizziness and the stars that she sometimes saw before her eyes. However, Jacione seemed not to fake her high blood pressure. I saw her on days where she was very preoccupied and uneasy with her symptoms. She had expected to have her caesarean section at the big hospital, Barão de Lucena, in Recife to which all 'high risk' pregnancies were transferred from the health post for antenatal examinations. However, not being able to get an agreement for sterilisation beforehand at the Barão, she decided to use the local hospital. Her mother worked there, and she had arranged for the surgery.

One day Jacione was not at home when I came to see her, and I went to seek her in her mother's house. The mother was alone and I was invited to stay while I waited. Jacione's mother was tired. Not just from a hard day's work (she cleaned at the hospital), but from years of struggle, it seemed. She told me about the arrangement she had made for her daughter. That it was a necessary solution, because Jacione had a good husband, who had but one defect: He was not interested in work. Not that he was lazy; he was just satisfied with doing nothing. In that situation two children were more than enough for Jacione, her mother said. She herself had 7 living children. The eldest had been 11 years old when her husband passed away. After three years of hunger she had got a chance to work at the local hospital. "It was a filthy place, and the person who gave me the job doubted whether I would take it. However, with 7 hungry kids at home one has to, and after a while I learned to eat when I ate, and clean when I cleaned," she said. "I had filled up the house with children. Jacione does not need to do that!"

Apparently, Jacione was not as convinced as her mother, because when I met her a year later, the arrangement had failed and she was not yet sterilised. She had not searched for sterilisation again though Brazil had just passed through a period of elections in which other women of her age had achieved their operations in exchange for votes. She was either indifferent or for some reason too preoccupied to talk about it. I never found out. However, I always had the impression that it was her mother who was the prime motor, and now that the immediate uneasiness due to the high blood pressure had disappeared, Jacione seemed in doubt. "I like to have children," she once told me. "I find it beautiful to expect a child. To be worried, to feel the belly harden, that weight. It is so good, when one feels the child moving within the belly. It is such an excitement!" Jacione had to find her way between the mother's interest in her sterilisation, her own worries about her household economy, her health that really troubled her, the joy of having a baby and her unwillingness to visit the hospital again. My experience was that she was not alone in facing such a dilemma.

Sterilisation was a matter of responsibility towards one's nearest. A woman ought to consider the future of the children she already had and the burden she added to her family, especially her mother, before getting pregnant again. Seeking sterilisation was therefore essential for one's worth as a caring and responsible mother and daughter. The surgery was perceived as obtainable for those who really wanted it, and there was no excuse for a woman who 'did not care'. Obtaining a sterilisation was therefore a status giving sign of being in control in the community of mothers. Thus, when Luzia felt threatened in the *mulherada* around Neide, her striving for a sterilisation also seemed to be a manner of regaining respect. When finally she failed and had to "go through the pain", she, an adept in 'face' work, told everybody that it was in accordance with my wish, which rescued her from embarrassment.[16]

However, having a baby was also longed for and many of the women I talked to appreciated the love evoked by a small child. As a woman said: "I think I will miss these small ones. The size of them now, I like it, and my husband likes it, too. When he leaves work, the colleagues stay drinking, but he says, 'I'll go home to see my kids'." A baby was valuable as a trigger of maternal sentiment, confirming the mother's worth to herself and to those around her. Only when children grew older did troubles arise. The saying *parir é facil, criar é difícil* (to give birth is easy, bringing up is difficult) conveyed both the dilemma and the resignation leading to sterilisation. One had to be practical and responsible. Some women acted promptly, others like Jacione waited for a chance to come – a matter of temperament rather than anything else, it seemed.

Being married

A fulfilled woman was, according to the man quoted earlier, a woman who had obtained what she wanted: a man, a home and some children. And in fact, man, house and children *were* interdependent elements of a proper woman's life. Having children with neither man nor house meant continuing to live with one's parents as a daughter; having children and a house but no man meant economic suffering and to some extent a lack of respectability;[17] and having a house and a man but no children with him meant that he might not feel responsible for the household. Hence, getting married,[18] formally or informally, was the entrance to adult status as a sexual individual and giving birth to a man's children was a way of securing him,[19] especially when formal marriage was not a possibility.[20] Marital relationships were 'knots' of economic, sexual and emotional interests. However, due to the different perspectives on life and marriage held by men and women, these interests were not easily satisfied.

Disunited couples

Gender categories in Brazil are based on a hierarchical structure of patriarchal domination in which masculinity and femininity are defined in terms of their fundamental opposition. Ideally, men are active and controlling, women passive and receptive (Parker 1991). Men and women therefore have very different, but complementary bases for establishing a gender identity successfully (Scott 1996). For most women the home and the private sphere is fundamental, and as Parry Scott writes "it is in relation to her home that a woman constructs a self-evaluation of her status" (1996:292). For a man, the ability to control his home and provide for it economically is essential. Men are supposed to show their care and attention by *não deixar faltar as coisas em casa* (not to let things be lacking at home), which however is an almost impossible task in a situation of widespread unemployment and poverty. As Pedro Nascimento notes in his study from the neighbourhood, that man was valued who returned home from work every night with a bag of food and walked directly to his home (1999: 21). However, such a man did not fall to every woman's share.

Many of the men had difficulties fulfilling their culturally ascribed role as providers. The women complained about the men drinking too much, gambling, having other women, and thereby spending their sparse income on amusement outside the home. They would return home late, throw their dirty clothes on the floor for the woman to wash, and demand sex and food just in order to leave again the following morning. If he stayed away all night, no longer wanted sex, or if the provisions for the house were diminished, the woman could be certain that he had another woman to care for. Women had to be on guard, always watching for small signs of infidelity.

However, as both Scott and Nascimento indicate, low income men are under double pressure, marginalised both outside and inside home. The ideal of the patriarch who demands and controls, which dominates Brazilian notions of masculinity, is hardly attainable for a man with a low-status job who returns home after work to a wife who complains, supported in her self-righteousness by her female network. The women's complaints were many: no food in the house, children suffering from lack of male authority, their own unmet need for affection, and projects that should have been completed long time

"I don't like to depend on a woman".

ago. "In these conditions men are seen disparagingly by women as 'slow and without initiative', representing and embodying their own failure outside the home" (Scott 1996:290). *"Que homem parado"* (what a standing still man) a woman would nag. The men who suffered the most in the neighbourhood were logically those whose wives worked and had to provide for them. Thus when we expected Sonia and her husband Edilson for lunch one day, Sonia came alone as she and Edilson had quarrelled about the bus ticket that Sonia had to pay for him. And Jairo, Irene's unemployed husband, once said,

> I don't like to depend on a woman. Not that I am a macho guy, no, I just don't like it. I don't even like it when my wife asks for something from any other person. It is better if she asks when I am not present, because I don't like it. I prefer to say, "Is something missing here?" and then I act. If I do not get what is missing, I wait till the end of the month, till any day. I already make the effort for things not to be missing, I do the possible and impossible, but it is difficult for us to agree, because she is worried as soon as something is missing.

Facing his incapacity outside home and as a provider for the family, a man may turn to violence. Or he may start drinking, staying away from home as often as possible leaving a void behind where the caring father and husband was supposed to be. Young women, especially, expressed an unsatisfied need of *carinho*[21] in their relationships. As Rebhun writes in her monograph on love in the town Caruaru in Pernambuco, ideas about marriage in urban Northeast Brazil no longer include only the customary marriage based on decency and co-operation. The romantic marriage with its emphasis on personality, sexual attraction and intimacy has entered people's evaluations of their own and others' relationships (Rebhun 1999).[22] These new ideas seemed to tear relationships apart in the neighbourhood rather than create the intimacy they prescribed. Women expected men to engage themselves more affectionately in the marriage. Men on the other hand seemed to think more like Jairo, who expressed his expectations to marriage as follows: "Imagine, I arrive in your house and you are with that angry face (*cara feia*) and say, 'Oh, I don't want anything [sex], my head is full of problems.' The head full of problems – it has nothing to do with it!"

For the men marriage seemed to be closely related to sex, which again was cast in terms of pleasure, desire and aggressive assertion.[23] It certainly had nothing to do with problems. Aware of his impressionable audience Jairo's friend, Roberto, explained it as follows:[24]

> The gender role of the man is to hunt, generally a man does not have any interest in a woman who is always standing over him, he likes more that one which is more distant, that thing of hunting, of conquering, that thing of approximation, that is the most important [...] When a man finds another woman outside home (*na rua*) ... sometimes he is weak, lacking incentive, lacking fantasy at home, and he meets another woman who will satisfy this fantasy, [he says] "I will go out with that married woman, it is a danger and I will eat that woman, because it is a woman of another home!" It's the instinct.

In her study about love in Caruaru Rebhun writes that infidelity is often an integral part of male networks as going out 'drinking and womanizing together' is a common activity among friends. He who is not willing to engage in these activities may lose not only personal status but also the economic opportunities available through such networks (Rebhun 1999: 192). Jairo once told me how important it was to be a good friend, always sharing what he had with his companions. He told me that a good friend is someone who others call for when a job has to be done. A good friend is also someone who is offered drinks when he is broke. I knew how Jairo felt at ease in good company and how he sometimes got a job for a day or two through his friends. How could he be the man he wanted to be without it? However, I couldn't help seeing it from Irene's point of view. She had to go without the little money he earned and she was tired of Jairo's fooling around with his friends. Once she threw him out of the house as he drank too much and apparently had another woman. It was as Rebhun writes: "[W]ith increasingly divergent interests, men and women find it even more difficult than it used to be to achieve the consonance of understanding and interests necessary for affectionate cooperation" (Rebhun 1999: 126). This was also Carmen's predicament.

Carmen's predicament

Carmen wanted a life she could not get. She was 26 years old and stuck in her present situation. The only step forward available to her seemed to be a sterilisation. It would allow her some possibility of steering towards her aim, but not the company of her husband that she longed for.

Five years ago Carmen had lived close to the neighbourhood with her parents and two brothers. A young man had courted her, and without thinking much she had married him. The couple moved into a house next to Carmen's family-in-law. Carmen had a job in a shop in Recife which she quit while she was pregnant. She gave birth to her first child, a daughter, but soon after her husband left her to live with another woman for a year. In the time that followed Carmen was helped by her mother, now widowed, and her family-in-law. She began to work again, now cleaning private homes, and one day while she was away, her husband returned. Without a word he had just put his clothes back. Carmen had to accept, she said, as her parents-in-law found it normal: ordinary problems that couples had to deal with. Carmen had no support for her anger. Since that day their relationship had never been the same. She had matured, she said, and understood that she would rather live alone than with a man who left her alone anyway. But she felt she could do nothing in order to change her situation.

The following is part of a conversation I had with Carmen one day in her kitchen. When I visited her rumours about her marriage had already reached me: that she was too weak and did not fight for her respect; that her husband had other women whom he met right in front of her door and so on. Luzia had informed me. She knew it all from Leda, her sister-in-law, who used to share her days with Carmen. Apparently, their ways had parted, as Leda could not respect Carmen's passivity, at least according to Luzia. In Luzia's opinion men could seldom "eat from only one plate" but they had to nevertheless respect the wife and keep their affairs away from her home. If a man did not respect these rules, his woman should fight for her dignity. Those were the rules of the game. However, when I met Carmen, she was almost resigned. She had too many worries. Recently, she had given birth to her second child, one she had not wanted, without getting the sterilisation that she had hoped for. On top of it came her husband's affairs, which were not new to her, but which meant the loss of other women's respect. And then there was her lack of economic freedom; she wanted to buy things for her home, her children and herself. When she told me about her situation the unobtained sterilisation was not even mentioned. Other concerns were more pressing, other projects more important:

Carmen: As I told you, I have my aim, and I will reach it. I do not know how, but there will be some manner of reaching it.
Line: Carmen, why is it that here so many more women than men want to study, make a small shop, make some little thing in order to improve the life of the family?
Carmen: Men do not care about that, because as I told you they are very careless. They care about... they are more like... There are persons, older ones that have this viewpoint that a woman has to handle the stove, only take care of what is inside the house. The husband has to put the food into the house, and then he can do what he wants, but the woman

cannot. Then today, the women of today are fighting for this freedom, are fighting for this space and are struggling to show themselves that this is the reality of life. That it is not just to stay inside the house with the hair in the air, all horrible, cleaning the stove, only taking care of the children. That the woman in herself can be useful for other things. This, exactly this, is how things are more and more in Brazil. In some countries it is already different. Like it passed in *Faustão* [a television programme] on Sunday... there was a woman... No, two women and two men, all talking about this in relation to the woman, that today the woman has already conquered this space. She wants to have her privacy, her freedom, things that the man is not searching for. At least ... I answer for myself... at least my husband, he is careless, and he does not care about these things.

Line: Do you think that it is because he already has what he wants or is it because he does not want to struggle?

Carmen: That is it! He never learned, because he always had... his father always gave him what he needed, he never learned to struggle, do you understand? He never learned and he never tried to say, "I want to struggle to get this for me and my children". And that is precisely what I want. But at the moment... I am not ... at times at home I become dizzy from reasoning, reasoning and not having any solution at the moment, because it is good to have one's own space. My freedom I have, but what I mean is: My economic freedom!

Line: But now you have the children...?

Carmen: The children...

Line: Because it is also a struggle to bring up the children...?

Carmen: It is. I have to calm down in order to do something. Now it is because I am so... from being stuck at home, I am agitated. From trying to obtain something that at the moment I cannot reach I feel suffocated. That oppression ... I become rather... Don't know, in a strange way, rather nervous, and I have to lower my standards even more.

Line: There are many women who become nervous...?
Carmen: There are.
Line: And your husband, can you talk with him about that?
Carmen: Yes I can.
Line: And what does he say?
Carmen: He talks, but he is the person that when one talks... it
           seems as if it enters one ear and leaves the other, because
           I speak and he continues doing exactly the same thing...
Line: He does not understand that you are suffering?
Carmen: No, he is not a man of many words, he is not *carinho-
           so.*[25]
Line: When you cry over something in life, does he give *carin-
           ho*?
Carmen: No, in no way.
Line: Is there no situation in which he is *carinhoso*?
Carmen: No
Line: Never?
Carmen: It is really bad. One is talking about something depress-
           ing, and he doesn't even say, "What is that you...?" Talk
           together... never! It is always me who explodes, who cannot
           take it, and then BLUF ... all out! I am seeing it like this:
           My God in Heaven, what did I do in my life?
Line: Sometimes women don't want to have sexual relations with
           them, because there is no *carinho...'*
Carmen: That is how it is, Lini... As in my case: even if I have, it is
           not a good relation. It is like this, as if one has a television
           in the front, as if one sees everything that he does with
           one...do you understand? My relation is like that.
Line: Isn't it good for you?
Carmen: No, because ...one day I said to him "Look,...." He just
           satisfies himself and not me...
Line: Did you say that to him?
Carmen: I said. When I sometimes talk with him, I say: "You just
           satisfy your needs and mine are left"...I did not want a
           man just for, let us say... Just for that moment of having
           sex. I wanted a man for all moments. Good moments, bad
           moments, in weakness, in everything, but that I don't

have. I am dying from envy, God forgive me, but...when I see a nice couple walking hand in hand, joined, I find it lovely. Sometimes I look like ...sometimes I ... till people say that I am looking at the husband, but it isn't so. It is because I find it beautiful. I want that relationship and that relationship I do not have. Even in the *novelas*, I stopped watching the *novela*, because when I see a couple which is really together and has a nice relationship I say, "It is one of these more or less that I wanted." In reality I do not have it.

Line: Do you think that it exists in reality?

Carmen: It exists.

Line: Are there women here who have a good relationship with their husbands?

Carmen: Yes, there is the daughter-in-law of Dona Laura.

Line: She who lives down the road?

Carmen: Yes. Shirleide. She has a beautiful relationship with her husband. It is lovely, lovely. And I say to God, God bless it every day, because they are joined, they share... We sometimes talk and she even says, "Look, Carmen, Bertinho and I, we combine everything!" Everything has to be combined. It is very lovely. He lives for her and the children. Mine doesn't, he lives more for the street, for the friends, for the ball than for anything at home. And such a relationship is bad.

What Carmen wanted was a partner with whom she could share life and affection. This goal belonged to a view of marriage that neither her parents-in-law nor her husband shared with her. Carmen had assumed the values, the feelings and the aims of a romantic universe in which men and women construct the future together – just like the neighbour couple – in agreement about everything. Carmen did not know how to engage her husband in this romantic universe and unable to pursue what she longed for, she opted for a minor goal: the sterilisation. With a sterilisation she could sooner or later start school again or begin to work and become economically independent. She would be less vulnerable in case he left her. According to her own view, she would even be better off if he left her. However, a life on her own was not what she wanted. It was just a solution to an immediate situation.

Being an active individual
The women were totally entangled in social relations and commitments that posed serious troubles to them and with which they were unsatisfied. They longed for something more, but this 'more' was constantly denied them by their present situation. When Neide's son wanted to buy sweets and she had no money for him, the situation confirmed her need. She needed money in order to let Tiago buy the sweets in order for him to be happy in order for Neide to be happy, too. Not having the money for him made her feel guilty – she was a bad mother. Carmen wanted a man she could trust, but in the present situation she had a very unsatisfying sexual relationship with him, and that was it. Complaining just made things worse, she feared, and therefore though he ignored her needs she had to go through with it whenever he wanted. In these tense relationships sterilisation played a significant role: as non-medical reasons for undergoing sterilisation women mainly mentioned either that having children was difficult or that they had problems with their husbands. Sterilisation reduced the pressure in both relationships.

Some women very firmly stressed that they themselves actively sought the sterilisation. It seemed a matter of autonomy for them. Fátima thus proudly said, "I was 23 when I was sterilised. I knew what I did; I was already an adult. I was very clear." And Neta: "It was I who decided it, I who obtained it, he … he did not even need to sign anything. I decided it and pronto. That means: He did not sign a paper, nothing, nothing, nothing. I sorted everything out alone." Maybe because of that, husbands feared the independence of sterilised women. The women told me so, but Pedro Nascimento, my colleague and assistant, also found his (male) informants to perceive sterilisation as a threat to male control.

A sterilised woman was free to have sexual relationships with other men than her husband, the men said. Neta put her husband's words like this: "He always said, 'And now you can just get another, as you will not be thick by anybody anymore.' That was what he threw into my face. 'You just want to make a ligation in order to find another, because you will not become pregnant. You can have sex with cats and dogs.' That was what he said." However, very few women told me that they actually enjoyed this freedom.[26] Extramarital sex was seldom a possibility to consider,[27] and sex with the husband was constrained by ideas about 'proper' sex within marriage[28] and the women's general disappointment. "The woman lives tired of life" they said; how could she feel sexual desire?

Nancy Scheper-Hughes suggests that the Alto mothers' refusal to grieve for the death of their infants could at times be seen as a gesture of defiance, a way of saying, "You can make me pregnant, but you cannot make me love all of them" (Scheper-Hughes 1992:428). What I saw and heard made me think of sterilisation in similar terms. "You can have sex with me, though I don't like it, but you cannot make me pregnant" seemed to be many women's response to their unhappy relationships.

The idea that after sterilisation women became 'cold', unable to feel pleasure in sex, was widespread.[29] When I asked if a woman changed after sterilisation, women would often refer to this idea. Sometimes in order to deny the truth of it, as when Rute said, "No, I did not change.... I have always been in that way... cold!" However, as Sonia said, frigidity was often a result of bad relationships rather than surgery: "What leaves me cold is not the ligation, but the man. Saturday and Sunday nobody sees the face of him, it is just football. He only gives attention to his friends, and they only talk about football, because they do not care about anything else. Doesn't it give disgust? Doesn't it make one cold? And the ligation? I cannot say that it is the ligation, if I am despised in my home. When he arrives he falls on the bed and then pronto! No conversation at all and how can I say that it is the ligation. Is there any love? The children sleep ... is there any sexual relationship? No, because the man is at the street corner talking about football. Many women say, 'After I ligated, I became more cold,' but what is that? When a woman has two, three children, the man turns his back on her. It is no longer the same thing. Then the woman says, 'Oh, it is because I became colder.' It is the distress within, and then she says that she does not want any more."

Several women told me, like Sonia, that being 'cold' had nothing to do with the body. It was a "problem of the head". It seemed to be a relatively new idea in the neighbourhood, as the women were very persistent in their efforts to convince me about this correlation between psyche and sexuality, and as those who promoted it were mainly younger women. In a study of reproductive rights in Brazil Diniz et al. propose that ideas about sex as a source of pleasure and health for women is partly associated with exposure to women's groups and political activism (Diniz et al. 1998:51). In the neighbourhood no women besides Josenita were politically active, but, nevertheless, ideas about women's rights to self-determination and sexual and emotional fulfilment circulated. According to the women themselves, debate pro-grammes and especially *telenovelas* broadcast critical questions related to the woman's role in society, and even though not at all feminist they touch upon women's concerns and dissatisfaction. Several women, for instance, enthusiastically described a male figure from a *novela* who, when his wife returned from her job, would have a new dish ready for her, everyday. He would serve her and do anything she liked.

Sonia, Neta, Carmen and the other women had thus engaged in a search for recognition mediated by images from the television, but without doubt corresponding to unfulfilled needs in their marital re-lationships. As Rebhun writes, the emphasis on romantic love in the media strikes a chord with poor women's disillusion due to "what they see as the unloving abandonment of their economically faltering men" (Rebhun 1999:185). Referring to Tania Salem (1980) Rebhun argues that working class women in Brazil suffer, in Salem's terms, from a "double indeterminacy". They see men "as their supporter, protector, and agent in the world" and when the men fail to fulfil this role, the women are left "adrift to confront both the powerlessness of poverty and the unreliability of men" (Rebhun 1999:181). The women I met wanted to decide on their own whether they would have sex, buy a dress, or divert themselves in one or another way. They wanted au-tonomy and intimacy at the same time, since both would allow them more freedom to act. However, they felt they had neither in their present situation.

In the complex web of relationships in the neighbourhood, women's relations to children and husbands were the most complicated and stressful of all. While their husbands did not give them the attention

A lazy midday in the shadow.

and care they longed for, the children, on the other hand, represented emotional demands that the women had difficulties fulfilling. In neither of these relationships did they experience themselves as the women they wanted to be; too often their inferiority was demonstrated to themselves and others. They wanted more than they felt they had. Sonia got angry, Carmen resigned, Anita struggled hard to make her pots and her baby shine, Jacione watched more television, Neide found a way out but was overtaken by misfortune, Fátima moved to Carpina in order to escape gossip when her husband betrayed her, Neta faked sexual pleasure in order to keep her marriage going, and Luzia ... I wonder what has happened to her. They all endured, knowing that life could be more than it was. Dreams about a little luxury, about being an interesting person, or about living in an impressive house merged these longings for autonomy and intimacy in an unbearable waiting for things to happen.

While the time passed the *mulherada* sat in the shade of the noon and shared their laziness. As a mother between mothers each was recognised – more or less – and being sterilised was prestigious. But nothing really changed due to that. "I have one and a half real. What do I do with that?" Neide once said, sitting in her usual company with nothing else to do. The others laughed at their common misery and Neide bought a packet of cigarettes, and so the chatter continued.

Few women regretted their sterilisation.[30] Looking back upon their situation, I think I understand. To be sterilised meant that one had at least done something.

Chapter Seven

Conclusion

[I]t is impossible to say just where historical forces end and ours begin, and strictly speaking the question is meaningless, since there is history only for a subject who lives through it, and a subject only in so far as he is historically situated.

(Merleau-Ponty 1962:173)

Through the description of the social relations in which women in the neighbourhood live I have linked personal action, hopes and longings to historical processes and forces of power and economy. I have situated fertility within these relations and described sterilisation as a means to control life rather than simply a method of birth control.

I have drawn on the notion of the subject as both acted upon and actively engaged in its life-world in order to make plausible and recognisable some women's wish for sterilisation in a world of poverty and disrespect. Through the focus on recognition as a human need I have described the women's desire to be valuable in others' eyes and the dependency on others that this desire implies. I have argued that they can be controlled because others matter to them, and I have shown that relations to particular others are mediated by ideas and expectations belonging to worlds that reach beyond the everyday life-world. But first and foremost, I have argued that the wish for recognition motivates action and that in particular cases – when recognition turns into a matter of physical survival of oneself or those dearest to oneself – this motivation is strong.

Human beings belong within their world. According to Merleau-

Ponty, we are beings-in-the-world before anything else, and through our engagement in the world meaning is produced. The coming to awareness is a cultural phenomenon and through it "all psychological motivations may find their way into the web of history" (1962:171). Through self-consciousness – in Hegel's terms – the individual human being acts back upon history as "a person trying to endow his life with form, loving, hating, creating or not creating works of art, having or not having children"(ibid.).

For Foucault the subject is equally a historical being, though not a creative agent as much as a result of historical processes inscribed on the individual body. "Power reaches into the very grain of individuality, touches their bodies and inserts itself into their actions and attitudes, their discourses, learning processes and everyday lives" (Foucault cited in Lyon and Barbalet 1994:49). As Nick Crossley (1996b) points out, the individual being in Foucault's analysis is acted upon, while Merleau-Ponty concentrates on the active aspect of subjective life, the reaching out into the world. Crossley, however, proposes that these two approaches enrich rather than exclude each other: for the individual to be acted upon, an active agent is presupposed who is willing to engage in social life and employ the cultural devices referred to by Foucault. For the active body-subject to incorporate history a surrounding cultural world is needed and, as Merleau-Ponty points out, it would be meaningless to ask where one world ends and another begins, if it were not for our need for explanation.

The present work is organised in such a way that the interplay between historical forces and individual experience is kept as fully alive as possible. The historical situation in which the women live is present in their narratives and in my analysis; if we accept Merleau-Ponty's conceptualisation it forms part of every aspect of life. The particular historical situation described here is, however, violent and oppressive. I introduced the field with a narrative about some murders that happened during my fieldwork, not only because the violent events laid bare for me the extent of maternal suffering, but because the everyday violence of life became the primary context for my understanding of women's wish for sterilisation. The routinisation of human suffering that Schepher-Hughes describes (1992:16) also shaped the world that I became part of for a time. The normality of violence – the media focus on murders, the brutal attitudes of the hospital staff, the beating of children and the frustrated marital relationships – were characteristic of the situation of constrained agency in which people lived.

However, I have sought to also describe the transcendent responses (Scheler cited in Kleinman and Kleinman 1996:188) – the endurance, aspirations, humour and irony – that in spite of constraints made life go on in the neighbourhood. I have described modern medicine as a means to grasp some sense of control, even though restricted to certain areas of life and reserved for women. And I have focused on metaphors through which the painful and humiliating is worked upon and sometimes transformed. People's perception of a unity between house and body mediated by the self is put forth as a symbolic reality in which individuals operate and in which sterilisation becomes meaningful as an act of 'autoconstruction'. In their unwanted pregnancies and the swelling or drying out or nausea due to contraceptive pills female bodies betray the expectations of responsibility and self-control that people seek to live up to. Surgical intervention becomes a means to cope with this weakness, and through changing their bodies women strive for recognition as worthy members of the very society that so often treats them with neglect and violence.

Simultaneously, I argue that they are drawn into society by the dream of happiness in consumption as presented to them by the media, the market and the attitudes of better off Brazilians with whom they are in contact. In the longing for participation in the 'good life' and the exclusion from it that poverty represents, inner and outer merge and a sense of second class citizenship develops. As sterilisation is also perceived as a consumer good, it signifies worth and participation in this imagined happiness of consumption.

However, sterilisation and recognition are more than matters of control on a symbolic and imagined level. In the social relations of the neighbourhood recognition is crucial for social and physical survival and sterilisation becomes a resource in negotiations of status within close relationships. The individuals that I describe inhabit the same empirical space, but their lives follow different story lines as they participate in various abstract communities that each offer the means to organise thought, feeling and action. Not only do the individuals differ from each other; they differ from themselves at different points in time according to their orientation towards others (Briggs 1991:151). The striving for recognition from significant others therefore poses several often contradictory demands on the women, who have to steer towards what is possible in the immediate and leave unresolved what is not within their reach.

I have employed George Herbert Mead's notion of the 'generalised other' in order to turn the 'others', whose recognition the women depend on, into a 'mirror' bridging historical processes and individual experience. The "generalised other" Mead writes, is the mediating factor through which "the social process influences the behaviour of the individuals involved in it and carrying it on, i.e., that the community exercises control over the conduct of its individual members" (Mead 1965:155). The 'generalised others' who have been in focus in my work are the 'medical other' with its norms of responsibility and submission to medical authority; the 'consumerist other' that equates buying with control and happiness; the 'maternal other' who cares for her children and helps them to a better future; and the 'wife-other', attractive and cared for by her husband with whom she is building a home. The 'generalised other' of the group of neighbour women represents norms of loyalty and generosity, within which the troubles and doubts arising from the need to handle all the aspects of femininity can be discussed and legitimised in the mutual recognition of equals.

In this complexity of the women's life-worlds I have situated sterilisation as both a resource and a symptom of violent constraints. I have looked at women's use of sterilisation and described it as a result of a political neglect of women's wish for fewer children and the failure of the Brazilian state to provide alternative forms of contraception. But I have also proposed that only the tip of the iceberg is seen when sterilisation is studied in isolation. Behind the active striving for sterilisation lies a need to reduce fertility stemming from a deep worry about the future and dissatisfaction with the present.

The future in the present
For the women in my study the future was only relevant in relation to the present. Their aim was attractive and necessary precisely because it represented an escape from present constraints and worries. When everything runs smoothly, we all may dream and imagine a splendid

future for ourselves, but only when this imagined self with it's innate promises is contested and threatened do we act deliberately. As John Dewey writes, "The present, not the future, is ours [...] The occasion of deliberation, that is of the attempt to find a stimulus to complete overt action in thought of some future object, is confusion and uncertainty in present activities" (1957:194). Ideas about rational choice in demographic theory have been widely contested. I will not say, though, that the women I met were not rational in their choices. However, the rationality at play was rational in the sense proposed by William James: for the individual actor it provided a feeling of sufficiency in the present and banished uncertainty from the future (Barbalet 1998: 47). And at the core of it was the force and logic of emotion.

The women in this study wanted to be recognized as responsible mothers by friends, neighbours and authorities, not just out of vanity but in their striving for a sense of control in an uncertain world. A striving not just to *be* in the world of others, but also to define *what* they wanted to be in that world. Nobody wants to be irresponsible, inconsequential or dead. Theories of demographic transition based on the assumption of future economic improvement do not take this striving into consideration. Economist models cover only one aspect of human life, and cannot describe the basics of sociality: people's fundamental need of recognition from family, friends and society. In order to base our work on theories that do not contradict our own experience of what it means to be human (Wikan 1992), we must broaden our scope. Birth control is never an isolated event; in the neighbourhood I came to know it was pivotal to life here and now.

Matters of life and longing

The longing that I have described is directed towards imagined futures as a movement away from what is present and the future embedded in the present. The longing does not represent a conscious political stand in itself. It is shaped by and aimed at dominant ideals and springs from a wish to conform and be respected by the powerful. However, it acquires a potential force once it is mirrored by the other.

In my work I have posed a critique neither towards the women in focus, nor towards sterilisation as a method of birth control, but towards the conditions in which the women have to act. I have pointed out that family economies are shattered by unemployment, frustration and divorce and that women are often left with the responsibility for their children's future, and without the means to do what they know is needed. I have described the insistent consumer culture as disdainful towards those who cannot afford to buy. I have argued that poor people are treated with a violent negligence at the hospitals and that a sense of inferiority springs from medical encounters, which pushes women into a wish for caesarean sections and the drastic change of their bodies that sterilisation constitutes. I have identified the number of sterilised young women who despite immediate relief are at risk of regret later in life. I have pointed at the missing alternatives to sterilisation and at the extremely ineffective attempts to improve the conditions in which it is provided. And finally, throughout the book I have argued that the women's efforts to improve their lives should be recognised. Others have raised many of the same points of criticism. Nevertheless, with its particular emphasis on recognition my work may be useful for those who work to change the conditions of life in Brazil and if so, I will be grateful. Yet in my view, change has to be manifested in face-to-face encounters. Without recognition in the lifeworld citizenship is empty (Crossley 1996a:171). Therefore, I see the prime raison d'être of this work in the seeing, listening and recognition it may provoke.

Immersion in lived phenomenological worlds does not preclude the study of political economy, which must be perceived as integral rather than external to action and agency (Carter 1995:83). The notion of recognition constitutes a key to understanding this synthesis, as it is our striving to be valued by others that makes us part of political economy – or political economy part of us. Merleau-Ponty ends the *Phenomenology of Perception* with the words "Man is but a network of relationships, and these alone matter to him."[1] What has been important for me in this work is both to describe empirical relationships as vividly as possible in all their diversity, inner dynamic and motivating force, and to emphasize that life goes on it its various strange ways because others matter to us.

Epilogue

Kitchen stories

*One can lie on the ground and look up at the almost
infinite number of stars in the night sky, but in order
to tell stories about those stars they need to be seen as
constellations, the invisible lines which can connect
them need to be assumed.*

(Berger 1982:284)

I sat in a kitchen in Camaragibe – a kitchen I knew so very well.
The tablecloth, the cups, the battered tin cuscuz boiler. The kitchen
belonged to Sonia who had been a central figure in my fieldwork and
who, during the days we spent in each other's company, had become
my friend. Sonia and I were sharing a beer – one of these big Brazilian beers – and the plan was that I should tell her about my writings
in order for her to comment on it and let me know if my conclusions
had any relevance in her world. Two months earlier I had submitted
my Ph.D. thesis at the faculty in Copenhagen and returning to Brazil
after more than a year's writing with my version of people's stories
was actually scary. Had I during the time at the computer lost the
sense of life out there? Had I invented a probable world that suited my
own anthropological project, but without any anchoring in Brazilian
ground? I felt a commitment towards the people who had become
subjects in my study. They had trusted me, as I had trusted them,
and in my description of their lives I wanted to be faithful to their
experiences as they had passed them over to me.

I drank my glass of beer and began to explain how I had taken my point of departure in the violent events that occurred in the neighbourhood during my second fieldwork. I talked about the way criminal youth is cast in public discourse in terms of lack of education and failed parenthood. And I went on to explain how I had realised that mothers felt responsible for the death of their adolescent sons; how I saw self-blame and fear blend in women's hearts and create a strong urge to do something to better their lives, the result of which might very well be sterilisation. I wanted to continue and talk about being a *pé de chinelo* and how Sonia had let me see something about poor people's relationship to Brazilian society, but Sonia interrupted me. She was very upset and categorically said, "No, you are all wrong. Mothers don't blame themselves. When a son has died due to violence, which unfortunately happens, the mother is relieved. She will think, 'Oh, what a luck to get rid of him, he was a black sheep, he was dangerous and could cause harm to the family and the sooner he leaves this world the better.' Some children just are like that. They can spoil a whole family."

While Sonia continued her rejection of my interpretation about mothers' self-blame I thought to myself, "Well, that was it then." The basis for my argument was an invention and the rest of my analysis might very well show up to be the same: a mirage, a castle in the air. In *Death without Weeping* Nancy Scheper-Hughes has described Northeast Brazilian mothers' acceptance of child death in terms of folk fatalism. According to the mothers in her study some children had to die. They might cause pain to their mothers, they might suffer themselves, but they were not meant for living and the sooner they died the better. Did Sonia not repeat this fatalism? The acceptance of suffering and denial of any reflection on responsibility and guilt? I had found Scheper-Hughes' conclusions simplistic and had sought a way of representing people's lives that allowed space for reflections and contradicting emotions, the friction between what had to be done and what was desired, and the negotiation and strategizing that characterise social life according to my experience. I had focused on the process that leads to action, but I now had to ask myself: had I misunderstood the nature of that process? Did Sonia not tell me that this friction – this constant negotiation of truth that I had described – did not exist?

Discouraged I asked her if it wasn't so that people in the neighbour-hood usually blamed the parents and in particular the mother, when a boy got involved in violence and eventually killed. She said, "Yes, yes they do, but that is not true. They say that the mother should have done this and the mother should have done that, but what can a mother do? She has to defend herself against the guilt she feels by saying that the boy was a bad child. She argues and argues with herself and she cannot bear it."

I was back on track again! I had not misunderstood. I had just forgotten that Sonia herself had a young son, who was accused for being too friendly with the wrong kind of people. She was defending herself, while *I* thought we were discussing the general validity of my conclusions. We each had a project going, each wanted to know that she was right. Our talk continued, but we soon left my work for other subjects. In Sonia's kitchen the nature and importance of that which had been my joy and suffering through such a long time, my research, changed; my thesis became a story, a search for meaning among many others. The television was on, children walked in and out, we ate that wonderful cuscuz that Sonia makes with peas, sardines and garlic and life was just what it was. To be lived.

NOTES TO PROLOGUE

1   The 'invasion', the squatter area, is further described in Chapter Three and
     Five.

NOTES TO CHAPTER ONE

1   Next to Sierra Leone, Brazil is estimated by the World Bank to have the highest
     income inequality in the world. Thus the poorest 10 per cent of the population
     is estimated to earn 0.8 per cent of the total income, while the richest 10 per
     cent have the highest income share in the world, 47.9 per cent, at their disposal
     (World Development Indicators 1999). From the poorest, marginalized regions
     of the country in the North and Northeast to the richer, industrialised regions
     in the South and Southeast, variations in living standards are huge. For this
     reason Brazil is said to contain a developing country within a developed – or
     vice versa.

2   I use the term 'life-world' throughout this work in the sense proposed by
     Alfred Schutz: a reality that is lived, experienced and endured, and therefore
     necessarily subjective (Schutz and Luckmann 1983:1). Because subjectivity
     arises out of embodied social interaction (see Chapter Five) the life-world is
     also always a result of intersubjective life.

3   I use the word 'control' in a broadly existential sense, not distinguishing between
     real or imaginary control, as the experience of competence in the subjective
     life-world that enables the subject to steer through obstacles in what to him
     or her is a meaningful project (see Jackson 1998:17-22).

4   The numbers for China and India are from respectively 1997 and 1998/99 – the
     latest from The United Nations. Data on 'married' women include, when possible,
     those in consensual unions. Reproductive age is defined as from 15 to 49.

5   Male sterilisation in Brazil is almost non-existent. The National Survey of
     Demography and Health from 1996 (this is still the most recent information
     on levels of sterilisation in Brazil) establishes the rate of male sterilisation
     (vasectomy) at 2.4 per cent of all formally or informally married men (PNDS
     1996). Latin American men are found to reject vasectomy due to 'machismo'
     and the belief that contraception is the woman's responsibility, but reasons for
     low use of this method in the region may go beyond cultural values (Bailey
     et al. 1991:192). Commentators have proposed the failure of providers to offer
     vasectomy as a reason for the low use of the method (Ross 1992:190). Mass
     media campaigns of vasectomy in Brazil are thus reported to increase the de-
     mand for the method (Foreit, de Castro and Franco 1989; Kincaid et al. 1996).
     Vasectomy has been proposed as a means to reduce the high caesarean section
     rates in Brazil, as many caesarean sections are related to the use of tubal liga-
     tion (Bailey et al. 1991:207).

6   A study by Thomas Merrick and Elza Berquo (1983) shows that female steril-
     isation was directly linked with monthly income; hence in Pernambuco 40 per
     cent of all sterilisations were found in the highest income class, while only 9
     per cent were found among the poorest – a pattern that is common to the four

states mentioned in the study (besides Pernambuco, São Paulo, Rio Grande do Norte and Piaui) (1983:88). Another study from Pelotas, Rio Grande do Sul, supports these findings (Barroset al. 1991:169). This tendency seemed to be related to the ability to pay for a sterilisation. Based on data from the 1986 National Survey of Demography and Health Rutenberg and Ferraz thus write "Twice as many women in the upper classes are sterilised as those in the lower class; the use of other methods varies considerably less according to class. While motivation to use contraceptives may be similar across social classes, access to sterilisation may not be" (1988:64).

7   See the section in Chapter Four under 'The sterilisation-caesarean section circuit' for further explanation.

8   From 15 per cent of all deliveries in 1970, the caesarean section rate increased to 31 per cent in 1980 (Granada-Neiva 1992 cited in Berquó 1998:392). However, the rate varies considerably from region to region. In 1996 it was found to be highest (52.1 per cent) in São Paulo and lowest in Northeast Brazil (20.4 per cent) according to the National Survey of Demography and Health (PNDS 1996).

9   Maternal mortality is estimated to be at least 2.9 times higher for caesarean sections than for normal births, mainly due to puerperal infection and complications related to anaesthesia. In addition, premature birth is seen to increase in Brazil with the prevalent use of surgical deliveries, due to the high number of elective caesarean sections with wrongly calculated dates of delivery (in comparison with acute cases) (Faundes and Cecatti 1991). Caesarean sections within public health care raise the costs for deliveries due to the need for anaesthetics and longer stays at the hospital and detract resources otherwise available for improvements in antenatal care and normal births. Besides, as Berquó indicates, high rates of caesarean sections reduce the availability of beds for normal births (Berquó 1998:393).

10 While women undergoing sterilisation in the first part of the 1980s were rich or middle class women who could afford private health care, lower income women adopted the method in large numbers in the late 1980s. Besides the provision of sterilisation within public health care, internationally funded family planning organisations offered sterilisations especially in the poorer regions. According to Molina da Costa, Antonia Lisboa, a former Brazilian Health Minister Adviser, affirmed that from 1985 till 1988 Brazilian NGOs in the field of family planning received US$ 32 millions (Guerra 1991, cited in Costa 1995:72). However, the role of international funding of and influence on the Brazilian fertility decline has not been thoroughly examined. The fact is that while the use of female sterilisation in poorer regions of the country increased, it stagnated or may even have receded in richer regions (South and Southeast) (Martine, Das Gupta and Chen 1998:178). According to the National Survey of Demography and Health 1996, today female sterilisation is most prevalent among women with no or low education living in Rio (46.3 per cent of all married women using contraception), or the poor regions Northeast, North or Centraleast (respectively 43.9 per cent, 51.3 per cent and 59.5 per cent). Better off women use reversible methods, primarily the pill.

11 Besides, both Viera and Machado point towards separation and remarriage,
    pressure in the decision-making process and the death of a child as variables
    that influence the level of dissatisfaction after sterilisation.

12 As male sterilisation is still rare in Brazil (see note 5 this chapter) the legalisa-
    tion of vasectomy did not have any immediate importance.

13 These studies are Berquo and Arilha (1992), Vieira (1994), Vieira and Ford
    (1996), Serruaya (1996), Diniz et al. (1998), Kaufmann (1998) and Andrade
    (1997). Inaldete Pinheiro de Andrade's study is based on reproductive history
    interviews with 20 women between 23 and 75 years old, among whom 17 were
    sterilised. The interviews were conducted in a rural community in interior
    Pernambuco, mainly inhabited by coloured and black people. Andrade relates
    the sterilisations that these women have undergone to a control of poor black
    people's reproduction deliberately effected by Brazilian politicians' neglect in
    providing alternatives to sterilisation. Elisabeth Vieira's study of the provision
    of female sterilisation in São Paulo is mainly based on a survey supplemented by
    15 in-depth interviews with women who regretted the operation. To facilitate
    comparison Elza Berquó and Margareth Arilha based their research on focus
    group discussions with sterilised and unsterilised women between 26 and 35
    years old from São Paulo. Only Kaufmann's study is based on participant ob-
    servation. She lived in a *favela* in Belo Horizonte in 1988, where she conducted
    a micro-demographic survey on contraceptive use in general. The studies of
    Serruya and Diniz et al. are described in the text above.

14 See Table 1 in Chapter Four for data on infant mortality. Nancy Scheper-
    Hughes came to Pernambuco in 1964 and she visited her field several times up
    to the mid-1980s, a period spanning many major changes in living conditions
    within which her observations are not always clearly or explicitly situated in
    the book. However, the empirical focus of her work is high infant mortality – a
    fact that may have been constant till very recently. Infant mortality decreased
    later in Northeast Brazil than in the rest of the country, and in the mid-80s it
    was still alarmingly high. Besides, rural-urban differences in infant mortality
    play a significant role even today (Sastry 1997), which means that my data
    varies from Scheper-Hughes' not just due to the time difference, but because
    of geographical variation as well. Scheper-Hughes did her study among people
    with a rural background and employment in the rural economy, while people
    in my study generally are accustomed to life in the city and a relatively high
    level of medical health care.

15 My work is thus more in line with Nations and Rehbun's critique of Scheper-
    Hughes' notion of maternal neglect (1988). Nations and Rebhun describe par-
    ents with dying children as active, doubting individuals who on "an accurate
    appraisal of realities" use the means at hand as best they can; according to
    them "caring about and taking care of may be related but they are not the same
    thing" (ibid.:186), parallel to my argument that the women acted in accordance
    with many concerns and often found themselves in ambivalence.

Notes to chapter two

1   This is a crucial requirement of the programme as the prioritised actions are directed towards women and require a certain level of intimacy, as for instance in the promotion of breast-feeding (Gouveia and Portella n.d.:16).

2   We interviewed girls over 12, but did only included girls over 15 in the final material, as nobody under 15 was sterilised and as it seemed that the ACSs had forgotten to ask some of the youngest, simply not considering them of reproductive age. Besides, the National Survey of Demography and Health operates with women from age 15.

3   In the case where nobody was at home, the women would probably be working outside the home. In the rare cases where the family did not accept ACS visits, it would be wealthy enough to have a private health insurance. In both cases, it is probable that the woman would be sterilised. The survey therefore probably has this presumed relatively small bias.

4   I had to clean the data for several double notations that indicated lack of accuracy in the work of the ACSs. They simply did not always remember or note down, which houses were visited.

5   I had difficulties bringing them all together for a briefing and agreements on the method of questioning during the survey; they made too many double notations and omissions; and they had too much work in general and therefore worked slower than planned. However, they struggled with this work, which they in no way were obliged to do, and I am grateful for their help. The criticism is not directed to them, but to myself for not foreseeing these problems.

6   Ethical considerations were an integral part to all my approaches to the field, but as long as I was working alone, engaged in face-to-face relations I found it a matter of conscience rather than formal rights. However, having others working for me made the consideration of formalities more urgent.

7   In the first survey we asked for the woman's own mother's number of child births at respectively home and in the hospital. In the second survey we collected data on all women over 12. This gave us a picture of childbearing in all age groups of women.

8   The so-called Kristeller manoeuvre is a commonly used obstetrical procedure in Brazil in which the abdomen right below the ribs is pressed down by both hands, or as I saw it the arm, of the obstetrician or an assistant in order to 'squeeze' out the child. Wrongly or violently practised it can cause trauma on the abdominal viscera or the uterus, dislocation of the placenta or foetal injuries.

9   However, like me Pedro was soon positioned differently. Pedro started off doing interviews for me, but after my departure he continued doing his own fieldwork on which he based his master's thesis. He did participant observation in one of the bars to meet the men where they were, and Neide later told me that he had become a 'bum' hanging around in the bars all day long. "A pity, isn't it" she said. Anthropologists on fieldwork certainly are positioned! However, Pedro has later returned to the same neighbourhood to work on male reproductive health, a project I am looking forward to know more about, and I suppose he has had to change this public image of himself.

10   Being lesbian in Brazil is a fundamental threat to the dominant 'macho' ideology
      (Parker 1991). While among politically active middle-class women in Recife
      lesbianism seemed to be perceived as a positive alternative to male control of
      female sexuality, in the neighbourhood most people perceived sex between
      women as morally wrong and repulsive. However, as Scheper-Hughes writes
      about her assistant 'Little Irene', whose faults were overlooked by the neighbours
      as she was always a willing and courageous helper when authorities had to be
      approached, so was also Josenita generally accepted as 'courageous, but crazy'.
      It is striking, and a comment on the nature of our preoccupations, however, that
      we as anthropologists often find assistants among people, who themselves are
      outsiders in the local community.

11   In 'Minima Ethnographica' Michael Jackson writes about friendships estab-
      lished in the field, that "(w)hat is closer to the truth is that these so-called
      friends are simply individuals who happened to help the anthropologist salvage
      his self-esteem" (Jackson 1998:118). That might very well be true, but I wonder
      if friendships 'at home' do not to a large extent have much the same function?
      Why are we so afraid of acknowledging our basic need of recognition?

12   The symbolic violence in ethnographic practice springs according to Hastrup
      from the fact that mere presence does not lead to fundamental knowledge of
      any culture or person. A certain pressure has to be laid on informants in order
      to elicit information, which under other circumstances would have remained
      in silence as taken for granted. In fact, Hastrup writes that "the asymmetrical
      relationship between the anthropologist as author and the informant as con-
      tributor is of a peculiarly creative nature, provided it is recognized" (Hastrup
      1995:142-3), but the question remains who is interested in the anthropological
      'creations'. If they are irrelevant to the informant, how can we then justify
      keeping up the pressure? Rather than discouraging us from doing ethnography,
      the question may rightly serve as a reminder to reflect on the relevance of our
      work, and act accordingly.

NOTES TO CHAPTER THREE

1   *Maloqueiro* is "a common denomination for small guys who walk around in
      the streets, dirty and barefooted, often in groups, asking for money, practic-
      ing small thefts etc." (*Novo Dicionário da Lingua Portuguesa*, 2nd edition).
      Maloqueiragem is the kind of things that *maloqueiros* do.

2   Discourses of race in Brazil have traditionally celebrated the nation as a 'racial
      democracy'. The specific blending of indigenous American, Iberian and African
      people into one single national identity has been seen as an alternative to racist
      societies such as the North American (an excellent example of this discourse
      being Gilberto Freyre's *Casa Grande e Senzala*, 1933). However, as pointed
      out by recent studies (Goldstein 1999; Sheriff 2000; Silva 1998; Telles 1995) the
      wide social, political and economic gap separating blacks and whites in Brazil
      indicates an inequality that cannot be seen as accidental. Though poverty is
      multiracial it affects non-whites far more than whites, while the middle class

population is much more racially homogeneous. (Telles 1995:397). The wealth of certain 'public blacks' like the famous Brazilian football player Pelé keeps the myth alive – in the neighbourhood as in Brazil in general (see also Chapter Five, 'Low Status lives').

3   See Goldstein (1999:564) for more about 'whitening' as a strategy towards social mobility.

4   The exchange rate between the US dollar and the Brazilian real has changed dramatically since then. In 1999 when the indexing of the value of the real to the value of the dollar was too much out of step with the economic reality, the real devalued and prices went up. The instability of the Brazilian currency is a recurring theme in daily life, and having passed through periods of extreme inflation Brazilians are always sceptical about the value of their money (Rebhun 1999:52-56).

5   O pau canta means, literally, that the stick sings, and metaphorically that working there is almost impossible, as impossible as making a piece of wood sing, 'like pressing the sweat out of somebody who does not have more sweat to give' – so I was told.

6   The age at which young women married varied a lot. Some were only 15 when they got pregnant and began to live with their 'husband' within the home of either set of parents. Some married in church at the age of 25 and worked for another year or two, before they got pregnant. And between these extremes many women married, formally or informally, in their early twenties.

7   I write 'unskilled' in the sense that they do not have any formal education or training, but the women considered themselves to be skilled. Thus, a young woman told me with a certain pride: "The only thing I know is cooking. I do not know how to tidy up a family's home, because this I did not learn, no. But put me in a kitchen, and you can order me to do anything" (Dalva, 25 years old).

8   See Chapter Six 'Being married' for more about gender relations.

9   Research on masculinity in Brazil has increased during the last few years. See for instance Scott 1990, 1996; Parker 1991; Parker and Barbosa 1996; Nascimento 1999; Rebhun 1999; and Fonseca 2000.

10 At times a bird was sold to somebody else, maybe exchanged for some other object of desire and status, as when Edilson got himself a mobile phone. The most desired thing, a car or motorbike, was, however, out of most men's reach.

11 Olho grande generally has two forms; one is attributed to the individual and synonymous to ambition, another is always impersonal and seen as a malicious force caused by jealousy. In both cases it can be explained, at least partly, by the bitterness experienced by the less fortunate towards the successful (Fonseca 2000:110).

12 Fonseca mentions "a certain evident antipathy between fathers and their sons," a factor which is as relevant to consider as the tendency of female cooperation (Fonseca 2000: 66).

13 According to Fonseca, frequent contact between brothers is a phenomenon registered in several studies from lower income populations in Latin America (2000:67).

14   Claudia Fonseca writes about "a circulation of children" in which women often let others bring up one or another child for a period, while they still count themselves as the mother of this child and may later want to have the child back (Fonseca 2000: 53). This seemed to happen very informally, it was commonly accepted, in Fonseca's study as in mine, and was often due to re-marriage, too many children or social problems in the family.

15   Rebhun writes that "It is quite possible to reach old age in Northeast Brazil without once having been entirely alone; in fact, it is difficult to do otherwise" (Rebhun 1999: 57).

16   See Rebhun 1999 for a rich analysis of love as social duty in Northeast Brazil.

17   During the colonial period, especially after the abolition of slavery in the late 1880s, patron-client relationships developed between the big landowners and rural workers and tenants. However, as the plantation economy became less profitable and as national institutions expanded to marginal regions such as the Northeast, the paternalism of the landowners declined while clientelistic networks emerged around political office holders, the so-called *coroneis*. As the bureaucracy developed and was freed from the control of the elected parliament, people employed within the bureaucracy or the legal institutions became powerful through their control of resources and to some degree took up the position of the *coroneis*. Today lawyers, physicians and others offer services without immediate return, in order to create indebtedness, transformable into votes once they enter politics (Eisenstadt and Roniger 1984:104-107; see also Potter and Caetano 1998).

18   Cecília L. Mariz (1994) points out that a distinction between Catholicism and the Catholic Church is necessary when trying to understand religious experience in Brazil (1994:12). Brazilians generally live in accordance with the Catholic worldview, but as the Brazilian Catholic Church was relatively independent from Rome until about 1850, Brazilian Catholicism has integrated religious elements from several different religious traditions; the 'romanisation' and rationalisation of the church initiated in the middle of the last century has not yet turned Brazilian Catholicism into a controlled and homogeneous phenomenon. Therefore, many people live with a folk Catholicism that does not always find institutional frames in the Catholic Church. Some who call themselves Catholics may find these frames in spiritualist and afro-Brazilian centres (ibid.:13-14).

19   This pattern may be conditional on the practical problem of visiting church while having small children to take care of.

20   According to Eisenstadt and Roniger "strong similarities have existed between temporal *clientelismo* and the image of dependency on the spiritual realm" in the Northeast due to the fact that local Brazilian priests, historically subordinated to the big landowners, were preaching a popular Catholicism with emphasis on the need to rely on both divine and human protectors and benefactors (1984:102-5).

21   Teachers are very badly paid. They often work in all three shifts, morning, afternoon and evening, which leaves no room for preparation and rest; in addition, the supply of books and other materials is inadequate and irregular. All this leaves the teachers with a sense of not being respected for their work.

22 This pattern of formal education resembles the pattern for Pernambuco in general, only with a higher concentration in the neighbourhood of women reaching grade four (9 per cent higher), and a 4 per cent minor group finishing secondary schooling (FIDEM 1996).

23 Until 1988 illiterate people were not allowed to vote; they were "nonentities" (Scheper-Hughes 1992:84) and today literacy is still somehow tied to the notion of 'being somebody', of status within society. However, computer literacy seems to be more and more important. It is not without effect that computers have been used for voting in the latest political elections.

24 *Titanic* (pronounced 'Titaniki' in the neighbourhood) was a real favourite among the youth. I could not help but think that it represented the dream of love across class difference, which they so easily identified with. International movies were rented from the video shop at the *avenida* and I was often surprised to see quite new movies in its collection.

NOTES TO CHAPTER FOUR

1 I will not discuss in details the implications of religion in relation to women's choice of sterilisation, even though both Catholic and Protestant churches in Brazil have opposed the use of contraception, as this goes beyond the ambit of my research. However, I found, like Diniz et al. (1998: 65), that the women were ready to break with the church's prescriptions: by appealing to the beneficent personal God of popular religion directly, bypassing the clergy, some women like Ana found ways to explain their steps to control fertility. Others justified their sterilisations with considerations of personal health, a justification which somehow set aside religious concerns. According to Serruya some women find it sinful to "go against nature" and might thus prefer sterilisation to contraceptive pills, since sterilisation is a one time procedure, which does not daily remind of the transgression of religious norms or the order of nature though it is a dilemma that women may continue to live with in silence (Serruya 1996:154). This may be true in some cases; however, I found nothing pointing in that direction in my material. As I will argue later, women's dislike of the daily intake of pills seemed rather to be related to the discipline itself, notions of a mass growing inside, and the economic stress of continually having to buy pills.

2 Statistics from Recife show that this development has continued: in 1990 27.5 per cent of households were registered as female headed in the Metropolitan Region of Recife – an increase from 24.3 per cent in 1981 (IBGE-PNAD in Rocha 1995). However, in the survey on families with newborn babies in the neighbourhood we found no female headed households; this suggests that women are divorced or widowed later in life.

3 As Paul Rabinow remarks it is significant that "no one talks about a political or social miracle" (Rabinow 1992:263)

4   As with all other social indicators this number has varied significantly within
    the regions. Thus, the number of physicians per 10,000 was for the Southeast
    7.1 in 1960, 10.4 in 1970 and 15.2 in 1980, while in the Northeast it was respec-
    tively 2.2, 3.4 and 7.0 (Faria 1997/1998:187).

5   These are soap operas, normally in 150 to 200 episodes, screened six days a
    week. They are full of emotion and suspense. There is always a strong element
    of class difference in the *novelas*, often told through the upward mobility of
    a main female character. And when showed, poverty is always presented as
    nice and neat, beyond recognition (Tufte 1992:77). Besides, Fadul et al. (1996)
    note that conflicts between the woman as housewife and the woman in search
    of emancipation are common themes; that the woman of the *telenovela* has
    conquered her sexual freedom; that chauvinistic male characters are often
    negatively presented; and that sex in general is separated from the question
    of reproduction. In addition, due to practical circumstances, families in the
    novelas are always very small, with one or two children – all factors that may
    support the development I describe.

6   The difference between urban and rural areas is remarkably large; thus, while
    in the beginning of the 1990s urban Pernambuco experienced a fertility rate
    of 2.1, rural areas had a much higher rate at 5 (PNDS/PE 1996).

7   The prevalence of induced abortion in Brazil is unknown due to a lack of reliable
    data. The procedure has always been illegal except in cases of rape or risk to the
    woman's life, and therefore seldom performed in public institutions. However, it
    seems that most women know how and where to have it done (Kaufmann 1994:
    176). Only women in high income groups are able to afford safe clandestine
    abortions in private clinics. Poor women resort to more precarious solutions,
    mainly self-induced. Herbal teas and other homemade remedies have been
    used to induce abortions, or as women say, regulate menstruations (Leal and
    Fachel 1996). When these have shown themselves as inefficient, women have
    inserted catheters, twigs or knitting needles or sought help at quack abortionist's
    clinics (Saietz 1998). Brazil was the first country in the world, where a drug
    intended for treatment of ulcers, sold under the name Cytotec, was used for
    abortion. From its introduction in 1986 till 1991, when the sale of the drug was
    restricted, it became well known and widely used as abortifacient throughout
    Brazil (Barbosa and Arilha 1993; Costa 1998). While now restricted, the drug
    continues to be sold on the black market. Although not 100 per cent effective
    is has become a relatively cheap and accessible alternative to more dangerous
    methods (Saietz 1998; Costa 1998).

8   In 1999 the organisation worked in 147 of Pernambuco's 176 municipalities
    mainly through public health posts with a central clinic in Recife. Ultimately
    it has to a large extent incorporated the feminist critique and the general turn
    towards reproductive health and rights, and is now distributing a variety of
    methods with medical supervision.

9   Asked why they did not inform about family planning and contraceptive meth-
    ods, the nurse at the health post said to me, "We do not inform as in practice
    we have nothing to give. Why should we indicate possibilities that we cannot
    offer?" The lack of supply was a fact, however, the resistance to inform also

seemed to have to do with too many tasks and a general tiredness at the health post.

10   The same survey shows that 20.7 per cent of married women use contraceptive pills, while 4.45 rely on condoms, 3 per cent on periodic abstinence and 3.1 per cent on withdrawal. Only 1 per cent uses the IUD, while another 1 per cent uses hormonal injections (PNDS 1996). In Pernambuco the rate of sterilisation reaches 45 per cent, the pill 10 per cent, the condom 3 per cent and traditional methods 7 per cent (PNDS/PE 1996).

11   However, variations are many within each geographical area. In her study of the prevalence of caesarean sections within public health care in a three-month period between December 1994 and February 1995 Lynn Silver documented the percentage for each public hospital. She found for instance that in Caruaru one hospital, Casa de Saude Bom Jesus, had 90 per cent of 88 births performed by caesarean sections, while another Caruaruan hospital only reached 10 per cent. A hospital in São Lourenço da Mata, where some of the women from the neighbourhood gave birth, showed the percentage of caesareans to all births at 46; the local Hospital Geral de Camaragibe a percentage at 24; while Barão de Lucena, the modern hospital in Recife that women (and the nurse at the health post) preferred, reached 33 per cent in the same period (Silver 1996).

12   According to Faundes and Cecatti the rate rose in this period with more than 100 per cent within the births covered by the national health insurance. From a level at 14.6 per cent in 1970 it gradually reached 31 per cent in 1980 (Faundes and Cecatti 1991:150). See Chapter Five for a discussion of the high social status of caesarean sections that, as in USA, has turned surgical deliveries into attractive consumer goods.

13   In Pernambuco the Ministry of Health changed the conditions to be 25 years of age *and* 2 children, but before this a 20 year old woman, mother of two, had caused a furore at one of the major hospitals when she claimed her right to be sterilised.

14   This may have changed since 1996 as condoms are now distributed widely in Brazil to combat the spread of HIV/AIDS. However, IUDs are still not commonly used. For some reason the Brazilian medical system has been very slow to include IUDs in the services they provide. Talk about risk of cancer and many check-ups during use made this method seem very complicated to women with whom I talked. Injections were not provided by public services in Pernambuco and only women who could afford to pay the relatively higher costs would consider this method.

15   According to the PNDS the mean age for sterilisation has been around 29 in Brazil during recent years. This mean age places the country in a middle position between other Latin American countries, where sterilisation rates are high (28 years in the Dominican Republic in 1991; slightly above 30 years in Columbia in 1990 and Ecuador in 1994) (PNDS 1996).

16   Thirteen deliveries were registered without specifications and are therefore not included. Besides, it would clearly have provided more direct information on the caesarean section-sterilisation combination, if we had asked whether the

women were sterilised during or after giving birth. However, that would lead to further explanations and probably some confusion. I had to pose as simple questions as possible in order to facilitate the work of the ACSs, and as we considered it unlikely that a woman would give birth with a caesarean section and then obtain her sterilisation post partum, I chose to ask about last delivery in order to elucidate the combination. Due to this rashly undertaken decision, the presented data can only be said to demonstrate the probable percentage of sterilisations performed through caesarean sections.

17   Surgical vaginal 'tightening' is quite common in Brazil. Several women in the neighbourhood had been advised by a physician to go through the operation, others asked for it themselves, and some developed problems afterwards (for instance, pain during sexual intercourse). Perineum surgery has served in some (or many) cases to legitimise, or as a cover for, sterilisation.

18   The episiotomy is an incision made into the thinned-out perineal body to enlarge the vaginal orifice during delivery. Episiotomies are done routinely in Brazilian obstetrical practice.

19   In the survey we conducted among 192 women who had given birth within a recent two-year period, we found 28 women who had been sterilised since their last delivery. Out of these only two sterilisations were justified by a history of too many previous caesareans. In comparison, three women from the same sample had been sterilised on medical indications due to hypertension. Women with hypertension were transferred from antenatal care at the health post to regular examinations at a big modern hospital in Recife. In the neighbourhood these women were assumed to be a step nearer to the desired surgery as hypertension often served as an indication in itself and because, once enrolled at this hospital, a lucky few would be able to make a deal with the doctors in charge. I met several women, though, for whom this strategy had failed.

20   The women I met who had been sterilised at public hospitals had paid little or nothing. However, several hospitals have both a publicly paid section and a private, and some women I interviewed had been registered, it seemed, as private patients at a public hospital. One had paid ten *reais* for a sterilisation under such conditions, another 650 *reais*.

21   For work on the widespread use of sterilisations in exchange for votes in Northeast Brazil see Potter and Caetano 1998 and Caetano 2000.

22   *Marginais* are socially excluded individuals, in daily talk mainly criminals and drug users.

23   Bricks, sand and other material were common 'gifts' from political candidates. One day I passed Pedro's bar together with Sonia. Pedro worked in the campaign for Dr. Nadegi. He visited women, whom he knew wanted sterilisations and offered them the operation on behalf of Nadegi. He also drove women in birth pains to the hospitals in Recife and provided other significant services. When we passed his bar Sonia said, "Oh, I have to remind Pedro of that sand!" I asked, "Did he offer you sand?" She said: "Yes, sand for my wall around the house." That wall was Sonia's next huge project. I presumed that she voted in favour of Nadegi since Pedro owed her the sand, but she said, "No! He doesn't know whom you vote for, and one has to take advantage *(aproveitar)*." However, she

did not expect him to remember his offer as the election had already passed and Nadegi did not win the candidature that she was nominated for.

24   *Esterilização: Sintoma Social*, a study by Elza Berquo and Margareth Arilha from the beginning of the 1990s using survey and focus group discussions also points towards this perception of different kinds of sterilisation with varying efficiency. However, this study mentions three methods, that is, the cut, the knot, and the 'both-and' that is, both knot and cut in one surgery. Only the latter is perceived by users to be efficient. A seven year period is also mentioned as the period after which the woman may become fertile again (Berquo and Arilha 1992).

25   Failure rates of female sterilisation are nowadays generally low. Less than 1 per cent of women sterilised become pregnant again, often within the first two years after the sterilisation. Reversal surgery is available at public hospitals, but may prove ineffective for the majority of low income women presently sterilised. While success rates are often high in internationally published studies of female sterilisation reversal (see Machado 1998), reported rates can be misleading as they define 'success' as the achievement of tubal pregnancy, regardless of outcome (including pregnancy outside uterus and miscarriage), and do not include women who requested reversal but were rejected (WHO 1992:125). According to WHO the individual woman has few chances for having her fertility restored. Success of reversal is also dependent upon the method of sterilisation performed. Since many sterilisations in Brazil are performed in combination with a caesarean section, invasive and less reversible methods can be used due to the easy access to the tubes. Women in my study opted for the most radical solution as they wanted to feel safe; they preferred to be shown the pieces of tube cut out. In case of regret, they may find their tubes destroyed to a degree where recanalisation of the tubes is impossible and artificial insemination or a test-tube pregnancy may be their only option. These procedures are not performed within public health care in Brazil and thus have no implications for poor women (Commercio 1997). A new method of surgical sterilisation allowing for higher rates of refertilisation has been developed in Brazil very recently, but this has not yet practical significance for the women in my study. Besides, reversal of sterilisation is expensive for the health care system, varying from $ 5,000 to 10,000 (Machado 1998:12), which makes it impossible for public health care to meet all requests, if reversal becomes attractive.

26   The case of Microvilar was not a single phenomenon. Withdrawal of spurious or poor quality drugs happens once in a while in Brazil. Likewise with condoms: while I was doing fieldwork a huge consignment of condoms was withdrawn from public distribution due to suspicion of poor quality.

27   I always had difficulties when I wanted to know more about the women's understanding of medical knowledge. They seemed to know that they did not know what was right, and they often became embarrassed when I asked questions like: "How do you think the pill works?" I twisted and turned my questions, but without success. Sonia resisted answering this sort of question. "I do not know anything about these things" she said. With Carmen I ended up saying:

"Carmen, there is something that I want to know, but I find it embarrassing to ask you. Can we make it like a school? I ask you some questions, and you answer whatever you know. Doesn't matter if you say something you are not so sure about. I just need to know what women here in Brazil think about the pills, you see?"

28   In 1995 95.3 per cent of all deliveries in Pernambuco occurred at a hospital (Moreira 1998:125).

29   With one exception: Taciana, who was the daughter of a local merchant, educated at law school, and disappointed with her caesarean. She wanted a "humanized birth" – a notion that belonged to the new movement for quality of care in childbirth in Brazil. However, Taciana agreed that a caesarean section leads to subsequent caesareans and eventually a tubal ligation. Seen in this light she accepted her fate.

30   Here I use Mark Nichter's (1981) approach to idioms of distress. Nichter argues that feeling states like inadequacy, dissatisfaction or suppressed anger that otherwise could take the form of untenable conflicts are often in socially or culturally constrained situations articulated in culturally available modes of expression. These idioms of distress represent discontent as well as adaptation as expression is held within culture-specific notions of, for instance, female weakness and will therefore reinforce dominant and oppressive notions rather than provide alternatives. A study from Vietnam by Tine Gammeltoft clearly and compellingly describes women's strategic use of physical weakness, particularly related to IUDs, in daily coping with social and emotional pressure. As Gammeltoft concludes: "Thus, while immediately useful to individual women, somatic idioms of distress may be self-defeating in the long run and simply perpetuate the very gender ideologies from which much of women's everyday distress seems to emerge" (1999:247).

31   A study from a neighbourhood in Recife co-ordinated by Parry Scott from the Federal University of Pernambuco, shows the same characteristics of hypertension: fat, salted food and distress lead to headache, cerebral haemorrhage and paresis. A large proportion of those interviewed in this study also perceived that more women than men had hypertension due to women's worries and responsibilities in daily life (Scott 1996).

32   I suppose men could have taken their children to the health post as well. However, I do not remember ever to have seen a man on my regular visits to the post, except for a few old men. Men were expected to provide for the family, including the provision of health insurance if possible, but the actual visit to the doctor was the women's responsibility.

33   By this I do not mean that the women had not always been unknowing and inexperienced about their bodies in biomedical terms. According to the women's narratives they had very little access to information about reproductive matters in former times. Neide for instance told me that she never learned anything about sexual or reproductive matters from her mother, Lívia, as the mother felt shame. As Diniz et al. write: "Among rural and older women, the body is an unknown entity, not to be talked about" (Diniz et al. 1998:37). But Lívia on the other hand never submitted to any authoritative knowledge. She was the kind

of woman, as Neide said, who went pregnant to the river to fish and returned in the afternoon with a baby. Not even the traditional midwives, who used to help women in childbirth, had much access to the woman's body. The dreaded *toque* (intravaginal examination) was never used, the midwife, Beneditta, told me. The old women's disgust with anything that penetrated the body, even the tongue in kisses in the *telenovelas*, pointed towards an experience of the body where nobody knew her body better than the woman herself. That, however, infants died of "childhood one after the other" (often diarrhoea) and women died from "children" (in childbirth) was the other side of the coin.

NOTES TO CHAPTER FIVE

1   I use the English term 'ignorant' when translating the Brazilian *ignorante*. People often mean 'inattentive' rather than 'unknowing', but *ignorante* is used in both senses of the word in many situations, for instance, when referring to uneducated poor people, adults who hit children instead of talking with them and better-off people who do not consider the sufferings of the poor.

2   The low quality of care at public hospitals in Brazil is often mentioned as one factor pushing women into surgical deliveries. Serruya thus also writes that "with nobody attending them in the moment of normal birth, the women prefer in an inverted logic to be operated, in order to be better assisted" (Serruya 1996: 148, my translation). In a discussion of gender violence in health services Diniz and d'Oliveira write: "We believe that in Brazil it is not possible to hold back the caesarean epidemic without a radical change that humanises the assistance to vaginal delivery. In the present conditions, including tremendous obstacles to access, the disregard of women as individuals, their reification, as well as the succession of painful, useless and risk laden assaults on their body, there is no way of convincing women (and their families) that vaginal delivery has advantages over caesareans sections" (Diniz and d'Oliveira 1998:40).

3   I have used Hegel's *The Phenomenology of Spirit*, completed in 1807, and Alexander Kojève's influential and authoritative interpretation of it from 1969. Kojève renewed Hegel's relevance in recent times, but as Nick Crossley points out, he added to Hegel's notion of the struggle for recognition to a degree that may justify a relabelling of the philosophy to 'Hegel/Kojève'. While bearing this in mind I will, however, continue to refer to Hegel as the source of these ideas.

4   See Fukiyama (1992) for a historical overview and discussion of the relevance of this view to our contemporary world.

5   Hegel describes the struggle for recognition as a "fight to the death". He distinguishes human beings from other beings by their willingness to put their desire for recognition above the desire for self-preservation. The struggle for recognition thereby becomes a contest between the two, the result of which can be the death or total surrender of either one; this gives rise to a master-slave relationship, which will generate no more struggles. The struggle for recognition creates "historic dynamic", whilst the master-slave relation results in a standstill.

6   This balancing between Being and Not-being is exemplified by Honneth in psychoanalytical terms in relation to love: "in the tense balance between fusion and ego-demarcation, the resolution of which is part of every successful form of primary relationship, subjects mutually experience themselves to be loved in their individuality only insofar as they are not afraid of being alone" (Honneth 1995:176).

7   I paraphrase Pierre Bourdieu from *The Logic of Practice* (1990:73). I could have gained analytically from using his work on habitus and symbolic capital, had I not so decisively opted for the actor's point of view.

8   Sonia uses the Portuguese word *sociedade* which corresponds to the English equivalent 'society' with all its connotations. The *granfinos* are the 'high society', the important, rich people.

9   The shame of eating in the presence of people who are better off than oneself was something I never really understood. Being confronted with it whenever I invited people to eat in my house, or when, for instance, Sonia told me about her work as *empregada*, made me aware of the degree of shame in their lives. Perhaps the explanation lies in the fact that it "gives one away; it shows the extent of one's desires, the seemingly bottomless pit of one's needs" (Scheper-Hughes 1992:160). When poor people eat in front of others they are self-consciously aware of the stigma of being hungry and ignorant: "One can eat too quickly, too sloppily, or too much. One's table manners may be wanting; one may be expected to use a fork rather than a spoon, or one may encounter a strange food on the table and not know how it is eaten" (ibid.). Recalling all the meals I had eaten with people in the neighbourhood, especially, for instance, at the wedding where Luzia and her daughters urged me to eat ("eat, eat, Lini!") or when Sonia one day, stuffing her mouth with biscuits, said, "Fill up the belly, Lini!" Scheper-Hughes' conceptualisation of food as an equivalent to life in both a very real and a symbolic sense seems relevant. Food is life, but a life that the poor cannot approach without shame. They are once and for all, it seems, marked by their marginality.

10   The fairly egalitarian relationship between pastors and ordinary members has been mentioned as one reason for the success of the Pentecostal churches in Brazil. As Mariz writes: "The Catholic Church opts for the poor because it is not a church of the poor. Pentecostal churches do not opt for the poor because they are already a poor people's church. And that is why poor people are choosing them" (Mariz 1994:80)

11   For more on silencing of talk about race se Chapter Three, "Living conditions".

12   Advertisements constitute around 25 per cent of Brazilian television programming (Chaparral in Tauxe 1993:598).

13   The designation 'humble' was used by people to describe the poor, in which group they also included themselves.

14   Zygmunt Bauman proposes that in the consumer society even work is consumed, in the sense that work devoid of the capacity to excite – work "that does not offer 'intrinsic satisfaction' – is also work devoid of value" (Bauman 1998:32). One could see the unemployed young men who hung around the neighbourhood in this light. What was offered them was simply too boring. It did not even grant

the capacity to consume, as the rates for unskilled labour were generally very low. Sonia had a son, around 22 years old, who slept all day long if he was not playing soccer. She complained a lot, and did not understand why he did not find something to do. "There is always something for a man of capacity" she said. However, in my view, the capacity that her son wanted had nothing to do with hard, exhausting work. It is not surprising that many youngsters in Brazil today are attracted to the drug trade: "… tempting fate by challenging the forces of law and order may itself turn into the poor man's favourite substitute for the affluent consumer's well-tempered anti-boredom adventures, in which the volume of desired and permissible risks are cautiously balanced" (Bauman 1998:39).

15 Some parts of the neighbourhood, usually at the margins of the settlement, were inhabited by people who had come in from rural districts recently. They would often keep animals and grow some crops. Those who had settled on the place years ago and now lived in the centre of the neighbourhood had, as Sonia said, lost their knowledge of growing crops. They knew how to exchange goods and services.

16 Before progressing in this argument, I have to emphasise that I also saw and heard about doctors and nurses who treated people with care and attention, and I know that much is done these days in order to change the negative conditions I describe here. However, in order to understand people's mistrust and shame in relation to hospitals, the descriptions and discussions in this section are relevant and not at all rare. I would rather say they seem to be only too common.

17 Pizzini's interpretation is that "[s]having returns the woman to prepubescence by removing her pubic hair, which represents adult sexual traits. The ritual signifies purification from sexual 'sin'" (Pizzini 1989:6). Shaving before giving birth is also a manner of keeping the birth under control, framed as a medical event with no sexual implications (ibid.:6). This may be in the interests of both women and medical staff. See also Pizzini (1991) for a discussion of humorous handling of sexual taboos related to childbirth. When I asked women in the neighbourhood why they shaved or cut their pubic hair short, they answered that it was a matter of hygiene, that long hair was "disgusting" or "ugly".

18 Many adults from poor families lack some or all teeth due to poor dental care in their youth.

19 As Pizzini notes, the staff's free access to the woman's body indicates her status as patient: "The doctor, nurse and midwife come into and go from the labour room without warning, and approach the woman without any of the preambles used in everyday life, such as greetings or introductions" (Pizzini 1989:6). At the hospitals which were part of my study staff members just passed in and out without considering the woman's wish for privacy. However, it was only at the university hospital that the crowding in the delivery room seemed abusive; at the other hospitals there was some privacy around the delivery. In the labour room, on the contrary, women were everywhere exposed to the public. One woman was thus left in the middle of the hall in a bed with a bedpan, with legs spread open and her genitals revealed to anybody who happened to enter the door. Fortunately, the bedpan was removed and she had covered herself with

the smock when two workers entered in order to fix an electrical installation. Likewise, Anita told me about her wish to cover her nakedness: "I was without sheets in the bed, only a mattress covered with plastic, and I was only wearing that dress, and there was ... well, there were a lot of men passing as it was in the visiting hour, and I put my towel down there, because it was very near the door." A patient must have to struggle hard to sustain the depersonalised, medical definition of the situation under such circumstances. When I asked one woman how she managed not to feel shame, she said: "One forgets. The pain is so strong that one forgets." I guess it is partly true, and partly a way of framing an otherwise embarrassing experience.

20   The network, REHUNA, Rede para a Rehumanização do Nascimento, in which many women's groups participate, is presently involved in a very active political effort to improve conditions for birth giving at public hospitals in Brazil; they are also advocating for establishing a midwife education programme in the hope of de-medicalising procedures. However, this initiative has met with strong medical resistance.

21   At the three hospitals that I visited, women often rather routinely had an intravenous infusion established, just in case augmentation of labour should be needed, or in case the delivery ended up as a caesarean. Sometimes the procedure was used just to prevent dehydration, as women were not allowed to drink anything after admission to the maternity ward. This procedure was, once again, justified with the possibility of a surgical intervention.

22   The women I observed giving birth were all told to *"fazer força pra baixo"*, that is to "press downwards", early in labour. As a result they were often exhausted later when pressing was really needed.

23   For a description of the 'Kristeller manoeuvre' see note 8 in Chapter Two.

24   Violent treatment of patients is not restricted to maternity wards. An article in Folha de São Paulo (Brazil's most important newspaper) 8 July 1997 under the title "Doctors are not preoccupied with suffering" presents the results of a research project in which the attitude to patients' sufferings was investigated. It concluded that both doctors and nurses were generally not preoccupied with patient's pains, but rather, with the diagnosis of disease. The patients, for their part, were said to be resigned to facing the pains "as if they ought to bear them".

25   He made a joke because the woman in birth was preoccupied with her slippers that she had placed underneath the delivery table. The physician commented upon it and made the women's preoccupation with their slippers sound ridiculous. He apparently did not know that these slippers were bought especially for that day, that they had been quite expensive for the woman, and that they presumably were the only things familiar to her in an otherwise foreign and violent situation.

26   Till the very last minute they resisted the feeling of weakness, or as Scheper-Hughes writes, they refused to be negated (Scheper-Hughes 1992:18).

27   The Portuguese word *toque* is here translated into 'touch', and refers, in this context, to an intra-vaginal examination.

28   According to Faúndes and Cecatti (Faundes and Cecatti 1991) the caesarean

section rate in 1981 increased with the economic status of the woman. Thus, 16.7 per cent of the women from families with less than one minimum salary per month had caesarean deliveries, while 57.6 per cent of women from families with more than ten minimum salaries per month gave birth in this way. The same study shows that while the richest state, São Paulo, had a rate at 43.8 per cent, Pernambuco reached 17.9 per cent in the same period. By the time of the PNDS of 1996, these caesarean rates had increased to 52.1 per cent for São Paulo and 24 per cent for Pernambuco (PNDS 1996; PNDS/Pernambuco 1996).

29 Both women got to know the sex of their child during pregnancy. Prenatal ultrasound scanning is prevalent in Brazil, even in the neighbourhood where I worked. Women usually knew the sex of their children beforehand. However, buying clothes in the 'right' colour proved to be risky, as the prediction was not always in accordance with reality.

30 During my stay in Brazil a movement towards 'humanisation of child birth' gained popularity. Curumim, an NGO in Recife, started a big campaign about the tender and calm atmosphere needed for the woman to give birth, and it seemed that more and more middle class women were inspired by the natural childbirth idea. This movement among middle class women appeared to be reflected in the awareness within the public health care system of a need to reduce the high caesarean sections rates. However, the irony, in Teresa's view, was that in the efforts to bring down these rates poor women were made to feel even further neglected. Now that they had learned to appreciate caesarean sections, they had to suffer as they could not enter private hospitals and clinics where these were still willingly performed.

31 Sonia did not live inside the 'invasion' but on a small plot near the Protestant church. The plot was meant for a public square but Sonia decided to build a house on it, as she had nowhere else to live. She had raised her house during one single night, thus claiming the right to use the plot, which had been unused for some time. Some people had complained and wanted to throw her out, but in the end she had managed to stay.

32 The piles of rubbish, the network of muddy lanes in between houses, the houses that did not keep sounds and smells out nor in, the fleeting time where days had few fixed points, and the family members who would move in and stay temporarily; all these were manifestations of fluidity in time and space. Of course there where also structures; for instance, in the neighbourhood families living near the *avenida* had a wall around their house, and children had to go to school at certain hours. Victora proposes that the fluidity in this way of living also prevails in people's bodily experience. Women experience their bodies as penetrable by outer influence; inner and outer are not separated domains but form one whole. The *mãe do corpo* (body's mother) that Victora found to be an 'emic' organ of the female body in the shanty town, shows how women experience their bodies in concordance with their experience of the fluidity of time and space. The *mãe do corpo* moves on its own within the body during and after pregnancy (Victora 1996:147). It cares for the baby and misses it when it is born. It is a phenomenological experience of movements that cannot be transposed onto the fixed structure of a womb on the drawings of the female

body that health care workers use. Josenita and I asked particularly about the *mãe do corpo,* or *dona do corpo* as it was called in the neighbourhood. Younger women generally denied the existence of such an organ. However, when investigating more closely into their understanding of the female reproductive organs we found that many knew little about reproductive anatomy and that their experience of movement within and in and out of the body resembled those categorised as *mãe do corpo* by Victora's informants.

Notes to chapter six

1   Schutz defines the everyday life-world as that reality which a "wide-awake, normal, mature person" takes for granted, and which he or she can immediately act upon. Sleep, fictive worlds or fantasies, or changed states of consciousness are not part of the everyday life-world, but of the more inclusive life-world (Schutz and Luckmann 1973:21ff).

2   I use Mead's notion of a community engaged in a game in an abstract sense, as I do not refer to a specific group of persons as much as to the abstract category of 'mothers' or 'wives'. Thus, it is possible for an individual to be part of several communities or social groups at a time, that is, the individual may oscillate between several social selves or 'me's'. Mead does not develop his notion in this direction, but leaves room for such an interpretation as he talks about both 'concrete' and 'abstract' social classes or subgroups. As an example of an abstract social sub-group Mead mentions 'debtors' or 'creditors' and he writes "The given individual's membership in several of these abstract social classes or subgroups makes possible his entrance into definite social relations (however indirect) with an almost infinite number of other individuals who also belong to or are included within one or another of these abstract social classes or subgroups cutting across functional lines of demarcation which divide different human social communities from one or another" (1965:157). An abstract social group may thus be, as I propose, the group of mothers within which the individual mother sees herself reflected in other mothers; a group that may cut across class or nationality, so that, for instance, a middle class mother in a *telenovela* or a researcher from Denmark becomes part of the group.

3   *The Structures of the Life-World* encompasses Schutz's original thinking and work through 25 years. Thomas Luckmann has written the book as an edition of manuscripts left by Schutz at his death in 1959. Despite Luckmann's crucial role I refer to Schutz as the author of the ideas.

4   Schutz distinguishes between "in-order-to" motives and "because" motives, the former being motives related to a future goal, the latter being the motives seen from the opposite time perspective, when we look at the process as a completed act. In the "because" perspective "[t]he causes of action are sought not in projects, but in what is already given" (Schutz 1983:20).

5   Labour is divided into three stages: the first stage, when the pelvis expands, the second stage, when the foetus is pressed down and out, and the third stage, when the placenta is born. Pressing too early is not only unnecessary, it may also be harmful.

6   *Casa* (house/home) and *casar* (to marry) are almost the same word in Portuguese, as Parry Scott points out when referring to the popular saying '*quem casa, quer casa*' (those who marry, want a home) (1996:294).

7   This distinction is of course not exclusive to Brazil; it is found in many other societies, as Hess remarks (Hess and Da Matta 1995:14).

8   This gender hierarchy was first described in terms of "*rua*"' and "*casa*" by Gilberto Freyre in his book *Casa Grande e Senzala* (1933). Others have placed it in a comtemporary context (Nascimento 1999, Parker 1991, Rebhun 1999 and Scott 1996).

9   It is, however, interesting in this context to note that medical health care, children's school lessons and *telenovelas* structured the days to a certain degree. About the latter one woman thus said: "I am in the street talking, and then 'five o'clock, ai! It is time for my *novela*' and I rush home, I don't make any food, 'come children – have a bath' and then it starts and I am there. When it finishes we will have coffee, and with this I go on."

10   The women who worked outside had quite a different life. They had to do the housework, cook and take care of the children before and after their jobs. Often even if their husbands were at home due to unemployment.

11   "Face", Goffman writes, "may be defined as the positive social value a person effectively claims for himself through verbal and non-verbal acts in which he expresses his evaluation of the situation, the other and himself" (1995:222). The person can be said to be "in wrong face" or "out of face" in embarrassing situations where for some reason her self-presentation does not correspond with the social context. On the other hand, when a person is "in face", she responds with feelings of confidence and assurance. However, an important aspect of Goffman's conceptualisation is that "face" is intersubjectively produced and maintained, and "while his social face can be his most personal possession and the centre of his security and pleasure, it is only on loan to him from society" (ibid.:225).

12   In her study among working class Brazilians in Pernambuco Rebhun notes that women much more than men emphasised affection and personal contacts in their interaction with others (1999:246). In addition, Rebhun refers to another study (Salem 1980) from Rio de Janeiro which found the same tendency. In my experience it is probable that women have refined their skill in affecting others precisely because they – much more than men – are without the means to act independently and because they – much more than men – are forced to act due to their primary responsibility for their children.

13   According to Schutz, in "we-relations" the other is experienced as essentially "like me" (1974:61-64) and "I can always (again and again) find confirmation that my experiences of the life-world are congruent with your experiences of it" (ibid.:85). "We-relations" are thus relations within social groups based on mutual recognition and engaged in a shared project, a community (Mead's term) in which the "we" mediates the self-other relation.

14   For more on elopement see Chapter Three, 'The family'.

15   The figure of Mother Mary is prominent in Brazilian folk-Catholicism, as are ideas about self-abnegation and unconditional maternal love. However,

the women I talked with never referred to Mary as a mother like themselves (they actually never mentioned her except on the day of Maria da Conceição, when some of them would participate in the religious feast at the Morro da Conceição). They did, however, idealise motherhood, which resulted in many quarrels and sorrows in support of Rebhun's findings from Caruaru. Rebhun found that maternal sentiments as perceived by her informants were the "matrix" for any other love (1999:167) but that the idealisation of mother love lead to conflicts and disappointment in many relationships, as ideals were difficult to follow (ibid.:166-71).

16   "Luzia, caesarean no, normal! Let's go, my little black, let's try!" is what I am supposed to have said, to which she replied, "OK, Lini, I follow your advice," She reported this 'exchange' to my friend Carla, who interviewed her after the birth, explaining to her that she agreed with me "because Lini said to me: Look, Luzia, caesarean is very bad, both for you, the child and us who accompany you." Do I need to say that I did not recognise any part of this conversation as something that had taken place between us? I had the permission to accompany her at the hospital even in the event of a caesarean, so I never felt I had any preferences and even less did I express preferences. Besides, I would never have thought of calling her "my little black" (it is interesting and a bit shocking, though, that she put these words in my mouth). However, putting things this way made the birth much more interesting and masked the fact that she had not achieved what she wanted: a caesarean section and 'her ligation'.

17   Neide once told me about a time, when she lived alone with her children: "The life alone as a woman is bad. The other women become jealous with their husbands, because you are alone and do not have a husband...They fear that you take their husband and stay with him." A woman living alone is a sexual being with no one to control her sexuality. Referring to the *rua* as the space for the prostitutes Parry Scott writes: "A secure, cohabiting sexual partner confers status. Here the regaining of a home is the regaining of a cultural identity which frees women from the dubiousness of the *rua*" (Scott 1996:294); this was also Rebhun's interpretation: "Even more than a widow, a divorced or separated woman faces the possibility of sexual harassment as a nonvirginal but nonattached and therefore unprotected woman" (1999:123).

18   I use the terms 'marriage', 'wife' and 'husband' here to cover different marital arrangements: legal marriage, church marriage and unmarried co-habitation. See also Chapter Three, 'The family'.

19   In their study from Porto Alegre Leal and Fachel also found pregnancy to be a means to establish alliances: "In this popular class group's perspective, teenage pregnancy is not perceived as a 'problem', as it is from a strictly medical point of view. Teenage pregnancy is, in the first place, an adolescent woman's strategy for forming a union" (1996:5). They found that pregnancy in the strict biological sense was not regarded as pregnancy. When the 'natural' indicators are present (nausea, no menstruation and so on) an intense negotiation starts to see who will *assumir*, assume or recognize, the child. Until the father, the father's or the mother's family or the mother herself have recognised the child as theirs, the pregnancy is still ambiguous, perceived as delayed menstruation. In this

liminal period teas combined with abortive medicine can be used to 'regulate' the menstruation. This is a strategic period in the life of every woman (Leal and Fachel 1996:12).

20 Marriage would sometimes be impossible either due to economic constraints, or because the woman was already married. Some women wanted to secure themselves and their children with a pension from their former husband, whom they therefore did not divorce.

21 The word *carinho* was used by the women to designate tenderness, affection, or, in some cases caresses. *Carinhoso* logically means to be tender, caring and attentive.

22 The emphasis on romantic love and eroticism has spread from the middle class in the South to poor people in the North through the popular *telenovelas*. Sex and gender relations that challenge the traditional patriarchal gender system (female autonomy, more caring male roles, even women's extra-marital love affairs) are the common attractions in the *novelas*. Rebhun writes on romantic love, *lóvi*, also referred to as *amor de novela* (soap opera love), that it is the outcome of economic and social changes in Brazil influenced by the United States (Rebhun 1999:184; see also Fadul, Mc Anany and Morales 1996).

23 Agression here does not necessarily mean violence, but rather an assertive 'taking' (see Kalckmann 1998:93).

24 I had interviewed Jairo several times, but one day I asked him if he could get some friends together for a group interview. We met the next afternoon in a most beautiful sunset outside Roberto's house: Jairo, Roberto, Nado and I. As the discussion developed we all realised that I should have conducted more interviews with (groups of) men as their viewpoints had important implications for the women and their lives and as they liked to be heard, too.

25 See note 21, this chapter.

26 A few women told me that their sex life had improved after the sterilisation due to the absence of the risk of pregnancy. "I love it," a woman said, "because I no longer have that fear, that ghost, that fear of getting pregnant. I love it."

27 In the Brazilian gender hierarchy a man is supposed to control his wife's sexuality. Consequently, female adultery insults the husband's masculinity and respect from others. Pedro Nascimento found that his informants perceived the woman as always potentially unfaithful. Therefore, they preferred keeping their wives at home, even though that might make them boring. As a man said, "The woman of the house is like a chicken from a farm: it is healthy but without taste" (Nascimento 1999:49). According to Nascimento, the men saw their duty to provide food and sex for the woman as a way of keeping her faithful. "A hungry woman cuckolds her man," a young man said (ibid.:50). Therefore, the threat of adultery can also be used to express dissatisfaction with a man's capacity to provide for the house (see also Rebhun 1999:199).

28 In Brazil, traditional patriarchal attitudes to sex prescribe the male role as sexually active, dominating and experimenting, while women are supposed to be innocent and passive, and preferably virgins at marriage (Parker 1991). To this universe belongs the sharp division between the *mulher da casa* (woman of the house) and the *mulher da rua* (woman of the street), who are respec-

tively honourably boring and interestingly erotic. Today a discourse based on sexual pleasure has entered women's expectations from their sex life (Diniz, Mello e Souza and Portella 1998) and my informants complained about boring sex as a reason for having lost sexual appetite. However, some of them clearly expressed that they did not want to experiment (unusual positions, anal sex or in one case just a caress on the thigh beneath the table while others were present), since they were not whores.

29   Diniz et al. write that the women in the study from Pernambuco (compared to those from Rio de Janeiro and São Paulo) more directly linked frigidity to sterilisation as they were eager to free themselves from the burden of unwanted sexual intercourse (Diniz, Mello e Souza and Portella 1998:60).

30   In the structured interviews with recently sterilised women we asked if they knew about other women who had regretted their sterilisation. We heard about very few, always distant acquaintances, which could in fact have been one or two that everybody knew of. Asking around in the neighbourhood and among the ACSs, I met a young woman, who was being examined for refertilisation at a hospital in Recife. She was in her early twenties and had been sterilised at the age of 16, when she was already a mother of two children. Her mother had arranged the sterilisation, and she – the mother – was registered at the hospital instead of the daughter due to the daughter's young age. Later, the mother took care of the children, and now as the young woman lived with a man, she wanted children with him. Another woman, a 40 years old widow and mother of three adolescents lived with a young man of 28 and wanted to give him children. However, she had not yet planned to opt for refertilisation. And then there was Diana (see Chapter Four 'Early Sterilisation'), who was sterilised at the age of 19, and who now hoped that the surgery was badly done. However, she would not go through another surgery, she said.

Notes to chapter seven

1   From A. de Saint-Exupéry, *Pilote de Guerre,* cited in Merleau-Ponty 1962:456.

Bibliography

Abu-Lughod, Lila
1991   Writing against Culture. In R. G. Fox (ed.) *Recapturing Anthropology: Working in the Present.* Santa Fe, NM: School of American Research Press.
1993   *Writing Women's Worlds: Bedouin Stories.* Berkeley: University of California Press.

Andrade, Inaldete Pinheiro de
1997   Os nós da esterilização. Universidade Federal de Pernambuco.
Centro de Ciências Sociais Aplicadas, Mestrado de Serviço Social. Master's thesis.

Ardener, Edwin
1989   Comprehending Others. In E. Ardener and M. Chapman (eds.) *The Voice of Prophecy and Other Essays.* Oxford: Basil Blackwell.

Avila, Maria B. de M., and Regina M. Barbosa
1985   *Contracepção: Mulheres e instituições.* Recife: SOS Corpo.

Bailey, Patricia E., Marcos P. P. de Castro, Maristela D. Araujo, Bernadete M. de Castro, and Barbara Janowitz
1991   Physicians' attitudes, Recommendations and Practice of Male and Female Sterilization in São Paulo. *Contraception* 44(2): 191-207.

Barbalet, Jack M.
1998   *Emotion, Social Theory, and Social Structure: A Macrosociological Approach.* Cambridge: Cambridge University Press.

Barbosa, Lívia N. de H.
1995   The Brazilian Jeitinho: An Exercise in National Identity. In D. J. Hess and R. DaMatta (eds.) *The Brazilian Puzzle.* New York: Columbia University Press.

Barbosa, Regina M., and Margareth Arilha
1993   The Brazilian Experience with Cytotec. *Studies in Family Planning* 24(4): 236-240.

Barros, F.C., J.P. Vaughan, C.G. Victora, and S.R.A. Huttly
1991   Epidemic of Caesarean Sections in Brazil. *Lancet* 338(July 20): 167-169.

Bauman, Zygmunt
1998   *Work, Consumerism and the New Poor.* Philadelphia, USA: Open University Press.

Berger, John
1982   Stories. In J. Berger and J. Mohr (eds.) *Another Way of Telling.* New York: Pantheon Books.

Berquó, Elza
1998   The Reproductive Health of Brazilian Women during the "Lost Decade". In
       G. Martine, M. Das Gupta, and L. C. Chen (eds.) *Reproductive Change in
       India and Brazil.* Delhi: Oxford University Press.

Berquo, Elza S., and Margareth Arilha
1992   *Esterilização: Sintoma social.* Campinas: NEPO/UNICAMP.

Bourdieu, Pierre
1990   *The Logic of Practice.* Stanford: Stanford University Press

Briggs, Jean L.
1991   Mazes of Meaning: The Exploration of Individuality in Culture and of Cul-
       ture through Individual Constructs. In L B. Boyer and R. Boyer (eds.) *The
       Psychoanalytic Study of Society.* Hillsdale, NJ: Analytic Press.

Bruner, Jerome
1987   Life as Narrative. *Social Research* 54(1): 11-32.

Burdick, John
1993   *Looking for God in Brazil.* Berkeley: University of California Press.

Caetano, André J.
2000   Sterilization for Votes in the Brazilian Northeast: The Case of Pernambuco.
       Faculty of the Graduate School, University of Texas, Austin. Ph. D. disserta-
       tion.

Carranza, Maria
1994   De cesáreas, mulheres e médicos: uma aproximação médico-antropológica ao
       parto cesáreo no Brasil. Pós-graduaçâo em Antropologia Social. Universidade
       de Brasilia. Master's thesis.

Carloto, Maria C., Jacira Melo, Matilde Ribeiro, Nalu F. Silva, Nilde F. Balcão, Maria
       T. Citeli and Wilza V. Villela
1994   *Esterilização feminina.* São Paulo: Sempreviva.

Carter, Anthony T.
1995   Agency and Fertility: For an Ethnography of Practice. In S. Greenhalgh (ed.)
       Situating Fertility. Cambridge: Cambridge University Press.

Carvalho, J.A.M., and L.R. Wong
1998   Demographic and Socio-economic Implications of Rapid Fertility Decline
       in Brazil: A Window of Opportunity. In G. Martine, M. Das Gupta, and
       L. C. Chen (eds.) *Reproductive Change in India and Brazil.* Delhi: Oxford
       University Press.

Casey, Edward S.
1996   How to get from Space to Place in a Fairly Short Stretch of Time. Phenom-
       enological Prolegomena. In S. Feld and K. H. Basso (eds.) *Senses of Place.*
       Santa Fe, NM: School of American Research Press.

Clifford, James
1986   Introduction: Partial Truths. In J. Clifford and G. E. Marcus (eds.) *Writing Culture*. Berkeley: University of California Press.

Commercio, Jornal de
1997   Desistência de ligações chega a 40%. November 30th.

Costa, Aurélio Molina da
1995   The Determinants of Tubal Ligation in Recife, Northeast Brazil. University of Leeds, School of Medicine, Division of General Practice and Public Health. Ph.D. dissertation.

Costa, S.H.
1998   Commercial Availability of Misoprostol and Induced Abortion in Brazil. *International Journal of Gynaecology & Obstetrics* 63(suppl. 1): 131-139.

Crick, Malcolm
1989   Shifting Identities in the Research Process: an Essay in Personal Anthropology. In J. Perry (ed.) *Doing Fieldwork: Eight Personal Accounts of Social Research*. Victoria: Deakin University Press.

Crossley, Nick
1995   Merleau-Ponty, the Elusive Body and Carnal Sociology. *Body & Society* 1(1): 43-63.
1996a   *Intersubjectivity: The Fabric of Social Becoming*. London: Sage Publications.
1996b   Body-Subject/Body-Power: Agency, Inscription and Control in Foucault and Merleau-Ponty. *Body & Society* 2(2): 99-116.

DaMatta, Roberto
1997.   *A Casa & A Rua. Espaço, cidadania, mulher e morte no Brasil*. Rio de Janeiro: Editora Rocco.

Dewey, John
1957   *Human Nature and Conduct: An Introduction to Social Psychology*. New York: The Modern Library.

Diniz, S. G., and A. F. d'Oliveira
1998   Gender Violence and Reproductive Health. *International Journal of Gynaecology & Obstetrics* 63(suppl. 1): 33-42.

Diniz, Simone G., Cecília de Mello e Souza, and Ana Paula Portella
1998   Not Like Our Mothers. Reproductive Choice and the Emergence of Citizenship among Brazilian Rural workers, Domestic Workers and Housewives. In R. P. Petchesky and K. Judd (eds.) *Negotiating Reproductive Rights*. London: Zed Books.

Eisenstadt, S.N., and L. Roniger
1984   *Patrons, Clients and Friends: Interpersonal Relations and the Structure of Trust in Society*. Cambridge: Cambridge University Press.

Fadul, Anamaria, Emile McAnany, and Ofelia T. Morales
1996   Telenovela and Demography in Brazil. Paper presented at the 20th Scientific
        Conference of the International Association for Mass Communication Re-
        search, Sidney, Australia, 1996.

Faria, Vilmar E.
1997/1998 Government Policy and Fertility Regulations: Unintended Consequences
        and Perverse Effects. *Brazilian Journal of Population Studies* 1: 179-206.

Faundes, Aníbal, and José G. Cecatti
1991   A operação cesárea no Brasil: Incidência, tendências, causas, consequências e
        propostas de ação. *Cadernos de Saúde Pública* 7(2): 150-173.

FIDEM
1996   Monografias municipais. First series. Recife.

Fonseca, Claudia
2000   Família, fofoca e honra. Etnografia de relaçoes de gênero e violência em grupos
        populares. Porto Alegre: Editora da Universidade/UFRGS

Foreit, Karen G., Marcos P. P. de Castro, and Eliane F. D. Franco
1989   The Impact of Mass Media Advertising on a Voluntary Sterilization Program
        in Brazil. *Studies in Family Planning* 20(2): 107-116.

Foucault, Michel
1980   *Power/Knowledge: Selected Interviews & Other Writings 1972-1977.* New
        York, Toronto: The Harvester Press.

Foucault, Michel
1984   The Means of Correct Training (from Discipline and Punishment). In P.
        Rabinow (ed.) *The Foucault Reader.* Penguin Books.

Foucault, Michel
1994   *Viljen til Viden.* København: Det Lille Forlag.

Freyre, Gilberto
1992(1933) Casa Grande e Senzala, 32nd edition. Rio de Janeiro: Editora Record.

Fukuyama, Francis
1992   *The End of History and the Last Man.* London: Penguin Books.

Gammeltoft, Tine
1999   *Women's Bodies, Women's Worries: Health and Family Planning in a
        Vietnamese Rural Community.* Richmond, Surrey: Curzon Press.

Geertz, Clifford
1973   *The Interpretation of Cultures.* New York: Basic Books.

Giffin, Karen
1994   Women's Health and the Privatization of Fertility Control in Brazil. *Social
        Science and Medicine* 39(3): 355-360

Goffman, Erving
1995   On Face-Work: An Analysis of Ritual Elements in Social Interaction. In B. G. Blount (ed.) *Language, Culture, and Society*. Illinois: Waveland Press.

Goldani, Ana Maria
1990   Changing Brazilian Families and the Consequent Need for Public Policy. *International Social Science Journal* 126: 523 -537.

Goldstein, Donna
1999   "Interracial" Sex and Racial Democracy in Brazil: Twin Concepts? *American Anthropologists* 101(3): 563-578.

Gouveia, Taciana, and Ana P. Portella
n.d.   Políticas sociais de saúde: Uma questão de género? O caso das agentes de saúde do municipio de Camaragibe/PE. Recife: SOS Corpo.

Haraway, Donna J.
1991   *Simians, Cyborgs, and Women: The Reinvention of Nature*. London: Free Association Books.

Hardy, E., L. Bahamondes, M.J. Osis, R.G. Costa, and A. Faúndes
1996   Risk Factors for Tubal Sterilization Regret, Detectable before Surgery. *Contraception* 54: 159-162.

Hasse, Cathrine
1995   Fra Journalist til "Big Mamma": Om Sociale Rollers Betydning for Antropologers Datagenerering. Tidsskriftet Antropologi 31: 53-63.

Hastrup, Kirsten
1995   *A Passage to Anthropology*. London: Routledge.

Hecht, Tobias
1998   *At Home in the Street: Street Children of Northeast Brazil*. Cambridge: Cambridge University Press.

Heede, Dag
1997   *Det Tomme Menneske*. København: Museum Tusculanums Forlag.

Hegel, G. W. F.
1979   *The Phenomenology of Spirit*. Oxford: Clarendon.

Hess, David J., and Roberto DaMatta
1995   *The Brazilian Puzzle: Culture on the Borderlands of the Western World*. New York: Columbia University Press.

Holston, James
1991   Autoconstruction in Working-Class Brazil. *Cultural Anthropology* 6(4): 447-465.

Honneth, Alex
1995   *The Struggle for Recognition*. Cambridge: Polity Press.

Hopkins, Kristine
1998   Under the Knife: Caesarean Section and Female Sterilization in Brazil. Faculty of the Graduate School, University of Texas, Austin. Ph.D. dissertation.

Jackson, Michael
1989   *Paths Towards a Clearing*. Bloomington: Indiana University Press.
1995   *At Home in the World*. Durham: Duke University Press.
1996   Introduction. Phenomenology, radical empiricism, and anthropological critique. In M. Jackson (ed.) *Things as They Are. New directions in Phenomenological Anthropology*. Bloomington: Indiana University Press.
1998   *Minima Ethnographica*. Chicago: University of Chicago Press.

James, William
1950 (1890) *The Principles of Psychology (1)*. New York: Dover Publications.

Junqueira, Eduardo
1997   Mãe Natureza. Entrevista com João Luiz Carvalho Pinto e Silva. *Veja* May 14.

Kaufmann, Georgia
1998   Gender and Reproductive Decision Making: The Contraceptive Choice of Women in a Brazilian Favela. In G. Martine, M. Das Gupta, and L. C. Chen (eds.) *Reproductive Change in India and Brazil*. Delhi: Oxford University Press.

Kendall, Carl, Chizuru Misago, and Walter Fonesca
1999   Combining Qualitative and Quantitative Research in Fortaleza. *Anthropology in Action* 6(3): 11-19.

Kincaid, D. Lawrence, Alice P. Merritt, Liza Nickerson, Sandra de C. Buffington, Marcos P. P. de Castro, and Bernadete M. de Castro
1996   Impact of a Mass Media Vasectomy Promotion Campaign in Brazil. *International Family Planning Perspectives* 22(4): 169-175.

Kleinman, Arthur and Joan Kleinman
1996   Suffering and its Professional Transformation: Toward an Anthropology of Interpersonal Experience. In M. Jackson (ed.) *Things as They Are. New directions in Phenomenological Anthropology*. Bloomington: Indiana University Press.

Kojève, Alexandre
1969   *Introduction to the Reading of Hegel: Lectures on the Phenomenology of Spirit*. New York: Basic Books.

Langer, Susanne K.
1953   Feeling and Form: A Theory of Art. London: Routledge & Kegan Paul.

Leal, Ondina F., and Jandyra M. G. Fachel
1995   Male Reproductive Culture and Sexuality in South Brazil: Combining Ethno-

graphic Data and Statistical Analysis. Paper presented at the seminar Fertility and the Male Life Cycle in the Era of Fertility Decline, IUSSP, Zacatecas, Mexico, 1995.

1996   Abortion in South Brazil: Contraceptive Practices and Gender Negotiation. Paper presented at the seminar on Socio-Cultural and Political Aspects of Abortion from an Anthropological Perspective, Trivandrum, India, 1996.

Leavitt, John
1996   Meaning and Feeling in the Anthropology of Emotions. *American Ethnologist* 23(3): 514-539.

Leder, Drew
1990   The Absent Body. Chicago: The University of Chicago Press.

Lehmann, David
1996   *Struggle for the Spirit. Religious Transformation and Popular Culture in Brazil and Latin America.* Cambridge: Polity Press.

Lewis, J. Lowell
2000   Sex and Violence in Brazil: Carnival, Capoeira, and the Problem of Everyday Life. *American Ethnologist* 26(3): 539-557.

Lock, Margaret and Patricia A. Kaufert
1998   Introduction. In M. Lock and P.A. Kaufert (eds.) *Pragmatic Women and Body Politics.* Cambridge: Cambridge University Press.

Lyon, Margot L.
1995   Missing Emotion: The Limitations of Cultural Constructionism in the Study of Emotion. *Cultural Anthropology* 10(2): 244-263.

Lyon, Margot L., and Jack M. Barbalet
1994   Society's body: Emotion and the "Somatization" of Social Theory. In T. J. Csordas (ed.) *Embodiment and Experience.* Cambridge: Cambridge University Press.

Machado, Katia M. de Melo
1998   Fatores associados à solitação de reversão de laqueadura tubária no CISAM – Recife. Universidade Federal de Pernambuco. Recife. Ph.D. dissertation.

Mariz, Cecília L.
1994   *Coping with Poverty.* Philadelphia: Temple University Press.

Martine, George, Monica Das Gupta, and Lincoln C. Chen, eds.
1998   *Reproductive Change in India and Brazil.* Delhi: Oxford University Press.

Martine, George
1998   Brazil's Fertility Decline, 1965-95: A Fresh Look at Key Factors. In G. Martine, M. Das Gupta, and L. C. Chen (eds.) *Reproductive Change in India and Brazil.* Delhi: Oxford University Press.

Mattingly, Cheryl
1994 The Concept of Therapeutic "Emplotment". *Social Science and Medicine* 38: 811-822.

Mead, George H.
1965 (1934) *Mind, Self and Society.* Chicago: The University of Chicago Press.

Mello e Souza, Cecilia de
1994 C- Sections as Ideal Births: The Cultural Construction of Beneficence and Patients' Rights in Brazil. *Cambridge Quarterly of Healthcare Ethics* 3: 358-366.

Merleau-Ponty, Maurice
1962 *Phenomenology of Perception.* London: Routledge.
1968 *The Primacy of Perception and Other Essays.* Evanston, Ill.: Northwestern University Press.

Merrick, Thomas W., and Elza Berquo
1983 *The Determinants of Brazil's Recent Rapid Decline in Fertility.* Washington, D.C.: National Academy Press.

Moreira, Morvan de M.
1998 O Sistema de Informações sobre Nascidos Vivos e a Declaração de Nascido Vivo, no Nordeste – algumas Evidências Relativas aos Estados de Pernambuco e Ceará. In P. Teixeira (ed.) *Mortalidade Infantil.* Recife, Fundação Joaquim Nabuco: Editora Massangana.

Nascimento, Pedro F. G. do
1999 Ser homem ou nada: Diversidade de experiências e estratégias de atualização do modelo hegemônico da masculinidade em Camaragibe/PE. Pós-graduaçâo em Antropologia. Universidade Federal de Pernambuco. Master's thesis.

Nations, Marilyn K., and L. A. Rebhun
1988 Angels with Wet Wings won't fly: Maternal Sentiment in Brazil and the Image of Neglect. *Culture, Medicine and Society* 12: 141-200.

Nichter, Mark
1981 Idioms of Distress: Alternatives in the Expression of Psychological Distress: A Case Study from South India. *Culture, Medicine and Psychiatry* 5: 379-408.

Notas Sobre Nascimento e Parto
1998 Editorial: Parto normal "a pedido". 3(5).

Observatório PE 2002
2002 Jovem e moradia. Power-point presentation by Jan Bitou for the conference "Os jovens e a cidade", Universidade Federal de Pernambuco, Recife. March 5-7.

Parker, Richard G.
1991 *Bodies, Pleasures, and Passions.* Boston: Beacon Press.

Parker, Richard G. and Regina M. Barbosa, eds.
1996   *Sexualidades Brasileiras.* Rio de Janeiro: Relume-Dumará Editores.

Patai, Daphne
1991   U.S.Academics and Third World Women: Is Ethical Research Possible? In S.
       B. Gluck and D. Patai (eds.) *Women's Words. The Feminist Practice of Oral
       History.* London: Routledge.

Pitanguy, Jacqueline
1994   Feminist Politics and Reproductive Rights: The Case of Brazil. In G. Sen and
       R. Snow (eds.) *Power and Decision. The Social Control of Reproduction.*
       Boston, Mass.: Harvard University Press.

Pizzini, Franca
1989   The Expectant Mother as Patient: a Research Study in Italian Maternity
       Wards. *Health Promotion* 4(1): 1-10.
1991   Communication Hierarchies in Humour: Gender Differences in the
       Obstetrical/Gynaecological Setting. *Discourse & Society* 2 (4): 477-488.

PNDS
1996   *Pesquisa Nacional Sobre Demografia e Saúde.* Rio de Janeiro: BEMFAM,
       IBGE, DHS.

PNDS/PE
1996   *PNDS 1996, Pernambuco.* Recife: Secretaria da Saúde de Pernambuco,
       BEMFAM, Fundação Joaquim Nabuco.

Potter, Joseph E., and André J. Caetano
1998   Clientelismo e Esterilização no Nordeste Brasileiro 1986 – 1995. Pa-
       per presented at the XI Encontro Nacional de Estudos Populacionais da
       ABEP1998.

Prefeitura de Camaragibe
1999   Unpublished data on infant mortality.

Rabinow, Paul, ed.
1984   The Foucault Reader. An Introduction to Foucault's Thought. London: Pen-
       guin Books.

Rabinow, Paul
1992   A Modern Tour in Brazil. In S. Lash and J. Friedman (eds.) *Modernity and
       Identity.* Oxford: Blackwell.

Rattner, Daphne
1996   Sobre a Hipótese de Estabilização das Taxas de Cesárea do Estado de São
       Paulo, Brasil. *Revista Saúde Pública* 30(1): 19-33.

Rebhun, L.A.
1999   *The Heart is Unknown Country. Love in the Changing Economy of North-
       east Brazil.* Stanford: Stanford University Press.

Ridler, Keith
1996 If not in Words: Shared Practical Activity and Friendship in Fieldwork. In M. Jackson (ed.) *Things as They Are. New Directions in Phenomenological Anthropology.* Bloomington: Indiana University Press.

Rocha, Edileusa da
1995 *Situação Sócio Econômica das Mulheres – Região Metropolitana do Recife.* Recife: SOS Corpo.

Rocha, Sonia
1995 Metropolitan Poverty in Brazil: Economic Cycles, Labour Market and Demographic Trends. *International Journal of Urban and Regional Research* 19(3): 383-394.

Rocha, Maria I. B. da
1998 Significados Históricos e Políticos da Regulaçõa da Fecundidade. In C. Batista and M. Larangeira (eds.) *Aborto: Desafios da Legalidade.* Recife: SOS Corpo.

Rosaldo, Michelle
1983 Toward an Anthropology of Self and Feeling. In R. A. Shweder and R. A. Levine (eds.) *Culture Theory: Essays on Mind, Self and Emotion.* Cambridge: Cambridge University Press.

Rozemberg, Brani, and Lenore Manderson
1998 "Nerves" and Tranquilizer Use in Rural Brazil. *International Journal of Health Services* 28(1): 165-181.

Rutenberg, Naomi, and Elisabeth A. Ferraz
1988 Female Sterilization and its Demographic Impact in Brazil. *International Family Planning Perspectives* 14(2): 61-68.

Sanjek, Roger
1990 On Ethnographic Validity. In R. Sanjek (ed.) *Fieldnotes. The Makings of Anthropology.* Ithaca & London: Cornell University Press.

Saietz, Dorrit
1998 Brazil: Population Growth Almost at a Standstill. In L. Nordahl Jacobsen and N. Rasmussen (eds.) *Women's Voices, Women's Choices: On Reproductive Health.* Copenhagen: Sex & Samfund.

Sastry, Narayan
1997 What explains Rural-Urban Differentials in Child Mortality in Brazil? *Social Science and Medicine* 44(7): 989-1002.

Salem, Tanja
1980 Mulheres faveladas: 'Com a venda nos olhos.' *Perspectivas antropológicas da mulher* 1: 49-99

Scheper-Hughes, Nancy
1992   *Death without Weeping: The Violence of Everyday Life in Brazil*. Berkeley: University of California Press.
1997   Demography Without Numbers. In D. I. Kertzer and T. Fricke (eds.) *Anthropological Demography: Toward a New Synthesis*. Chicago: The University of Chicago Press.

Schutz, Alfred, and Thomas Luckmann
1973   *The Structures of the Life-world I*. London: Heinemann.
1983   *The Structures of the Life-World II*. Evanstone, Ill.: Northwestern University Press.

Scott, Parry
1990   O Homem na Matrifocalidade: gênero, percepção e experiências do domínio doméstico. Cadernos de Pesquisa 73: 38-47.
1996a   Matrifocal Males: Gender, Perception and Experience of the Domestic Domain in Brazil. In M. J. Maynes, A. Waltner, B. Soland, and U. Strasser (eds.) *Gender, Kinship, Power*. London: Routledge.

Scott, Parry, ed.
1996b   *Saúde e Pobreza no Recife*. Recife: Universidade Federal de Pernambuco, Núcleo de Saúde Pública.

Secretaria de Imprensa
1998   *Guia da cidadania*. Camaragibe.

Secretaria de Planejamento
1997   Regionalização administrativa. Camaragibe. Report.

Serruya, Suzanne
1996   *Mulheres esterilizadas: Submissâo e desejo*. Belém: NAEA/UFPA/UEPA.

Sheriff, Robin E.
2000   Exposing Silence as Cultural Censorship: A Brazilian Case. *American Anthropologist* 102(1): 114-132.
2001   Dreaming Equality: Color, Race and Racism in Urban Brazil. New Brunswick: Rutgers University Press.

Shweder, Richard A.
1991   *Thinking through Cultures*. Cambridge, Mass.: Harvard University Press.

Silva, Denise F. da
1998   Facts of Blackness: Brazil is not (Quite) the United States... and Racial Politics in Brazil? *Social Identities* 4(2): 201-234.

Silver, Lynn D.
1996   Monitoramento e avaliação rotineira da qualidade e distribução da assistencia obstétrica hospitalar: Estudo do potencial do sistema de informação existente. Unpublished report.

Sjørslev, Inger
1995   Det Metodiske Forløb. *Tidsskriftet Antropologi* 31: 177-183.

Skidmore, Thomas E.
1999   *Five Centuries of Change*. Oxford: Oxford University Press.

Stacey, Judith
1991   Can There Be a Feminist Ethnography? In S. B. Gluck and D. Patai (eds.) *Women's Words: The Feminist Practice to Oral History*. London: Routledge.

Säävälä, Minna
1999   Understanding the Prevalence of Female Sterilisation in Rural South India. *Studies in Family Planning* 30(4): 288-301

Tauxe, Caroline S.
1993   The Spirit of Christmas: Television and Commodity Hunger in a Brazilian Election. *Public Culture* 5: 593-604.

Telles, Edward E.
1995   Race, Class and Space in Brazilian Cities. *International Journal of Urban and Regional Research* 19(3): 395-406.

Thomassen, Carsten
1992/93 Sorte Børn "Unødvendig Produktion". *Kontakt* 8: 36-38.
        Townsend, Nicholas Reproduction in Anthropology and Demography. In D. I. Kertzer and T. Fricke (eds.) *Anthropological Demography: Toward a New Synthesis*. Chicago: The University of Chicago Press

Tufte, Thomas
1993   Everyday Life, Women and Telenovelas in Brazil. In A. Fadul (ed.) *Serial Fiction in TV: The Latin American Telenovelas*. São Paulo: School of Communication and Arts, University of São Paulo.

UNICEF/IBGE
1991-1996 *Indicadores sobre crianças e adolescentes*. Brasilia/Rio de Janeiro: UNICEF.

Van Maanen, John
1988   *Tales of the Field: On Writing Ethnography*. Chicago: Chicago University Press.

Victora, Ceres
1996   Images of the Body: Lay and Biomedical views of the reproductive System in Britain and Brazil. Brunel University. Ph.D. dissertation.

Vieira, Elisabeth M.
1994   Regret after Sterilization among Low Income Women in São Paulo, Brazil. Ph.D. dissertation.

Vieira, Elisabeth M., and Nicholas J. Ford
1996   The Provision of Female Sterilization in São Paulo, Brazil: A Study among Low Income Women. *Social Science and Medicine* 42(10): 1427-1432.

WHO
1992   *Female Sterilization. A Guide to Provision of Services.* Geneva: WHO.

Whyte, Susan R.
1997   *Questioning Misfortune: The Pragmatics of Uncertainty in Eastern Uganda.* Cambridge: Cambridge University Press.

Wikan, Unni
1992   Beyond the Words: the Power of Resonance. *American Ethnologist* 19(3): 460-482.
1995   The Self in a World of Urgency and Necessity. *Ethos* 23(3): 259-285.

Wolcott, Harry F.
1995   *The Art of Fieldwork.* Walnut Creek: AltaMira Press.

Wood, Charles H., and José A. M. de Carvalho
1988   *The Demography of Inequality in Brazil.* Cambridge: Cambridge University Press.

Index